# The Political Dance

Nathanael Michael Gibson

# DEDICATION

This book is Dedicated to Amanda, who loved me when I was unlovely, carried me when I could not stand, and helped me smile when so much was taken from me. If who you are is determined by what you do, then this is the best way I can to introduce her to you.

# CONTENTS

*The practice of morality being necessary for the well being of society, He [God] has taken care to impress its precepts so indelibly on our hearts that they shall not be effaced by the subtleties of our brain. We all agree in the obligation of the moral principles of Jesus and nowhere will they be found delivered in greater purity than in His discourses.*

*- Thomas Jefferson*

The Writings of Thomas Jefferson, Alberty Ellery Bergh, editor (Washington D.C.: The Thomas Jefferson Memorial Association, 1904), Vol. XII, p. 315, to James Fishback, September 27, 1809.

# Introduction: In The Kitchen

Notions like these begin around the dinner table. They begin in long car rides. These are the kinds of notions that come from conversations in moments shared. Perhaps it was a reaction to something I heard while listening to the radio or television. It could have percolated through the things said at a family get together. Recently, one of the kids described encountering their first taste of college life. First encounters with a world of new approaches and ways of doing things were the core of that conversation. There were questions. Now, Place yourself in my shoes. The worldview that had been presented by community and home went from being the only view to one of many worldviews. What do you tell the young collegiate about the differing world views being encountered?

I think the resulting conversation we shared is probably a fairly common conversation to be had at that age. If you've been around kids entering the beginning of adulthood you probably also realized it was important how you answered questions. That period in a young person's life isn't just important because it's when they usually get their first real taste of their own independent life. It is also when they first start developing awareness of their own differences. That's when they begin to develop their own opinion. It's fun to watch. They really do grow up so fast. One minute a couple might pick out which room will be the nursery. It feels like the very next moment that couple is now helping their kids do the very same thing.

Not much will fill you with as much satisfaction as investing in another person. And young ones grow so quickly. You could almost say investing in their lives is instant gratification. Year after year we watch as the child grows to take on more and more responsibility in maturity. Simple concepts become more complex. When they're young it seems every concern is either personal, immediate, or both. Apple juice is serious stuff. How does the young one who used to petition for juice at the family table go on to be concerned for the plight of the poor in Africa? It may have taken years, but it happened so fast. This concern, I think, is a sign of maturity. The capacity for awareness of and concern for others seems to reach its fully matured, most manifold state, somewhere between eighteen and twenty four in our culture. Fathers I've known who were, and still are, especially protective to their daughters put the number at no less than thirty years of age. Of course, the process of continually refining and developing mature judgment continues from there. But, that span of years seems to be the age when we first have all the pieces in place to "grasp at the reins," so to speak. I've heard mothers joke that kids don't totally become adults until twenty five. I tend to place a lot of weight on a mother's observations. There may be reason why the mothers I've known have been inclined to pick that number, even in jest. They've noticed their child take the final personal steps necessary, at about that time, to become able to care for others.

Yes, somewhere in that special time comes the capacity to form more developed opinions. But, not everyone shares this personal experience, and the resulting view that comes from that experience. Fewer still are willing to rest upon the anecdotal. If you prefer a statistical case, consider marriage. The question of marriage is one of the most important decisions a person will make in their lifetime. It is also a decision many feel tremendously motivated to make. Some think about it from the time they are very young. But, when does the decision to marry most commonly occur? According to the U. S. Census Bureau, the median marriage age was 25.9 between 2005 and 2009. The desire and drive for a relationship, for many, had been there for years. But, practically and legally speaking, the decision could have been made at a younger age. So why the relatively high median age, which is years after the earliest opportunity to fulfill the desire of marriage? It's not until the capacity to form a mature opinion develops that one can comfortably begin making, what our society considers, mature decisions. Leaving the care of parents to start a life caring for another is most certainly a decision which requires maturity to end well. Where desire for lasting companionship meets the hefty weight of living to fulfill the dreams of another, an age in years is found.

The importance of this age is not limited to romantic overtures. The ability to form a mature opinion also carries with it another ramification with which we are most familiar. With maturity comes a decision about how to care for one's self. A personal course in life is charted from this choice. What we will work to achieve in life, what we will work towards the existence of, flows from this place. When one of the kids raised questions on how people develop opinions, I realized it was the beginning of a new and very special time in life. We had a conversation. Secretly, I smiled to see someone I bounced on my knee so many years ago coming of age. I listened with pleasure as the footprint was traced, ever so lightly, where this young adult would begin to carry the weight of personal understanding in society. I also wasn't surprised at all to learn this new inductee into the adult world had also been asking family members questions about marriage.

It is interesting to see someone develop their opinion in the broadest sense of adult capacity for the first time, which they will refine and enhance for the rest of their life. It is of keen interest how opinions, and the method of making them, improve with age. When the father of my darling first asked me what I thought about people on the other side of the political aisle, I told him. An hour later, we were both still fervently and pleasantly engrossed in conversation. Since that time we've had many such conversations. Some were brief. Others lasted over long car rides. There weren't any fireworks in these conversations. That is to say, no roiling emotions remained at their end. There was passion, to be sure. We often both left the conversation with something new to think about.

As I've often said, the only person who wins an argument is the one who comes away from it learning something new. I think we all feel strongly about our convictions. When we share a firmly held opinion, some driving impetus within leads us in giving voice to what we believe to be important. Hopefully, this is a process through which we learn from one another.

No one knows everything. Even if there was a person who knew everything, they couldn't apply themselves to every endeavor simultaneously. We don't all place the same priority in the same areas, so, we don't spend our limited time developing a thoroughly informed opinion on everything. There just isn't enough time to do so. It follows that we need each other to fill out ideas we are either disinclined to pursue ourselves, or lack the time to explore fully. Hearing another's point of view can expand your world view, if you're willing to listen. Sadly, unlike the case of my conversations with my elder, comity does not always take place. Others may not be open to what they perceive as unconventional input, including what you value. It can be confusing, even painful, when your convictions are overlooked or dismissed. That others spend their time and resources on what you consider to be frivolous may not seem to make sense. It may make even less sense that they would ignore what you consider vital. I once heard a priest ascribe the number one cause of pain in this world to cognitive dissonance. As strange as that may seem to some, I think that must be right.

I've felt my share of pain in my lifetime. I've been hungry with no expectation of food, save what is minimally necessary for survival. I've been wounded with no time to stop and heal. I've had to endure hardships without knowing when, or if they would end.  It's not something I like to discuss, but I think I may have endured the equivalent of a few other people's share of hardships as well. But, my hardships were all mine to endure. I'm not complaining. It has been good to grow up in the U. S. The point of all is to provide personal assurance that physical pain is secondary to emotional pain and the questions which follow. Questions like:

"Why?"

"Why did she leave me?"

"Why did he hurt me?"

"When will it stop?"

"What could I have done differently?"

"How is it possible that these good people don't understand?"

These are questions that can remain long after our bodies have healed. It is amazing the resiliency questions like these can have. Sometimes, an emotion or memory triggers them years later, and they still have the ability to cause us pain. On a personal note, I am thankful I do not currently suffer in any great measure, my little daily difficulties not being worth mention. I am grateful for healing. But, some do suffer greatly. And, given the nature of life, it is a safe bet I will again. Even when questions are put to rest, more will arise. But what happens when there are certain veins of interest which do not ease, no matter how much we salve our concern?

A question one of my grandfathers who fought in World War II carried, perhaps, is a prime example of the tenacity of questions. "Why did I live when so many others died?" It is one carried by many who were trained to endure intense physical pain, but now battle on the field of emotions. Some continue to battle this question well into their post war lives. Yes, questions can be tenacious. A tolerance can be built up to physical pain. Medication can be prescribed to ease what training and experience cannot. Questions, however, are different. I'm not sure how you build up a tolerance to internal questions, or that it would be healthy to do so. Denial certainly isn't desirable or healthy. I've never heard of a pill that provides an answer. Without real answers, questions run the risk of remaining. Medication cannot cure "Why?" Only answers which fit and fulfill our questions can bring our ease and release, that, and trust.

I'm not asking you to start by trusting me. I've found people who ask for your trust without building their credibility in your mind through actions either lack the sense which commonly comes from experience, or think you do. I find answers do help, though, even when delivered through the kindness of a stranger. What else is there? There is no easier way. So, in lieu of convenience, we are left with struggle, the struggle for answers. We must grapple with concepts to form understanding. Otherwise our cares and cognitive dissonance will drive us, making for a hard task master. Some deny this master, and rebel from being driven. But this is a short sighted course. The only avenue left to these is distraction. Through this fickle aid rebels from daily and personal concerns seek to occupy their hearts and minds. But, distraction is like meat thrown to a junk yard dog. All distractions run their course, and are finished. Their ministration is fleeting. They all prove vain. That junk yard dog will eventually finish his meal. Then he'll be less hungry, and you'll still be in *his* yard. Those rebels, us, we still try to flee cognitive dissonance. Our flight takes many forms. For those with affluence, there is a constant stream of people wishing to offer ways to occupy the mind. For those with less means, there is work. Work gives as it takes, time and health are traded in return for satisfactions and means. For those who do not find that work gives commensurate to what it takes, there is dissipation. But why, may you ask, do all distractions ultimately fail? Distractions give no fuel for answers to the questions which remain when they have left us? It's like playing building blocks without the blocks. After our time is spent our questions remain unanswered. Worse yet, questions may grow in insistency over time while distractions wane in charm. We, who have not traded wisely for our time, find ourselves no richer at the end to pay the toll for these questions we carry.

It seems there is a particularly insistent question lying at the root of our culture. It is a question which has been answered before. But, it seems we are destined to ask the question again in our time. Perhaps, there is merit in this. A wise and erudite person once told me there comes a point when we expand our understanding less, and deepen our understanding more. Questions can also serve useful purposes. They are not one sided things. We may garner a greater understanding in asking a question. We humans seem to need to ask questions. We need to ask even when we are already presented with an answer. We do it for ourselves, for personal reasons. It just seems to be a part of how we learn. Both in healing old wounds and developing new understanding, we need our questions. When we come to the place where our experience begins to venture forth into the unknown, we create a question. Questions are the explorers sent out by our desire. In this magical place, where we understand what we need well enough to form our desire into words, learning can take place. The space where desire, understanding, and limitation intersect we call a teachable moment.

I guess you could say our nation has come to a teachable moment. For those who are unfamiliar with the term, I'll explain it a bit further. A teachable moment is the point when you're willing to take more time, and pay more attention than you were previously. I'm reminded of the story of a man named Archimedes, who experienced possibly the most famous teachable moment in history, culminating when he stepped into a bath. Archimedes, like many of us, had stepped into a bathtub more times than he could count. For most of us, nothing about the act of stepping into a bath comes off as vital or pressing, except when someone fails to bathe frequently. But this time, Archimedes had something on his mind.

Someone Archimedes knew had given a goldsmith pure gold to create a votive crown. It was feared the goldsmith was stealing by removing some gold, then mixing in another metal to maintain the right size, then passing off the impure gold alloy as the real thing. At the time when Archimedes lived, people didn't know how to determine the purity of metal in an irregular shape. A gold brick, yes, but gold shaped into a crown is a no. It was a real concern that the goldsmith had kept some of the pure gold, replacing it by mixing in another less valuable metal. This kind of theft had been potentially costly and undetectable until the metal was later melted down again.

Archimedes stood like a soppy statue, dripping and thinking. He had watched the water rise as he got into the bath. It fell again as he pulled back up to standing. He noticed that water raised an amount equal to his volume as he stepped in his bath. It occurred to him that he could measure the volume of an irregular object by measuring the amount of water it displaced. Knowing the volume would provide Archimedes with half the ratio needed to determine the density of the crown, since gold has a very specific density, thereby proving or disproving the crown's authenticity. Eureka, shouted Archimedes, as he leaped from the bath! Legend has it Archimedes was so excited he immediately raced out into the streets to test his theory. He was so excited he forgot to dress himself on the way out.

Eureka means I have found it. It was made famous by a man whose life experience came into contact with challenges, and caused him to look at an everyday part of life in a different way. Eureka was the cry of someone seeing what was always in front of him in a way he never saw it before. Awareness was focused by need, creating a willingness to pay more attention where one normally would not. We're not always this fortunate. Sometimes, we watch these moments pass by with a spectacular degree of ignorance. Yes, I'm speaking from experience. Our questions teach us to look at life in ways we would never have otherwise imagined. Should we fail to develop this newfound willingness, or lack the life experience needed to recognize answers in that moment, we'll experience the cost of a real world education. I can tell you that's a much steeper cost. That kind of an education can cost its weight in gold.

I do believe we humans are the only species to give each other awards for spectacularly missing these teachable moments. A man named Foxworthy built a career on relating such tales. It could be said that a man named Darwin tried to view all biology in terms of the ability to adapt. A teachable moment is certainly one measure of our ability to adapt. Given the magnitude these moments carry, I've tried to make it a priority to recognize them. After watching enough moments pass by it has become my desire to be more attentive. But, desire and results aren't always congruous. To use a metaphor, my rearview mirror seems clearer than my windshield. I'm firmly confident Mr. Foxworthy could find a funny story or two in my life worth relating to paying audiences. I've learned a certain amount of personal effort is needed to catch a few more of these moments as they pass by. These days I simply hope my life's story doesn't lend well to invoking the name of Darwin by way of explanation.

There seems to be a transitional point between pressing questions and teachable moments, teachable moments and painful questions. In this space there is room to move, time to see, time to act. There is the time to choose a new direction, if you know the way, before another direction sets in. Rather than transitioning to somewhere between Foxworthy's next great hit and validating Darwin's theories on adaptation, let's aspire to finding an answer which heals and fulfills our pressing question. Why does our current political division occur? This one question gives way to more questions like branches on a tree. What effect is political division having on our society? How are people using an understanding of this division to profit at our expense? When will it end?

I've waited while these important questions lingered. Some people have answered the effects, the branches of the root question in a most satisfactory manner. But, treating symptoms rather than a cause is never truly final. Treating symptoms incurs the cost of added maintenance, and we are quickly becoming bankrupt. I am a simple man of humble means. I was sure by now someone else would have provided the answer. I don't wish to stir from my little world. My problems have been great and my hands are so small. I get by on grace, I live on it entirely. Putting these words to page takes time. Again, my grasp is so small. My hope was that perhaps someone wiser and wealthier, whose reach is greater, would provide a better answer already. But, no answer has been forthcoming, and people are suffering. Some don't even know the cause, but simply accept their pain as hazards of life, or as caused by opposition. Hopefully, my humble answer will sustain our needs until my betters attend to this cause. Because of the dearth of an answer to our communal question, I aspire in my little way to provide some relief.

To start, to open our conflict to widest and fullest range of input from which to create solutions, we must frame the body of our desire with words. Why haven't we, as a society, found the answer behind the current polarized political environment? It's not an easy question to answer. Our culture and governmental system is unique in human history. When you gather together governmental elements from throughout time, and build them on one foundation, it's not as though there's an owner's manual to consult. Our governmental system has protected and fostered liberty at an unheard of level in our lifetime, or any lifetime preceding us. But our lives have become filled with other cares. We've been content to be entertained. In certain ways we've given up on our own education. The media we have trusted for news has taken to forming an entertaining narrative. We even let someone else define for us what they feel we need to know. It is simplest to say that we've been distracted.

But, to be fair, that's not all that's going on. There's a principle at work here, waiting to reveal its value as comparable in worth to gold. Now that you've got to know me a little, let's get to work in our effort of exploration. Please, use the following pages as a starting place for positive change. Digest the reasons and take on the hard questions. Form an opinion. Then, talk about it with the people you care about. You would be surprised the effect this can have. A man named Confucius was respected in China as an authority on positive social change. On the topic of where positive change begins, Confucius is attributed with saying:

If there be righteousness in the heart,
there will be beauty in the character.
If there be beauty in the character,
there will be harmony in the home.
If there be harmony in the homes,

there will be order in the nation.
If there be order in the nations,
there will be peace in the world


    Join with me in broadening the debate. We'll find reasons for hope. So bring your life experience and your desires for the future. Find food for the kind of thought that starts conversations in cars, kitchens, and down through generations. But, before harmony, order, or encountering the world, I hope you enjoy.

# Past is Prologue

It has been said that one of the most severe curses to come out of China is, "May you live in interesting times." We live in a fast past era of reality television, the twenty four hour news cycle, and instant messaging. Billions of dollars are spent every year on entertainment in a never ending search for interesting. As the "fifteen minutes of fame" add up adoring fans love every hour. It may be hard for the current generation to understand how this could be a curse. Where I grew up there was corn and cows. If a car went by that day it was rush hour. Of course, you wouldn't recognize the village I grew up outside of by my description now. Over time country roads have been eaten by suburban sprawl. I still remember I nearly cried the first time they painted the roads. The old farm that sat on a hill just outside of town is gone. It has been replaced by a subdivision. Even the hill the farmhouse stood on is gone, leveled. I'm not that old, at least I don't think so. The sleepy village just turned into a growing town that fast. Now everything seems to happen faster, including the speed at which information travels. There a lot of interesting out there to choose from. Like a lot of people I find enjoyment in sentiments and places that are interesting. If you know of a new hot spot for food, or a good product at a better price, I'm usually interested. The word interesting itself is one of my favorite words, just not when used to describe the affairs of a nation. Interesting being used to describe a new line of liquid hand soaps that won't clog up and then squirt your clothes in embarrassing places when you try to use them is good. Interesting events in a nation end up making the evening news. Think about what you see covered in the news. The majority of what I see coming out of the news media is what you might describe as bad news. It would also qualify as interesting. If you could sign up to randomly have one of the stories from the national news desk magically happen to your life, would you do it? You're not likely to want to be involved with that kind of interesting personally. But, it's a different kind of interesting. Wars, famine, flood, scandals of corruption in our government, and other national disasters, these qualify as interesting on a national scale. I like my nation best when it is boring, reliable, and safe. And why wishing interesting times on another person is considered a severe curse. Me personally, I've got enough interesting to keep me busy in my own life. When it comes to the activities of powerful people and others whose actions can affect my life I prefer simple to interesting. Simple pleasures rarely disappoint. But interesting, that's dicey. If you watch the news, though, that doesn't seem to be the national mood. Lately I've been feeling that my sentiment is one which places me in the minority. Before we get too carried away, there's more to this gem of eastern wisdom. A second curse is known to be paired with along with that first curse I quoted. The second curse is, "May you get what you wish for." It seems both curses have been coming true in the millennial United States of America.

I'd love to tell you everything is going to be fine, that everything we're facing has happened before. All this has happened before. Two occasions readily come to mind from our history. The culture became polarized. Issues created clearly visible lines of division between the populace. Then the population divided into groups in ways that went beyond normal disagreements or competing interests. Each side believed something they desired greatly was being challenged. The saw in the issues of the day a window into their own most dearly held desires and beliefs. After that the polarization became heated. Each group's worldview and body of thought coalesced into political statements which defined their disagreements. The lines that had merely defined separation grew into chasms. Each side peered over the pit with disdainful glances at their opposition. Putting their disagreements into artfully crafted words provided support for those who wished to pull the other side onto their side or into the chasm, and claim supremacy. When the finesse of statecraft and words meant to mollify failed, force prevailed.

Division occurs every day. I've found as a general rule that when there are exclusionary groups of Us's and Them's, the Us's eventually become the Them's. That's why I'm not a big fan of exclusivity. In some cases I recognize the need. A secret barbecue recipe needs to stay a secret or the restaurant that owns it will have a harder time staying in business. Or, consider your personal banking information. It belongs to the exclusive club of your household and your bank. If an identity thief gets access to your personal data then your standard of living could change for the worse. But even the kind of exclusivity I care less for can exist without causing deep cultural divisions. There are people banding together around pursuits and causes all over the nation on a regular basis. They can range from helpful to harmful to just entertaining. What lines of division drive the kind of intensity that heats a fiercely oppositional environment? What defines the scale? What makes the difference between escalation and de-escalation? Not every issue is universally motivating. Not every cause rallies mass support. Even dire offenses can be, and often are overlooked in our culture. Why do some arguments carry when others fail? I ask these questions because the United States in our time has become polarized.

We're getting "wave elections" where everyone from U. S. senators down to the lowest office on the ballot will get thrown out of office one election year, and then go back to normal voting trends the next election, only to have another wave hit the election after that. The parties on Capitol Hill talk about getting along using the same language the U. S. State Department and the U. S. S. R. used for talking about getting along during the cold war. The division we face even seems to cut right through the parties themselves. Those in the Republican establishment try to fight the label of progressive for fear they'll be beaten in a primary by a more conservative candidate. Those in the Democrat establishment try to look the most progressive for fear a challenger from the left will defeat them in their primary. Meanwhile, the government leaders in both parties are upsetting the public because they have only achieved the curtailing of rights to representation through lawless abuses of power while adding trillions in spending. The number of times the Supreme Court has ruled the president's actions as unconstitutional is in the double digits at this point. The Senate simply stopped voting on bills the House of Representatives sent them if the Senate leadership decided those bills were contrary to their political agenda. The House responded by burying them in paper to accentuate the bottleneck, but that didn't move the gridlock.

There is a saying that it takes two to tango. It can also be said in the U.S. that it takes two legislative bodies to send a bill to the president's desk to be signed into law. For a while the Democrat political party courted the liberal/progressive wing to gain the kind of energized political support that contributes to wins in the voting booth. As the Democrat energy level rose from this fresh infusion the Republicans gave in to liberal demands for a while. But, the conservative wing of the Republicans got tired of the word "compromise" being used as a euphemism for unconditional surrender, and the string of concessions the party leadership was making. "No" became the operative word in Republican politics. "No" provided an opposing pole to the Democrat demand of "Now." And, that's where we are today. Institutions and groups we've looked to over generations to guide our nation into continued prosperity no longer conduct even the basic functions of budgeting or oversight. Each side seems to be growing in the strength of their polarity, even as the number of those who identify with either party drops and the unsatisfied middle swells. I can't form an answer logically as to whether we're looking at polarization which will grow or fade. Others may claim to know. History seems less certain. There are some concerns which can be expected to find purchase in the hearts of those sufficiently motivated to drive a nation. But, no matter what the forces or concerns, this war will first be waged on the battlefield of ideas. Before conflict progresses or regresses, the seat of human will is where the decision must inevitably be made. If we address the heart, we may ameliorate our concerns.

If our premise is true we should look to the disposition of our will. Perhaps the answer lays less in predicting the future and more in knowing ourselves through study of our past. The divide we face now is political, politics being the action of a people's collected will. Since our hearts are at play here, perhaps the best hope really is better understanding ourselves. To tackle the polarization at present, we arm ourselves on this battlefield of ideas by learning the roads our very human hearts took us down in previous generations. To understand what is happening now we need to start with what has happened before. Our political environment is heating up now. One sure way to prevent a fire is to move its source of fuel to a safer place. To learn about fuel we can look at examples of what has fueled polarization before. Let's start our self education with two of the most heated and pivotal examples from our history. Hopefully these examples and paths our nation's hearts tread back then will instruct us now in our need.

The first time of extreme polarization in our nation's history, to which I find my thoughts drawn, is the time of our birth and the Revolutionary War. What violent pangs of labor, which saw so many die and yet an enduring nation was founded. Some recall this only as a history lesson about a conflict between a colony and a crown. That dynamic existed. But, there was also another battle taking place on a battleground unconstrained by geography. That battleground was the hearts, the will, of the colonists. There were those called loyalists who believed in fealty to a king. They saw the attempt to govern themselves as lacking in the virtues which make up fidelity. The power of the Crown's military also carried the promise of security against the threat posed by other nations. Liberty was a thing they were willing to surrender in exchange for the classic feudal compact. The king has an army. And, there was the threat of invaders and the like who would take what they wanted with violence unless there was the credible threat of violence in return. The invaders may not leave anything, but the king will let you keep a little if you agree to call yourself property of the crown. Mixed in with fealty was also fear of the king himself. Again, the king's got an army. Rebellion would bring dangerous reprisal. The Crown would not abide a challenge to its rule. That kind of challenge would not be allowed to find a peaceful resolution. This transaction of freedom in exchange for the protection of a ruler had been employed around the world for thousands of years. Everyone was using their sense knew the penalty imposed by the king for throwing off his rule would be violence.

There were also those among the colonists who were starting to believe in something new. They were willing to question the way things had been done as far back as anyone could remember. They were willing to comb through history looking for exceptions, to learn from these exceptions, and to eventually become the exception to the rule of monarchy in their time. Those on the opposing side from the loyalists were calling themselves patriots. These idealists believed in the principle that a king is not born any different than the rest of us. He is therefore not any more entitled to rule over others than the next person. If there no inherent claim to power exists, then consent must be required to rightfully obtain the fruit of another person's labor. Without such consent, and the means by which to express or withhold this consent as fully as political is capable of allowing in government, they insisted a law of nature was being grossly violated. Our predecessors, who eventually successfully defended their claim to freedom and shaped a new nation, believed war was preferable to living contrary to their nature.

How does this help us? Before a nation which would stand as an advocate for the self evidence of liberty was founded, a battle of ideas polarized its people. The polarization grew heated. When the British troops moved to put down a revolution, they marched into a growing civil war in the colonies between patriots and loyalists. Polarization certainly has the power to change the course of history. It also creates interesting times.

Next up for consideration is the time of polarization which culminated in the end of slavery in the United States. It also saw us embroiled in a war that killed more U. S. citizens than any other war in history. Again, polarization came from firmly held beliefs that were being violated and liberty withheld. The birth of the United States had been based on the assertion that some liberties are natural to existence and self evident, not for anyone to infringe upon. This challenge to the way nations had been ruled was a grand experiment. Before the U. S. Constitution it was believed by many that without a ruler to regulate them, the people would fall into anarchy in barbarism. By the time of the Civil War the experiment had been a grand success. The colonies had endured in their united form without a monarch, and prospered. This success gave credence to the claim that all mankind is endowed with the right to life, liberty, and the pursuit of happiness, for both them and their posterity.

Upon those of good conscience, this proof in practice also imposed an unavoidable duty. A nation where men ruled themselves was not only a possibility, it was a reality. The premise had been proven. The unavoidable conclusion was that humanity is born with rights. This includes the freedom of people to determine their own conduct in the manner of their choosing so long as it does not grossly interfere with the liberty of others. Included in this understanding is that everyone has ownership over the produce of their labor. That people have the natural right to rule themselves was no longer in question. The laws of nature had borne this claim out. But if this natural right exists, it is incumbent that the same liberty must be extended to all. This was not the case. Another practice that was as old as monarchy and needed struck down still existed.

In the southern states slavery had become a way of life. Some lived in comfort on the produce of other's work, which they took for themselves. This practice had become so common that a significant portion of the southern state's economy had become dependent on slavery. They were fighting change, too. The growing industrial revolution in the northern states and in Europe offered an alternative to slave labor, but the south still refused. They clung to the millennia old practice of enslavement. The southern states moved in congress to block any effort which could gradually remove slavery from their way of life. The Homestead Act was an example of the maneuvering which took place in the national government. Lincoln eventually passed this act in 1862. The act gave land to people who couldn't otherwise afford it. Before it passed the South understood that easily affordable land would mean more homesteaders who couldn't afford to pay for slaves. This would have meant unsettled lands would be populated by those who were not cultural inclined towards slave ownership. Eventually, those lands would become new states. The U. S. government is set up so that people and land that exists as states equal votes. The amount of members in the House, and their allotment between the states, is based on population. The amount of members in the Senate is determined by the number of states. If people who aren't able to afford slaves expanded into unsettled territories, spurred on by the promise of building a home, it could have tipped the balance. The Homestead Act meant adding new votes in a way which would shape the future. The country would have eventually grown its way out of slavery. That's why the southern states opposed the act. It's not that crazy a theory. Some people say that although the issues have changed, this political maneuver is still being employed today. Democrats have arguably been working to stymie hydraulic fracturing and coal. If these industries were freer then there would be more development in the states where the resources are plentiful. More development means more population. More population means growing majorities in congress for these states. If you haven't noticed, there seem to be more states which typically vote Republican holding these resources than typically Democrat states. And, there certainly are many Republican leaning states out west with a large amount of land designated as government lands. For example, President Bill Clinton famously led a nineteen ninety-six federal land grab in Utah. The president converted lands holding low emission "compliance coal" to federal lands under the logic that this would make them off limits to mining and development. His side of that debate claimed that banning mining of this clean coal was good for the environment. There were other voices in that debate who claimed designating those one point seven million acres as federal wilderness area was a political maneuver. Without drawing a comparison between the issues in the eighteen sixties and the nineteen nineties, it is clear to see that controlling land and development has always impacted the future of this nation. Clearly we weren't the first ones to figure this trick out in our time. People who think they have something to lose with time to learn tend to find and use what works in any time. The proponents of the Homestead Act envisioned the country growing in ways which would relegate the barbarism of slavery to the past. Agents of the South also saw where this act would lead. The South was firm in their opposition, determined to stop the Homestead Act. They successfully prevented its passing from the 1840's all the way until 1862. The Republicans were only able to pass the bill after secessionists left congress. The passage of the Homestead Act at that point was possible because the polarized nation was now in what would be its most lethal war. Those of good conscience could countenance waiting no more. They matched ability with opportunity. The spoils won through the practice of slavery were about to be paid in blood.

 Grave injustices were ended in each of these two instances of polarized times. That's great. That's more than great. Each time things go interesting polarized conflict laid the foundation for a tremendous improvement in human welfare for generations to come. The first example was a promise of freedom for all. The second example opened the way to begin fulfilling that promise to an entire race within our borders. Since those times we've made it our business to broaden the application of that promise in successive generations. The positive consequences have reached around the world to lift people up. But, the cost has been very high. Obviously, the cost was not too high to pay. People judged by our history to have lived lives worthy of serving as moral compasses, like George Washington and Abraham Lincoln, did not shrink from the high cost. They served us with honor and distinction in the times of the Revolutionary and Civil wars, respectively. Their record speaks for itself. If faced with a high cost we must personally pay to win freedom for our neighbor, it would be a worthy and amazing accomplishment to follow their example. But, we must never forget the cost. Is it possible that we can do great good without suffering a great evil? It's a worthwhile question to ask. Especially since some say the times we live in are becoming more and more interesting. Personal willingness to carry a burden for a neighbor should not be questioned over the desire to first try and find a plain, simple, less interesting but equally effective solution. Blessed are the peacemakers, after all. If anything, a solution which lifts the human condition while inflicting less harm to precious life could be celebrated, could it not?

I've often said, anyone can complicate something, but it takes a genius to do simple. We need to do some research first, though, before we can find our simple solution. Success isn't a spark that ignites. It is a slow burning hot coal that flares hotter when attended. Perhaps, if we go a bit farther back in time, even before the founding of the United States, we can find a peaceful example which will serve our need. What kind of example do we require? From whom do we learn? Well, we need to start with a time in history when a culture was suffering from polarization. That much is readily apparent. But let's go deeper. It can't be just any culture. The culture whose example we learn from need not be identical. But, there must be strong points of similarity. In addition to a cultural example, we also need a personal one. We need an example of someone who served by working against polarization, even when faced with great personal cost. We need a success story to learn from, someone whose service stood against the cultural tide of division and brought about healing. But who could that be? I believe I have a culture and a person in mind. The time is not that far removed either, when measured against the span of our time here on this earth. The pertinent period can be found in the time since the birth of the western world, at least by Greco-Roman standards. The best part is that we don't even need to have the connections of a classically trained historical scholar to get our hands on the relevant documents from the time. The collected writings in question and their study are nearly ubiquitous. But, I'm getting ahead of myself.

In roughly the thirties A. D., the culture in and around what was then the Roman occupied nation of Israel had become polarized. Why Israel, you may ask? There is a great relevance to be discovered here. In the House

Chamber, where laws are crafted, a face is shown in full relief. That person is Moses, lawgiver to Israel. His image graces the north wall, and is flanked by important images on the eastern and western walls. All reliefs, including Moses, "…depict historical figures noted for their work in establishing the principles that underlie American law," according to The Architect of the Capitol in their February fourth, two-thousand fourteen update on their website *http://www.aoc.gov/capitol-hill/relief-portrait-plaques-lawgivers/moses*. These images which flank Moses on either side are shown in profile rather than full relief. They portray people such as Hammurabi, who is credited with creating the first systematic written collection of laws in recorded history, Solon, who is considered to be the father of Athenian democracy, and Thomas Jefferson. Whether they came before the time of Moses or after, all other figures are positioned facing Moses. That's enough about Moses for now. Hopefully, I've piqued your interest. We need to more firmly establish the link between the U. S. in the modern era and ancient Israel before getting back to Moses. That means we'll start with examining the similarities between both paths of polarization as they played out in our two cultures.

Some put the date of this highly polarized period to which I'm referring in Israel we'll be studying as early as nineteen A. D. But, most sources I've seen or heard put it around the early thirties. We'll be going with period circa thirty AD. So, that means we can narrow the window of time in which the events we will examine occurred to less than a decade. Thankfully for us, the time in or around the thirties is about as precise a point in history as we need for our purposes. If you think about it, being able to narrow the dates down to within a decade shows just how amazing the work is that archeologists and scholars have been doing. These events happened two thousand years ago, almost four thousand years ago if you include Moses. There are days when I can't remember what I had for lunch the previous day, and I was there for that meal.

What we're looking for here is the way a culture was divided. In its time, this culture was deeply polarized between two competing major political groups. Not sure whether I'm talking about Israel or the U. S.? Wait for it, the similarities get even stronger. The Israelites didn't always have the same governmental system as they did at that time. They started under the rule of a tyrant. They became free. Then, they organized under the thinnest coalition that could be called a government with maximum freedom and some theological requirements. If they had all cooperated and lived by the laws they had under that system it would have worked beautifully. But, they didn't do so well. Some behaved very badly, and as a people they were often embroiled in more conflict rather than cooperation. So, after a while they demanded a more centralized government power. That demand was fulfilled and they switched to a monarchy with the hope that they would have the ability to maintain the rule of law interiorly while repelling foreign invasion. That went well while they had a good king, but didn't go so well the rest of the time. Eventually, they were conquered under roman rule and ended up with a governing body headed up by a chief leader since the Romans had learned from Alexander the Great to let the locals keep their territories in check. Basic functions of government would remain largely the same, as much as the roman ruler assigned to them would allow, except money there was a massive "Property of Rome" stamp on the land. Any time that stamp or the understanding of what it meant began to fade in the minds of the people the Romans would come back in and stamp it down hard again.

Those who know U. S. history are probably paying a little closer attention by now. These people would know that what we started with was called the Articles of Confederation. Although the Articles of Confederation survived the Revolutionary War, a time when a common enemy and common task unified the patriots, they wouldn't last much longer. Shay's Rebellion from seventeen eighty-five to seventeen eighty-six proved this system too weak and ineffective. Our founders called a constitutional convention and looked back through history for an answer. They looked at Greek democracy and republics like Rome for the basic structure, but made some modifications to widen how representation took place. They looked at monarchy too, but decided the potential tyranny presented in monarchy wasn't the way to go. They also knew getting too close to anarchy would leave them vulnerable to all manner of ills, from both within and without. All these considerations and more went into the system we enjoy today. If you'd like to get a look at the types of actual conversations they were having I recommend reading The Federalist Papers. The Federalist Papers Number Nine talks about a lot of what we're covering at the moment. I'll avoid venturing into what some may consider a dry discussion by letting the curious get into that research for themselves. A good teacher could reveal the electrifying nature of the time. I'm just your average person muddling through. And, good teachers assign homework. We'll fast forward a bit and look at the end result of those discussions. We've established a bit of the form, but we've yet to determine how our government was intended to function.

Our system of law in the modern day U. S. is based on what's referred to as the Judeo Christian system of values. The Judeo Christian system of law was based on Mosaic Law, named after the Jewish leader Moses. For those who are interested there is a great 1956 Cecil B. DeMille movie with Charlton Heston, Yul Brynner and Anne Baxter called *The Ten Commandments*. It's not a bad choice to watch if you're unfamiliar and would like to be introduced to Moses in a dramatic, less formal manner. When designing our government the founders were heavily influenced by Jewish law through this Judeo-Christian values structure, also referred to as Mosaic Law, or the Law. As you can see from the quote at the beginning of this work, Jefferson preferred the Law as it was taught by Jesus, which is where the Christian component of Judeo-Christian come from. As I mentioned earlier, there are the useful comparisons between how the Israelites moved from relative anarchy to monarchy and what early America went through. When our nation ratified the Articles of Confederation they experienced some of the same pitfalls as early Israel in that this earlier civilization experienced weakness and a lack of unified power as well. Our first official attempt at confederacy had also fallen apart, and we determined the need for a stronger executive power. When Israel experienced the problems that come from not operating in a unified fashion they wanted a king to unify them. They chose a king over warnings and protestations about what a king would do once in power.

There's an interesting account detailing the warnings they were given. I paraphrased for brevity, but it goes something like this.

> The king will draft your sons for his army. Some will be forced to plow and harvest his fields, and some will make his weapons and equipment. The king will take your daughters away from you. He'll force them to bake, cook, and make his perfume. He will take for himself the best of your fields, groves, and vineyards. He will give them to his subordinates. He'll also take a tenth of your harvest and distribute it among them. He'll take the best of your livestock for his uses, and also demand ten percent of your flocks. You will be the king's slaves. When that happens you'll beg for relief from this king you are demanding, but won't find any.

They didn't listen. Don't judge too harshly, we're not that good at listening either. That's what power gathered to one person or group has always brought about from the dawn of time. There are still those who clamor to give a ruling few more power. It may seem hard to believe for some, but we can be every bit as stubborn and blind as people were thousands of years ago. Technology changes, styles change, but human nature doesn't change. They were tired of foreign invaders and domestic criminals raiding, causing problems, and generally behaving badly. They had some leaders who were set to succeed the current leadership and who did not look promising. They looked around at other nations which had kings and perhaps thought that was the expedient solution. The whole monarchy thing went badly in the beginning for them. The first king looked great on the surface. He had great looks, was tall and handsome. He came from a good family with standing. But, he was still a human with the power of life and death in his hands. He made some mistakes. His health didn't hold up, you could say he went crazy while on the throne. If you believe the account of the story, it could be opined this was part of the plan to let Israel know just what they were getting into by investing that much power over themselves in one person. When the right leader rules in the seat of a king they take limited actions within the power at their disposal to further the health of their society rather than ruin it, and things are good for a while. But, even good leaders die eventually, or become compromised before their death. The more power they have at their disposal, the more harm one bad leader can inflict. Anyway, after him things went great for a while. The next king was great, and the king after him did some really bold things. Then things went badly again as king after king did not live up to the examples set in golden age Israel. All this is important because it paints a picture of what happens in a powerful, tightly centralized government that can shift the pain of its mistakes onto the backs of others. The potential for awesome power and even good is there. But, humans don't have that great a track record. We don't always know what to expect from others once they have power over us. Most of the time, the results aren't what a reasonable person would consider good. In a society there are certain rights that must be upheld. If not, failure will ruin the health of that society. This is true even when we are the ones ignoring our own rights. The power that was given to kings in that time was power no person or group of people had the authority to give to rulers, even over themselves. The founders also considered monarchy. Some wanted George Washington to be our first king. He was an amazing leader. He probably would have been a good king. But, someone would have taken over after him. The people back then were experiencing the perils and shortcomings of monarchy firsthand. They wanted the unifying, rallying power to defend themselves but sought to place restraints on the power and reach of government in their daily lives. These restraints on government power became known as checks and balances. Each extreme of the spectrum ranging between anarchy and totalitarianism had downfalls worth avoiding which were weighed in crafting the U. S. government. Great political minds worked to create an enduring system which balanced liberty and security. As a founder of our nation, famed inventor, accomplished writer, businessman, international diplomat, and co-signer of Constitution, Dr. Benjamin Franklin was one of those minds. Seriously, any time you think we've got the market on clever cornered over people who relieved themselves in outhouses just look up the life of Benjamin Franklin. We've talked about forms of government and systems of law. If the representative republic method of government is the vehicle, then the moral law in the culture that system relies on to function is the destination. In order to understand where a founder like Franklin envisioned the Constitution taking us we have to understand not only the government system embodied in that great document, but his understanding of morality as well. On the topic of morals, Benjamin Franklin wrote:

> As to Jesus of Nazareth, my opinion of whom you particularly desire, I think the system of morals and His religion as He left them to us, the best the world ever saw or is likely to see. - Benjamin Franklin

> Works of Benjamin Franklin, John Bigelow, editor (New York: G.P. Putnam's Sons, 1904), p. 185, to Ezra Stiles, March 9, 1790.

That's high praise from an eminent figure. We know Thomas Jefferson was also one of our founding fathers. Among his accomplishments are writing the Declaration of Independence, and he was the third president of the United States. Jefferson was off doing diplomacy for the States overseas, so he couldn't take part in drafting the Constitution in the Constitutional Convention of seventeen eighty-six and seventeen eighty-seven. But, Jefferson was very influential in developing our system of law in practice, our governing philosophy in theory, and the thought on which they were based. This obviously makes his opinion valuable to us. We're starting to get an idea of where influential founders came down on the teaching of morality. We could go on, but we've got to stay on topic and I'm such a fan of giving homework. This is a bit ironic, if you talk to any of my teachers from high school. But, I'm also a fan of irony in most cases, especially this one. The problems we're facing now point to a system that isn't working. It is my contention that this is user error. Some people claim this is what the tech world calls and ID 10T user error, but I won't go that far. If you don't get it just remove the space. When things aren't working in an ideal fashion, it can help to go back the beginning, the foundation on which successive generations have built. Understanding the design behind a system and the intentions for which it was brought into being, can give guidance towards whatever correction is necessary. Thomas Jefferson considered the life and moral teaching of one Jesus of Nazareth to be important. So much so, that he attempted to compile them into a book called, wait for it, "The Life and Morals of Jesus of Nazareth." I would reference passages from it to give you an idea what the book is about, but the title is really self explanatory. Jefferson's interest was the life and morals of Jesus of Nazareth. It is hard not to see the similarities between the way Jefferson wrote the Declaration of Independence, and the way freedom is protected in Ten Commandments, which are central to Mosaic Law on which Jesus taught. Both have inalienable rights endowed by a creator, to use the Jeffersonian language. The Declaration affirmed the rights of humanity, the same as the Ten Commandments which outlined a free society and free lives in through that which they secure. Because it is so excellent, let's look at some of Jefferson's work from the Declaration of Independence:

> We hold these truths to be self-evident, that all men are created equal, that they are endowed by their Creator with certain unalienable Rights, that among these are Life, Liberty and the pursuit of Happiness.--That to secure these rights, Governments are instituted among Men, deriving their just powers from the consent of the governed, --That whenever any Form of Government becomes destructive of these ends, it is the Right of the People to alter or to abolish it, and to institute new Government, laying its foundation on such principles and organizing its powers in such form, as to them shall seem most likely to effect their Safety and Happiness.

There's a broad understanding of our answer right here. Our government in its function must be founded in our unalienable rights and operate on such principles and be organized in such form as most likely to result in our safety and happiness. But, let's not get ahead of ourselves. We still have to understand these unalienable rights. When the Ten Commandments declared you have a right to be free from being murdered, stolen from, or having your character assassinated through people lying about you these rights were rooted in the authority of God. When the Declaration of Independence claimed the right to life, liberty, and the pursuit of happiness, Jefferson asserted these freedoms came from our Creator as well. The importance the source of our freedoms holds in practical application, even to those who do not revere the deity, is that these inherent human rights we recognize are placed beyond human meddling. They come from an unchanging authority that no human can match, so no one can claim the authority to take them away from you. These rights are inherent to our nature and not negotiable or even debatable. They are part of the human condition. Any affront to these freedoms is therefore an affront to nature itself, and should be resisted with all the vigor that can be mustered. This understanding is clearly a moral one. Understanding the meaning of the Declaration of Independence makes it clear that Jefferson placed a great deal of importance on moral understanding. With Jefferson's approach, as well as others like Franklin, we can begin in earnest to consider the link between moral law and our very nature. This could get interesting....

# INSIGHT FROM HINDSIGHT

Understanding morality as being unalienable according to natural law is what formed the basis on which our founders declared their rebellion from a king and formed the nation we enjoy today. It was the foundation upon which they built our system of government. This could be the lead we need to find our answer, and begin to fix the polarization in our government and nation today. Could it be that simple? Has the answer been in our founding documents all this time, waiting for when we would forget ourselves, or maybe for a time when we were ready to go deeper in our understanding of ourselves? Has the answer been waiting there in front of us for over two hundred fifty years? It almost seems too easy. I'm used to working for things. This is like finding the hundred dollars you need to pay a bill that is due in the kitchen cabinet when you were sure the cabinet was empty. I'm not saying the founders didn't think we would go astray at some point. If you read the Federalist Papers then you know there were probably days when they wondered if this would last through their lifetimes. If you remember, their first try didn't go so well. But, the second try was a raging success. That success provides reason to believe their process is something we can learn from. So that's it, the answer was always available if not apparent. But, if the answer was always there, what changed in us to bring our attention back to those principles. Why in this time, and in this way? That may be a bit too deep, an answer for the historians to provide in later years. Let's leave a mystery out there for someone who knows better. For now, we'll concentrate on what we know.

 Maybe we need more than an answer. For example, we know mold has always been there. We humans missed the beneficial opportunities mold possessed for a long time. Please, don't take offense at my comparing our founding documents to mold. Just stick with me. How many lives has mold saved? Didn't penicillin come from mold? Until we learned to ask questions about bacteria, it was just mold. The penicillin was always there, we just weren't paying attention to it. Who wants to look at mold? It's not a pleasant experience. It took a lot of suffering caused by bacteria to get us to look closely at an area where we didn't want to look. When we began to learn bacteria caused problems, we began to ask how to solve those problems. As we learn more, we ask tougher and more complex questions. The opposition we face in life can take the role of a tutor, leading us to discovery. Granted, bacteria have killed a lot of people, and it still kills people today. We've seen a lot of improvement in health and lives save but haven't figured that problem out totally yet. The cost of learning through experience can be quite steep. That's the kind of motivation in an accessible environment which does provide an education. At some point we all reach a point in our lives where prior understanding doesn't cover what we're facing. After a painful failure, or a few, we gain a willingness to try new things and a keener interest in things we overlooked without a single thought in the past. An older teacher once told me that, after a while you don't broaden your knowledge base so much as work to deepen it. What I took from that is at first your learning is more comprised of new information. But, at some point you'll need to deepen your understanding of the areas you have already learned in order to learn more. The deeper we study a thing the more we learn about that thing and its connections with the world around us.

For those who are noticing that I repeat myself quite a bit, if I repeat something you should probably be paying a little closer attention to what is being repeated and the surrounding passage. It's like when the teacher writes something on the blackboard. You're likely to see whatever that teacher wrote on the test they give. Except, in this case I've either lost my mind and can't help repeating myself, or the test I'm trying to prepare people for is called life. Life is a self administered IQ test where anyone who knows how to look can see your grade. That's the kind of thing I say to tease friends when they are experience failure due to something right in front of them. You know what I'm talking about, you're looking at your BFF pushing on the pull side of a door and getting nowhere. They've got no idea why what they're doing isn't working for them. They're too busy complaining about it to you to notice the sign that says "pull" in big letters next to their hand. See, that right there is not a passing grade. It's funny with your friends, especially since you know you won't hold it against them. And, you usually know they just got done forgiving you for doing something even more stupid. But, that kind of joke loses most of its humor when you have to watch it play out in society. It's like the whole country is lining up on either side of a set of doors and trying to push the door on their side the wrong way. If both sides were to simultaneously apply their strength in the same direction, but on the other side's door we'd be getting somewhere. Instead, the leaders of each side have been doubling down by telling their people they just need to push harder. Those leaders don't want to enter in the right way, and they don't want anyone else moving past them in line, so they mobilize their following to keep pushing doors shut. That way anyone trying to push from the right side either gives up because they can't shift all those people pushing on the other side, or gets in line and helps push the wrong direction in the wrong place, hoping that eventually something will break.

A shifu I studied under taught me that learning rises, and then plateaus before rising again. He taught me not to be frustrated with the struggle when I thought I wasn't learning anything new. It was just the process of gathering my faculties and covering ground, so to speak, on the plateau before reaching the next elevation. Here's a fun thought. Maybe we didn't realize our answer because we weren't yet ready to ask the right questions until now. In our beginning, the nation was just getting started. The grand experiment of man ruling himself had just begun. We were testing a theory. We used the best knowledge available, and tried to broaden our understanding in a largely untested arena. Now, we've pushed the boundaries of discovery until we may have found ourselves on the precipice of discovery again. We must also keep in mind, given the dangerous nature of first-hand learning, that discovery is not the only precipice we're on. Many see our nation today as facing grave opposition. If we're not wise we may yet again be about to pay the wasteful and often tragic cost associated with discovery through trial and error. You see, a polarized environment heightens our awareness of need, but also raises the stakes. We could be in for some hard, costly work. But, as I've been getting at, there is hope. If we can find others who have plowed this furrow before us we may be able to reap benefits without the cost where they have toiled.

A note on hard work before anyone gets carried away and starts drawing conclusion based on my previous statement. It's not that I'm against hard work. I've been working hard and enduring hardship my entire adult life. I once worked a job where I had to walk approximately seventeen miles a day while carrying and manipulating equipment the whole time. I started working early, too. I didn't grow up rich, born to a life of ease. My first job was at fifteen. I had to work longer hours than were legal for someone my age to help my family make grocery money. That's not the sort of personal story you can really fact check, since none of the other parties involved are likely to admit being a part of what fits the legal definition for child labor. But, I'm telling you, for what that's worth, that I was proud to help put food on my family's table in our need. I did a lot of chores growing up so I was used to working. And it didn't last long. When times got easier for the family I went back to a normal childhood. I even got to play sports. My parents had to sacrifice a lot so I could have that opportunity, since schools were now charging students for their participation in school sponsored events like sports. I graduated high school and later on good jobs were hard to come by. After the Great Recession hit I stopped counting the number of job applications I put out when the number made it into the hundreds. At that time I had to work that much harder just to make ends meet. The point of all this is to say,

I've never had it easy. So, take it from me when I say that hard work isn't magic. The people I respected who set an example of working hard all said "Work smarter, not harder." That reminds me of a story....

A man decided to build a tree house for his kids. He started out, like many who have begun the same project, with a hammer, a tree, and some boards. The man wasn't a carpenter by trade, but figured nearly anyone could use a hammer to pound some pointy rods into wood to affix them together. This assumption was especially frustrating since every time he began to pound one of those "metal rods" into one of the boards, the board would just split and come apart. He started cursing the boards, then the hammer, and of course his fasteners. The tree even got some of his ire. It in the middle of one of these tirades that his neighbor came out of her garage and around the corner, a glass of lemonade in hand, a thick book in the other, and reading glasses perched on top of her head. She took one look at the spectacle and turned right around, heading into her house through her open garage door. An hour later the man was still splitting boards and carrying on his heated one sided conversation with wood based materials. Even though he had originally bought a large number of boards, all the boards he was dealing with now were much shorter than when the project started, and the outlook for the next hour did not look good. At this point the neighbor came around the man's fence wearing a tool belt and carrying a power drill. The man looked at her with a look of bewildered indignation. She smiled like he had just warmly invited her, and went on to explain that she would have been there sooner but had to charge the power tool's battery. Without further explanation she went to a board, drilled out an appropriately sized hole, changed her bit, took one of the pointy rods from the man, put the bit in the end of the rod and screwed it into the board without difficulty. You see, around each pointy rod was wrapped an inclined plane. The man had been working up quite a sweat, yes, but he was still hammering screws.

Some people believe hard work leads to success. This is not a true statement. There is no direct correlation between hard work and success.

34

There are actually a couple degrees of separation between the two. Hard work leads to the ability to capitalize on opportunity. The ability to capitalize on opportunity must then be met with opportunity. If there is opportunity in an area where you've been working hard, assuming you're wise enough to recognize opportunity and take it, that is when you can achieve success. So hard work doesn't lead to success, hard work, opportunity, and at least the minimal amount of wisdom does. If you doubt me, try learning an existing foreign language without access to study materials or anyone who speaks that language. Or, if you don't like that hypothetical try hammering screws. You can imagine how improbable success would be. Looking at the equation another way, perhaps "hard work equals success" is just an aphorism meant to encourage people who already know what they are doing. Perhaps the problem isn't the saying, but it is what we bring to the equation, and how we define success. When I look at the word success in the dictionary there are several definitions. One definition is the favorable outcome of an attempt. Another is achieving wealth, fame, and honors. Both meanings use the exact same word. Well, that could be why we're so confused.

I've known plenty of people who could paint a wall, wire an electrical outlet, or fix a c/v joint in an automobile. By one definition they were successful in their work. But, none of them got famous or wealthy from the effort, no matter how hard they worked. In fact, if they worked too hard and didn't work smart they could expect their bodies to give out sooner, the number of good working years in their lifetimes to be reduced, and the costly medical bills associated commonly associated with old age to begin earlier in their lives. What they got for their work was a wall that is sealed and attractive, an outlet that conducts steady power, and firm, reliable control of their automobile's steering through acceleration. None of these jobs will do themselves. Each job takes effort. In one sense a willingness to do hard work did equal success. But, only if you understand that you're taking for granted the skill of the workers, the availability of materials needed to do the job, and the knowledge it took to complete the work. Without wisdom hard work is thoroughly deficient to reach the end goal of prosperity which we seek for our nation. Wisdom is thinking and acting using knowledge, experience, and understanding. It is a keen awareness of what is, and insight into what results will be. So for the purpose of clarity I propose a new equation; hard work plus wisdom and opportunity equals success.

Our hope is that the troubles we face may be the guise opportunity wears to hide itself until we are ready. If we are assiduous in the process of discovery we may find success can be purchased at a gentler rate than the ransom this world so often demands in exchange for enlightenment. In reviewing history we hope to find experience which pays our price, if we are wise enough to look and adopt the good we find. Life is hard enough. Let's start with looking for a smarter way. Our conflicts and challenges have grown from a foundation which shares key elements with another culture. Because of this, we can find grounds on which to relate events founded in Mosaic Law. Let's look there. The moral understanding which was the basis for their law is the basis for ours. From that basis both of our cultures grew independently. The culture of the Second Temple period in Israel occurred in the past, where we can reflect upon those events and study them. It is often said that history repeats itself. Arming ourselves with the knowledge of what has happened before gives us reason to hope for what may happen from now on. In studying the polarization of that culture upon which our founders leaned so heavily for moral teaching, we may find that the answers which worked in Israel and abroad during their time may also work for us in ours. Times have changed. We live in the era of microchips and mobile mass media. But human nature doesn't change. So let's eagerly dive into the study of what has happened before, firm in our expectation. If we can find the good which prevailed before us during a very dark period we may also find the means to change our own destiny in our own age. We may find an answer which is not limited to the enlightenment of our people in our age. We seek to find tools which will change our polarization into integration. If we understand the arc of history correctly we may be able to trace the arc of our own history will take. It's a high aim. But, acting forewarned with this knowledge we will better know the work needed to change the tracing of the arc we will someday leave behind. Without assurance of what will transpire in coming years this is a necessary aim. Or else, as polarization increases history tells us we face certain fears of that which we do not desire happening again.

 Sometimes when I'm having trouble seeing what's right in front of me I'll ask someone who isn't as familiar with my task to come over and take a look. They will often notice things I missed because I was so used to dismissing those details as unimportant. Looking at how another nation we are less familiar with grew more polarized in a different time may provide us a new set of eyes. This could help us recognize the things we need to notice in our own time because they are the things which stand out against the unfamiliar background of another time. To study the mechanism of our polarization we need to learn how people thought back then. Let's focus on the way they formed their message in approach to one of their most highly contended issues. That should tell us a great deal. The points they choose to make, how they go about making them, what they leave out all may be important in our discussion. Sometimes a person will press an issue they are not as concerned with because it affects the things which do matter to them. The issue is not always the issue. Issues can be argued passionately for their intended side effects, or ramifications, rather than solely for their own merit. If you are astute you're probably starting to get the idea that moral understanding has a great deal to do with human behavior in government.

 Somewhere around the thirties A. D., polarization in Israelite culture was embodied by two groups. On one side were the Pharisees. On the other side were the Sadducees. There were other competing sects, but these two could be considered the dominant groups in that day. The Pharisees enjoyed popular support. That was their main advantage. Eventually they ended up becoming the ascendant group following the Diaspora. A lot of things changed after that. The Sadducees might not have polled as well if there had been polls back then. But, they had the high priest, which counts for a lot in a largely theocratic system. Having the high priest might be like having the presidency in today's terms. In that time these two substantial groups competed with each other for control of their form of government. Before we go further, let's look at the similarities. In our culture we call the two major competing groups Republicans and Democrats. We have other political parties, but these are the two parties which dominate U. S. politics. These two parties can be further defined by the most motivated groups within their parties. For republicans, the most motivated group would be conservatives. For democrats, the most motivated group would be liberals. In our lifetimes until recently these two more motivated groups have been represented by the republicans and democrats, respectively, and have come to form the base of each party. There's some tension between the political parties and their base from time to time. Motivated people are great for motivating other people and winning elections. But, once the election is won the motivated ones tend to be willing to pay more attention than the people who aren't as motivated, which political leaders don't generally like. That tension between the leadership of each party and their base used to end with the parties coming back to together to win elections as a unified group. Of course this all applies to those who are politically active. If you don't vote, no one in politics really cares about your opinion until something happens that motivates you to start voting. So our discussion will mostly apply to those who can be expected vote. Remembering our terms for the motivated groups in each party, our voting population is mainly divided between liberals on one side and conservatives on the other. The easiest way to explain the difference between a liberal and a conservative is by examining the issues used to by both major parties to divide the voting public and drive the public to vote with one of these two groups. That means looking at the issues which move voters to feel like they absolutely have to vote for one party or the other. When looking back at Second Temple Israel, the same holds true. There was more than one issue back then to choose from. If you'd like a fun extracurricular activity, try this. Compare the "Separatism" of the Pharisees with the "Isolationism" found in extreme conservatism. On the other side, compare the "Hellenism" of the Sadducees with the "Globalism" of extreme liberalism. The similarity is... eerie. But, for clarity, let's use what was arguably the biggest issue of that culture in that day.

I believe the division between the Pharisees and the Sadducees was seen most clearly when it came to their argument over whether or not there is a resurrection. That was their big wedge issue back then. If you're wondering how a theological issue presented itself in the fore of battles for control of government, you'll recall that their culture was now under Roman rule. The people knew the king was heavily influenced by Roman power over him. In hearts of the people those involved with the temple still had a great deal of sway. There were also traditions in the culture which elevated the role of theology in their daily lives. One might assume that issues like the resurrection are the sort of things which are debated in theology centered societies. Please keep in mind that there are plenty of people walking around now who are preoccupied with the concept of the afterlife. Whether you believe in life after death or not, what is important for our discussion is how the two groups each went about pursuing their side of the issue. Stay with me and I'll explain why a theological discussion of the afterlife in the time before Rome sacked Jerusalem matters in the present day.

Let's look at the Pharisees. They believed that everyone who ever lived would be resurrected at some point after death to face judgment for their actions during their time here on earth. They believed this just judgment would go beyond outward expressions. Final judgment would go to the very soul of a person, judging the disposition of his or her will. They would be punished or rewarded according to whether they desired to do what is good or to do what is evil in their lives here on this earth. The Pharisees measured this willingness to do good using a person's willingness to follow God's commands recorded in their scripture. They considered this as an outward sign reflecting the disposition of a person's heart. For this reason, personal conduct was most important to this group. They were known for making great shows of how set apart they were from those less inclined to follow the commandments. And, they considered the commandments which dealt with personal behavior to be the most important. Because of this they were known for prizing their own personal sense of purity most highly. Their main concern was that they avoid doing anything which could potentially sully their image. That was how the Pharisees and the people who believed the Pharisees evaluated worth. They weren't about to take any chances that could "get their hands dirty" or else they might lose reputation and influence. That approach to personal purity also shaped their worldview. They were known for adding traditions and crafting interpretations which brought them power while making the lives of the common people more difficult.

The Sadducees claimed there was no resurrection. They believed the most important thing was how we treated one another in this life. The logic here being, since our story ends at death the most important time to focus on is now. They held that this life is all there is, and they were more concerned with things which had a more immediate impact on human condition. That meant how you treat other people matters most, practically speaking. They were also known for being literalists in their interpretation of the Law. That meant if something wasn't literally spelled out in a collection of specific writings held dear by the Jewish faith, they felt it wasn't something they weren't bound to obey. That view excluded the traditions and interpretations of the Pharisees, which upset the Pharisees to no end. That approach to the Law shaped the Sadducees' worldview.

The concept of life after death, facing eternal judgment for how you lived in this world tends to affect daily behavior. If people think they are being judged on how they conduct themselves they'll act accordingly. If people think their life affected by how they treat others, then they'll act according to that understanding. The understanding people live with makes the more likely to accept certain laws and actions by their government, and less likely to accept others. The Pharisees of that time sought to leverage that first set of ramifications for the purpose of conforming others to their worldview. The Sadducees in turn dismissed the very premise from which those ramifications sprang. The way their strategy worked is that people would conform to the assumptions of their worldview because they would look for ways to invalidate the grounds of other sect's claims. This method is commonly referred to now as "Hobson's Choice." One side made demands of a person's conduct, the other side removed opposition. Both sides were fully committed to the struggle for power. Their prize was position, privilege, and the ability to systematize their worldview. The people of their nation were caught in between their power struggle.

Of course, this is a lay description of events from that time. Even if I were capable of writing a reference manual on Judean history, the point is to disperse the material in a way that will lend itself to eager readers holding it in their hands. To that end, I think it best to endeavor in making heavy material lighter. Anyone can complicate something. It takes a genius to do simple. Even a high estimation of my faculties would lead one to believe I have a quite a task cut out for me. So let's look at the big picture. And, if anyone gets picky I'll be playing the, it's my opinion, card right next to the, look it up for yourself, card. You can quickly see how the issue of the resurrection in that time was what we would call a wedge issue in politics today. It was an issue almost everyone found highly motivating which could be used to separate out supports for both sides from the general populace. We all expect to die at some point, right? Many people have questions, even trepidation as to what comes next. One respected group is telling you that you have to live their way or face punishment, and the other saying the first group doesn't know what they are talking about. If you don't think something like that could split a nation into two groups, consider today's debate over global warming, aka the coming ice age, aka man-made climate change. One side is claiming you have to change your behavior or face consequences from forces greater than yourselves. The other side is replying with the loud call of, "Rubbish!" You have to admit, it's kind of funny that the same side demanding gender neutral "inclusive language" decided to name one of their signature issues "man-made" as if women were either being ignored or excluded. Anyway, the ramifications of each side's stance on the resurrection trickled into every facet of life, providing channels for what people wanted to believe. Add the weight morality brings to any issue and you've got yourself a wedge issue. For intrinsic reasons inherent to the issue and reasons associated to the conflict surrounding the issue, this wedge issue could be used to separate a population into factions.

Ok, we know the how at this point. But, why did it work? The simplest answer is human nature. For a more involved explanation we'll need a credible teacher. Again, I'm just an average guy from the Midwest. The people who know me might even read that line and describe the estimation of as average ambitious. There are some days when the most impressive thing I do is tie my shoes in the morning, but that's usually when my back is giving me trouble. I'm only kidding. My friends are very encouraging, and I recommend you surround yourself with encouraging people, too. But, we really could benefit at this point from brining in a seasoned expert. We know we'll need a teacher who can answer the questions we've raised so far. We also know we should turn to a teacher who is respected on the subject of Mosaic Law. With all this talk about nature, we should probably choose a teacher who is a respected expert on the subject of human nature. We could probably use a teacher who can reasonably define what human nature even is. It would also help if this teacher was able to speak to the concerns in that time and in our time. That brings us back to the question, where would we find one?

Benjamin Franklin has already given us a hint. I'm sure it's obvious where I'm going with this, but let's go through the steps that due diligence requires. It's kind of like a math problem; we've got to show our work. Let's build on Franklin to develop our own proofs. We'll start in the oldest precincts where the study of human nature has historically been found. Years before philosophy, sociology, or any other "logy" studied the aspects of humanity, there was religion. Religion was useful, among other reasons, because it provided organizational structures where thought could amass and be debated. It functioned as a barn where we could store intellectual hay. Here is where humanity's early pursuits in answering the most basic questions of our human nature took place, and still continues today. Within this rational framework, answers were often found through the study of relationships. Of course, there were some people who burned at the stake or were dunked in water from time to time. Humans go in some very dark directions when they take on the power of a god to do what is right in their own eyes. Cullen Murphy puts the number burned at the stake in the inquisitions under the authority of those who called themselves physicians of the soul at several tens of thousands. You can find his article in The Huffington Post titled "The Top Ten Questions Everyone Has About the Inquisition," originally posted 1/23/2012 and updated 3/24/2012. But, this wasn't the only bad medicine in history being carried out in history. Medicine for the body was pretty scary too back then. Humans and mistakes, you know? The medieval period is a prime example of how high the cost of education can be. We don't always get things right, even when we know better. Sometimes, people with power aren't interested in doing better. Still, you're probably not going to discount MRI's because somewhere, at sometime, someone thought trepanning was medically solid. Don't look that one up if you've got a weak stomach. The middle ages were rough all around. They killed each other off from plague by dumping refuse in the streets when a couple hundred years before the Romans were improving hygiene using toilets with marble seats, and which were serviced by sewer systems with running water. During that same period Augustine was writing his "Confessions." Don't throw the good out with the bad. The good advancements and many of the ideas we have today were built upon solid foundations laid by those who came before us. People are a mixed bag. Sometime when you reach into the bag you come up a good quality. But, even some of the best people can fail to do what is good. History is made by people, so history is mixed too. I know I'm a mess, and if you're anything like me you won't be too quick to judge other people. Another thing my shifu taught me was to deal with people on their strengths. People are full of weaknesses. If you relate with them on the best they have to offer there will be the opportunity to see some real beauty. If you focus on their weaknesses you can tear down anyone, but you'll miss a big part of the glory of life. People are like stained glass in that respect. When there is light shining through they are magnificent. But, from when looked at where they aren't illuminated they are dark, ugly, and in some cases scary. Let's try to stay positive and focus on where the light has illuminated our human condition in religious history.

Perhaps two of the most important relationships studied in religion are: our relationship with the laws of nature which govern our existence, and our relationship with one another. Relating this study to our founding fathers makes it more apparent why they decided to choose as the basis of their claim for freedom, "the laws of nature and nature's God." This is obviously a religious phrase. If religious philosophy was reliable enough for our founders to base a system of law on, we should probably at least consider a teacher from the same religious background as they did. To use a figure of speech, why should we reinvent the wheel? We'll also understand their conclusions a little better if we employ the same lexicon. That brings us back to Jesus. Perhaps the most universally respected religious figure of all time is Jesus of Nazareth. Anyone who is reasonably rational would agree. Jesus is the expert on Judeo Christian morality. But that's not the only thing which recommends Jesus. There is the matter of methods and results, ends and means. In a few brief years of the thirty-some years spent walking among us on this earth, Jesus declared a non-violent message. The time Jesus lived in was rife with rebellion and oppression. It got so bad that about forty years after Jesus was crucified the Romans got so tired of rebellions in that part of their empire that they decided to end them by whatever force they deemed necessary. They marched in and sacked the Jewish Temple in seventy A. D. In 130 A. D. they marched in again. This time much of Jerusalem and the surrounding area was either buried or leveled, and the population had been dispersed. If they didn't want the people who came back to recognize a landmark as a prominent hill, they didn't leave it standing. We can be sure that in the time before Rome exerted its strength, if violent means were the answer then the public will to fight was definitely there. Many would have made Jesus their leader in war. But that wasn't the plan. Jesus chose to be tortured, publicly abased, and put to death rather than take up violent opposition. It may seem backwards to some, but there is a time and place for everything. What Jesus was doing was much greater than merely building an ancient military power on the Mediterranean.

Many died while pursuing the way of Jesus, killed by their governments. It was actually illegal in Rome to be a follower of Jesus for a while. To be a leader in this following was punishable by death according to Roman law.

There were times when the Romans were anything but lax when it came to discouraging the spread of what was being called a new religion. By Roman law, any religion that existed before the Romans showed up got to stay. Anything newer got branded a cult and stamped out. Judaism got to stay since it was older than the founding of Rome. Christianity was considered a new development. Christianity didn't even go by that name yet. They were just known as followers of Jesus, and after that they were called The Way. Roman law was against them. In the years that followed the Roman Empire was known, among other things, for killing. Many of the people they killed domestically died in very bad ways. I'm not even going to tell you what they did with molten gold. They were equal opportunity executioners. They didn't discriminate based on race, color, or gender. They "discouraged" practicing the message of Jesus wherever it flourished. That meant they killed you so you wouldn't do it again. I won't get into everything else they did, but they were very discouraging. It wasn't like you could get away easily, either. In their day, the reach of Roman power extended across what western society considered the known civilized world. But despite the disincentives, despite all the most powerful nation on earth did to destroy this small sect from nation that was no more, this way and this message carried on long after Jesus, the founder of this religious sect was brutally killed. The message of Jesus eventually overcame the message of the Roman Empire. Before the Roman Empire collapsed, as all empires on this earth eventually have done, following Jesus had even become the official religion of Rome. The Roman Empire converted to become the Holy Roman Empire. All this was accomplished without a war. What a powerful message. Speaking on the end of one's life, there is a big difference between dying for a just cause in civil disobedience, and killing at the extent of a full scale unjust war. If you can't discern the difference between a just war and an unjust one it is probably best to emphasize a message of peace. Revolution can be a very messy undertaking. If you read the Declaration of Independence then you know that Thomas Jefferson also wrote:

> Prudence, indeed, will dictate that Governments long
> established should not be changed for light and transient
> causes; and accordingly all experience hath shewn, that
> mankind are more disposed to suffer, while evils are sufferable,
> than to right themselves by abolishing the forms to which they
> are accustomed.

Not all revolutions end as well as the one which resulted in the founding of the United States. Even the rare case of a firmer future, the costs of revolution and the preceding offenses are so very high. Before that long train of abuses and usurpations plays out in our time, let's consider a contemporary example of someone who chose to do violence to his own selfish ambitions, rather than to his neighbor. Let's consider someone who carried as his weapon a message of peace and love so effective that it gave him the power to tear down injustice around him. Martin Luther King, Jr. is one of our national heroes. In our recent national memory he demonstrated the difference between personal sacrifice in service to others and armed insurrection. He could have advocated violent conflict in redress of grievances suffered by so many Americans based solely on the color of their skin. There certainly seemed to be enough fuel to start that fire. Instead, Martin Luther King, Jr. was willing to live a life preaching a message of love that would take him down to death. He did this, as he said in his famous "I have a dream" speech" in the hope that his children could live in harmony with all other children. And, he was also a follower of Jesus. Rather than war and hate, we enjoy the peace and unity that his life and willingness to pay the ultimate act of devotion bought for us. Ideally, we can hope of for nonviolence. The message of us doing violence to our own selfish ambitions so that we can live lives pursuing more dearly held and higher ambitions worked to bring about peace for Christians in Rome, and greater equality in the eyes of the government to the racially oppressed in the U. S. thousands of years later. Now instead of African American, Negro, black or any other name we can formally call all neighbors our brothers and sisters. This message of peace has been proven time and time again to be a successful and timeless method for societal reformation.

Polarization is a condition which creates separation. The most violent separations seem to have occurred in our history over injustices. The fuel of violating natural laws which were previously unrecognized has fired the most violent polarization which has ended in the advancement of justice, but on ground soaked with human blood. And, there's the possibility that it could have ended for the worse. Rather than an expansion of justice, we could have had greater tyranny. Those aren't the kind of dice you want to roll unless there's really no other choice left available. Thankfully, in the past at critical junctures we've received peace for our perils. But, before justice either finds our faults or breaks through the constraints we've crafted yet again, let us make every effort to find it first so we can leave a legacy of peace for our posterity. Let us be willing to sacrifice that which is holding us back in exchange for that without which we cannot prosper. Now that we've established firmly that Jesus has something to teach us, let's look at what he taught.

I mentioned earlier that the words of Jesus are available and widely disseminated. If it is possible, that may actually be a bit of an understatement. They are recorded in the Bible. It was the first substantial book printed on a western printing press by a man named Gutenberg in the year fifteen forty. Its texts, study materials, and supporting research has been widely circulated every since. An interesting note, the Chinese actually developed movable type centuries before Gutenberg. That's correct. The Chinese developed the first printing press. Why, you ask, did movable type not take off like it did in the west? Germans, Gutenberg was German, like the French and the English have a twenty-six letter alphabet. When you're printing with movable type you press one page at a time, making multiple copies of that page while someone else is laying out the next page of type. On the page you are printing you might need a bunch of "s's" and maybe a couple "q's." That means you can print pages and pages with only a few copies of those twenty-six letters in stock. The Chinese language comprises a list of characters numbering in the tens of thousands.

Depending on the page you're creating you could require multiple copies of one symbol. You can see how storing and retrieving enough characters for practical use could prove prohibitive. Needless to say the idea didn't catch on widely in the East. But, let's get back to the history recorded in alphabets more conducive to early printing, and a book that benefitted from early western printing.

The Bible is worth mentioning specifically. Included in this book are letters and personal accounts about our trusted teacher of moral principles. These were written by those who both witnessed the actions of Jesus, and knew Jesus personally. One of these people was a tax collector named Matthew. This man wrote his recollections of Jesus into an account, now simply called Matthew, or The Gospel of Matthew. Later on, someone came along and organized the various books, poems, songs, letters and everything else in the Bible by chapter and verse. Later the various bodies of work which are collected in the Bible were all referred to as books, so a letter or collections of wise sayings which each existed as their own literary work would then be referred to as their own respective book within the Bible. Some of these books can be very long. Before computers and word processors created searchable documents, chapter and verse was the means western minds used to keep track of what was said where in the Bible. That way you didn't need to be an expert on the system of mnemonic devices used in the time of Jesus to reference various passages. For example, if you were discussing Psalm 22 back then and you wanted other people to know what you were talking about you would start with the first line of the piece you were going to quote. That was expected recall that literary work to the memory of the people in the audience, and they would then know the rest. It's like asking someone to sing the first line of a song you know but haven't heard in a while. If that sounds familiar, it might be because the same technique is taught in speech class for reading and writing cue cards today. It is a way of memorizing topically rather than numerically. But, like I said, that's not something western minds in western society found facile. Sometimes, when you're not as familiar with the material the chapter and verse system is better. It's much easier and quicker than starting from the beginning of a big book when you're looking for something specific. There are downsides, too. If memorizing verses based on how they were parsed is all someone cares about, and due diligence is not paid to understanding the greater context, well, that's like memorizing the numbers in the Dewey Decimal system as a substitute for reading. What we need is specificity and context. Now that we've brought everyone up to the same speed on how to read the materials we'll be using, let's continue on.

What we're looking for is an instance where Jesus would have described the moral understanding of Mosaic Law, on which we loosely based our system of governance. Hopefully, understanding the basis of our system, through Jesus' understanding of the Law, will yield a clue to bring the peace and equilibrium to our polarized culture. And, I think I know where to find it. I believe what we're looking for is found in Matthew chapter twenty-two, verses thirty-four through forty. This passage describes a time Jesus ended up in the middle of a conflict between the Pharisees and the Sadducees. You'll remember we mentioned them earlier. As usual, they were competing for political power, just like the republicans and democrats of today. The Pharisees and the Sadducees often competed for influence by arguing as publically as possible. They would engage in heated discussions over the meaning of the Law. Each group was trying to force public opinion to their side. Winning in these debates would mean more resources at their disposal through moving public opinion in the direction they wanted to see their nation move. Is it just me, or does that sound a bit like cable news to you? The same people who were yelling at each other back then are the same types of people yelling at each other today, for the same reasons. We have our share of prime time partisans who are experts at getting a following through being outspoken. They do their debating on political shows, competing for points called ratings and public opinion. They work to increase their own personal brand so they can sell more books, increase the fees they received for speaking at events, and grow the public support that will make these and other activities possible for them in the future. It is big business, and it happens on both sides. Though they may hail from one side of the political aisle or the other, they share similarities. The preferred method for garnering ratings used by these wonks (the British term not the Australian slang) is trying to persuade viewers to share their worldview. The better ones are honest about what they are trying to do, the sleazy one are less honest. But that's probably true about every profession. Anyway, there's nothing new here. The whole process really is much less difficult to comprehend when you realize the discussions which occur every night on political news shows have been going on in some fashion or another as long as there have been politics, which is as far back as recorded history goes. If you want a simpler understanding, it's really not that much different from a sixteen year old trying to convince the parents to let them go to a party. Politicians want your resources so they can express their will, and of course party. With teenagers you want to help them develop their decision making faculties while protecting and nurturing their sense of self. When they want bad things I heard on person say you've got to break their will without breaking their spirit. If the kid wants to drink and drive, that's break their will situation If you don't teach them it is wrong and dangerous, who will? You want to prepare them for making decisions which will contribute to their happiness in adulthood. And, that's where the comparison ends. When politicians start thinking in groups and wanting to be emancipated from the electorate, you've got to remind them they exist as representatives and quash their sense of self every chance you get. That's a lighthearted way of looking at it, but you get the idea.

 The heavyweight thinkers in the first century were trying to score points with their audience as much as any modern political news show during sweeps week. Celebrity cameos weren't invented yet, but back then they had their own version of stunt casting. Their method of achieving this was drawing influential figures into endorsing some tenet of their side's worldview. Rather than dealing with tough as nails talent agents or paying hefty endorsement fees, they were very crafty in how they went about snaring people into their political contests. They would hunt down whoever had influence and start asking questions. Every question was loaded with peril if you were targeted for one of those crafty conversations. And, back then it wasn't about losing cool points. The person getting peppered with questions could lose more than a future speaking engagement or book deal. In those days political popularity games could end up being played to the death if you didn't have powerful friends backing. Before things went that far, though, the goal the major parties hoped for and worked to ensure was that these verbal challenges would end in one of two ways. First, that the influential person would support their side's worldview, or Weltanschauung, if you're a fan of German. Before anyone asks, I don't speak German. I just love the accent and a few specific words. Schnell is great too. Acquisition was a goal in these political struggles because acquiring someone influential would upset the balance of popular support between the two sides. It would also be useful to fold those influenced by the co-opted person into the acquiring party's side. Second, if acquisition failed then the major party would shift their argument to trip up the targeted influential figure. This would be done with the intent to destroy that person's credibility. The plan here was to do it in such a way as to decrease the likelihood that their target's influence would lead people away from one of the two main groups. That would leave the targeted figure's following with nothing else to do but stay home, or join another group. Of course, the most highly desired scenario by the acting major group was that the now embarrassed former influential leader's following would join their group. Either tactic could be employed at any time, making it nerve wracking, I would imagine, if you weren't entirely sure which conversation you were having. Really, it's just like primary season in presidential politics. All the primary candidates are up there on stage trying to influence the primary voters while trying to either destroy the credibility of the other candidates, or convince them to quit and support them by buying them off with Secretary of something or other, or even Vice President. It's an age old choice used in conflicts. Even drug cartels offer this choice today as a means of obtaining power. They refer to it as choosing silver or lead. They either buy you out, and then they own you. Or, they shoot you so they don't have to deal with you any more. There is not third offer. The beauty of the U. S. system of government is that our founders figured out how to mediate political conflict without the violent force that bullets embody. It's against the rules to buy candidates too. But, that's more challenging to police. The line between freedom of political speech and association which takes the form of political donations and blatantly buying results is one any number of those in political office have tried to bend, if not outright break. We have to stay vigilant against the blurring of those lines, since there still will always be people who are willing to push that boundary.

Jesus was considered influential with a large following. We would call it a grass-roots following today. Because popular support swelled the number of people who found him persuasive, Jesus was often targeted for these kinds of debates in a time before ballots replaced bullets, as Abraham Lincoln so succinctly put. The violence bullets embody, or in that time the sword, was very much still in play. The people targeting Jesus were playing for the highest stakes. A lesser nerve would have broken. A duller mind would have made a dire mistake. But, by all the accounts we have in the gospels, targeting Jesus publicly went uniformly bad for those endeavoring to politically arrogate or destroy Jesus. He was willing to die before being co-opted all the way up until the end. Incidentally, if you like watching hypocrisy getting called out publically, these accounts are for you. I bring all this up, not just to point out the rich similarities, but because one particular encounter between Jesus and these groups is especially important to our needs now, in our time. This one conversation is especially important for our needs because of the topic discussed.

When we explore the relevance of this conversation we're going to keep it simple. We could spend more time on the material. There's a lot that is amazing and profound for us to discover here. If we're not careful, we could be easily digress into a discussion of antiquity and get pleasantly lost. Rather than loose ourselves in past glories for a while, I'll recommend a couple resources so you can revel in the glory at another date. Despite the flaws, the culture of Israel was a beautiful culture. The Law was its crowning gem, standing out as a wonder. If you do find yourself wanting to seriously research that period, and are dismayed we won't be spending more time on it here, you could start by picking up a survey of the Old Testament. Mine is a second edition by Lasor, Hubbard, and Bush. There, you can find information germane to our conversation, such as supporting background information on the period of ambivalence recorded in the Bible in First Samuel, when Israel transitioned from a theocratic loose coalition of tribes to a centralized monarchy. As you will recall we discussed earlier, if you were a U. S. founding father who knew history, and wanted to find a happy medium between anarchy and monarchy, the way people reacted to their government back then could be considered useful. If you want to make a difference today, studying what they knew could help you too. But, not everyone is interested in books with sufficient heft to inspire mortal fear in passers by when placed precipitously on the top shelf. If you want to study the period on your own but favor yourself a more casual historian, I recommend "Killing Jesus" by Bill O'Reilly and Martin Dugard. O'Reilly and Dugard do an excellent job, revealing a great deal about the environment in which events pivotal to our study took place while telling a good story. In their account they describe events surrounding the foiled trap, which we are discussing at the moment. Let's continue with our discussion since the fallout of this Theo-political debate revealed answers to questions which have polarized us in America today.

Jesus had just brought the Sadducees to silence over that most important wedge issue of the resurrection. All of the Sadducees' art, all of their study, all of the time spent honing their arguments against the best opposition the Pharisees could bring had not prepared them for this. It would be like the average person on the street showing more political skill than a pundit who had dedicated their lives to politics in the best political think tanks. It was unthinkable for the ruling class back then, and yet it was happening. Like sharks sensing blood in the water, when the Pharisees heard their biggest political opponents had been beaten on one of the day's biggest issues, they closed in.

If the Pharisees could trap Jesus with a clever argument in this moment of victory over the Sadducees, they could then claim their worldview was superior to both that of Jesus and the Sadducees. Final victory was theirs to win. It was their moment to be had for the taking. The thought that a teacher from the streets could go two for two with the best of the best in the political class on the same day was inconceivable in their minds. No, they could hear the people saying it now, Jesus defeated the Sadducees, and the Pharisees defeated Jesus. They would have to plan quickly but soundly. Their tack had to perfect. The Pharisees met to put their best argument forward. They had to be hoping that at by the time people were getting ready for bed, they could claim public credibility as the last remaining viable choice for a major political following. This could be their end game.

But, what question to choose? It had to be a good one. Other highly educated men of who followed the same rigorous intellectual traditions had faced embarrassment attempting to confound Jesus before. After each failure by the ruling political class the number of those who believed Jesus swelled. The Pharisees would have to be careful but decisive. This was their moment and everyone who witnessed it had to know why they would put their trust in the Pharisees to run everything. To get that kind of broad accreditation they would have to choose something big. They went right to the source, the foundation of their entire system of law. They drilled down to from whence their society derived their very concept of morality. They went to the Ten Commandments. The question they posed to Jesus was, "What is the greatest commandment?"

Each major group desired to see the values they esteemed most highly carried out in the functions of their government and society. That's why each side made their intricate political arguments, and then struggled to defend them. Both Pharisee and Sadducee had placed the advocacy of their preferred values at paramount height. They had come to the point of excluding other values, no matter how valid or important, if it meant furthering their own preferred values. Whether or not the exclusion was intentional is irrelevant. They did what they did because they each had their own preferences, and struggled to see them implemented in society, just like in our time. Popular support gained from ruining the competition's credibility or by co-opting influential people like Jesus for their side could help with this aim. The question of which commandment was the greatest played to the Pharisees strength since they were cared most about personal purity. Everyone knew the first commandment is what Jesus would have to point out as the greatest. That was a commandment which dealt with the kind of life which led to the purity the Pharisees centered their claim to power around. By supporting that commandment Jesus would be supporting all the arguments which the people identified with them. If he did not point to that commandment as the greatest when everyone knew otherwise, they could use his answer to attack his credibility.

That is the way rule has been established throughout time. Depending on how a government manages their credibility the will of the people can be gained or lost. That will is the support required for a system of governance to maintain rule over time. Though not always recognized, this is the reality on which the governments and strength of nations have hinged for all time. Or founders recognized this reality, but were not the first to discover it. In China, five hundred years before Jesus confronted the political powers of his day, Sun Tzu considered public opinion one of the battlefields upon which war was fought. Our founders were the first ones who used this knowledge to establish a more perfect union, depending on how much credit you give the Magna Carta. The Pharisees and Sadducees in their time waged war on the battlefield of ideas with popular support as the prize. Through winning the prize of the people's will they sought to divert the time and energy of their nation into serving their worldview. This battle was their way of life for the ruling political class. It was the reason they used to justify their actions and acquire power in their culture. These were not the Rabbis of today who carry on the good in Pharisee tradition, teaching people to be good to one another and not generally holding positions of political power. The Pharisees of that day were competing for raw power. Under Roman rule power had been removed from the king in Israel and left to Roman administrators. That elevated the temple leadership in power, since their power had not been diminished in the same way as the king. As long as the public was pacified and the taxes came in on time the Roman administrators could be kept happy and less involved. The temple leadership had a great deal of power in their government, and much to lose if the Romans became grieved. Because they had become politically powerful in addition to being a theological sect, the power they gained was their means, and for some became itself an end. Of course, there were Pharisees recorded as being good people, like Nicodemus and Gamaliel. But, there were bad ones too who had taken over powers they were never intended to have. To put it succinctly, governing had become their business. For some, their standard of living depended on it. Even if they wanted to do things differently, well, there were some who believed different would be bad for business.

Those in charge believed that for business to continue as usual this man Jesus had to be dealt with. They didn't like competing for public sympathies or his favor with the people diluting their control. Most of all they didn't want anyone fouling their arrangement with the Romans. It was time to deal with this upstart. In the minds of the Pharisees, their question had forced Jesus, the greatly loved teacher, to a moment of decision. They were totally invested in their own way of thinking, and were sure Jesus would have to pick one of the competing, exclusive values systems developed by either the Pharisees or the Sadducees. Both sides had become very good at gaining popular support. Both sides had all the incentives this world has to offer, and generations of practice. They had made their business carving the broadest base of support possible from out of the people, and business was good. A newcomer like Jesus who won too many times at their game was bad for business. Co-opting the following of newcomers as the popped up, destroying their leaders, leaving their followers nowhere else to go but to one of the two major parties, that was good for business. Jesus had defeated the Sadducees on one of their most formidable wedge issues, the resurrection. The Pharisees were the only one choice left the populist following which had grown behind Jesus. He would choose a commandment on which the Pharisees built their influence. It would be the modern day equivalent of supporting a plank in the Pharisee campaign platform, or endorsing a candidate. Their side would retain Jesus' following. The Pharisees would be solidified as the dominant party of political and religious thought. The political balance would be tipped in Pharisee favor. But, just when they thought themselves at the apex of their power, Jesus again did the unthinkable and turned their game back on them.

Recorded in the Bible, in the book of Matthew chapter twenty-two, verses thirty-seven through forty is Jesus' answer. Jesus said the greatest commandment is to love God, and it comes first. But, living the commandment to love your fellow man is equally important in practice to the wellbeing of society. Jesus followed up by saying all the demands of their system of governance rested on those two commandments. With that bold move and deeper interpretation Jesus had undercut both major groups, shaking the foundation of everything upon which they had built their power. The political ruling class of that time created arguments that reinforced their own worldview and preferences. They used various parts of the Law to support their claims, each trying to gain the broadest support possible for their exclusionary systems. Both groups were going to the glue that holds society together and treating as their own personal bank account. With their divisive arguments they were making withdrawals from the stability of the nation, contributing to polarization, whenever they needed more stability for their party. For the political ruling class of that time, this was groundbreaking and terrifying. For many, it was also persuading. Co-opting Jesus had failed. Amazingly enough, discrediting Jesus had also failed. From then on, they began to understand loaded questions wouldn't get the job done and they stopped bothering with questions. They decided their best option was to kill him. And, by the hand of the Roman authority they did. But, as many people know, that didn't work out the way those corrupt leaders planned either.

Another man from that time period named Mark also wrote about this illuminating conversation. For really important things it helps to have more than one perspective. Mark recalled in his account that the legal expert who crafted the question for Jesus found agreement and common ground in hearing the answer with that man his peers wanted to destroy. Now that's a powerful message. I don't think it is too much to say that result is the hope for our time. In life, in death, and in new life Jesus showed us the power of living love. In love there is something held and something shared which can't be exhausted or taken away.

Love doesn't age, won't spoil, and never fails. By being love Jesus became our hope. If we merely acknowledge his sacrifice we have failed gravely. If we respond to his love by learning to let it resonate within ourselves there is hope. In learning to love in the way of Jesus we gain hope for ourselves, for our neighbors, for our society, and for the whole world.

# FOOD FOR THOUGHT

Before we go too much further we should get our terms clearly defined. If you look up love in the dictionary you'll see several definitions. Those definitions range from feelings like affection to activities such intercourse. This is why I feel the need to explain the chosen verb in the two commandments to love. After all, you might upset some people if you get it into your head that you're on a mission from God to go over to your neighbor's houses and love them according to the latter definition I mentioned. It may surprise some people, but this confusion is actually fairly simple to clear up. Having that one word hold this many meanings is a more recent development. The words of Jesus were recorded a couple thousand years ago. They used different terms for different ways to love back then. In the Greek used back then, which is a language in which the text was written, they had six or seven specific words for expressing the various meanings we assign to the that word love in the English we use now. To get what Jesus was talking about, our understanding has to match the understanding for the word that was used in that time and place. We have to know what the audience being spoken to would have heard if we really want to know what was being discussed. Without this certainty things would otherwise get confusing. Really, think about words we use in this modern age. For example, if I said something was wicked cool, someone from a hundred years ago might assume I whatever I was talking about had been chilled with an evil cold. Here's another example, something called gnarly could be good or bad, depending on the context and the way it is used now. That same person from a hundred years ago might think I was talking about twisted wood. If we spoke to someone from a thousand years ago they would wonder what language we were speaking, since modern English wasn't around yet.

Fortunately for us the language used in this text was very specific and commonly understood. It was the lingua franca, the language of commerce used throughout the Roman Empire. Much like English today, back then when two groups who didn't speak the same native language wanted to trade they could use Greek. At that time, if you wanted to reach the widest audience possible, or communicate in a language that could describe complicated concepts with less risk of your meaning getting lost in translation, you used Greek. These words which matter to us were recorded in the Greek of that day and had specific meanings which scholars have researched thoroughly in the intervening time between then and now. That means we can have a very high degree of confidence we know what Jesus was stating, even given the amount of time which has elapsed since. So what did Jesus mean when he gave us these two commandments that we love? The word love which was used in both commands is the Greek word agapē. This word describes an all giving, selfless love. The word charity when used in the context of a religious term comes close to explaining this kind of love. We understand charity as love in action. Charity is a kind of love which gives sacrificially and contributes to the wellbeing of the human condition. This is getting interesting, and a longer explanation is in order given the gravity of the subject matter we're covering. Here is possibly the best, most comprehensive definition I've seen for what love is.

Love is patient. Love is kind. Love is not envious, or boastful, or proud. It does not dishonor others, is not self seeking. Love is not easily angered, and it keeps no record of wrongs. Love does not rejoice about injustice, but delights when truth wins out. Love never gives up, never loses faith, is always hopeful, and endures through every circumstance.

Who wouldn't want to be the object of that love? I'll let you guess where I got that definition. The perceptive reader probably already knows. But for the rest, we'll just consider finding that passage more homework for those who would like to follow up on it. Those who read that and applied to themselves may find themselves reeling right now, recognizing the weight of the responsibility to love that is being placed on us and feeling a bit inadequate. We're not just objects of love. We must give love as well. Loving like this is what our teacher is commanding us to do, both in how we conduct ourselves and how we treat others. We live under a commandment to love like this. In a way, it's also encouraging. If this is our destination, who wouldn't want to be able to love like this? It is a useful exercise to ask yourself what it would be like to be known in the lives our families, dear friends, and others in need as love in all these ways. Here's a fairly popular exercise. Insert your name in the description of love I just provided. Everywhere you see the word love replace it with your name. Stay strong. Let's take this further by fast forwarding just a bit, to the end of your time here on earth. Pretend with me that your friends, family, and those who you have made an impact on in your life are giving your eulogy. A person who fancies themselves humble might say they don't want to be remembered. A truly humble person would say I want to love, and to be loved. I want my children, my grandchildren, cousins, nieces and nephews, friends and whoever else I've touched in my life to cry because I was worth missing, and smile when they think of me. I want to have been, and in my memory to continue to be a hope in their world and a light in their darkest hours. Most of all, I want them all to be inspired to go on to love that same way.

I think by now there is little question left as to what Jesus meant in these commandments to love. One way of loving covers how we conduct ourselves. The other love covers our conduct towards others. The Pharisees identified more with the first law of love. The Sadducees identified more with the second law of love. With a statement, Jesus

61

dismissed the whole system of exclusionary philosophies both groups had built on dividing the populace for the purpose of amassing political power. This teaching from Jesus breaks the strength of polarization within human morality by placing properly functioning society within a continuum comprised of both commandments. It was a wry trap that had been set. But, Jesus busted the trap by interpreting the Law at a deeper level than the best minds up to that point. No one had put it that succinctly before. The Ten Commandments sprang from two obligations on humanity. One is to love God with all you have and are. The other is to love others, to care for others, as you would be cared for or loved. So let's talk about love, starting with the first commandment as stated by Jesus. To put the commandment to love God simply, this means doing things God's way in your personal conduct. It's like doing what you know would make your mother or father happy when they're not in the room. You do certain things and don't do other things based on how your parents would feel about those actions, rather than how you may feel about your choices. Except in this case, your aim is to do things God approves of instead. It is a way of living which doesn't create harmful disorder, and helps clean up the messes we create when we don't conduct ourselves as well as we should. Trust me; I've made my share of messes. Some people only live this way in part. It's like kids that do different things depending on whether or not their parents are in the room. I'm reminded of the posters that come down off the walls in some college dorms on visiting parent day, but go right back up the next day. What I like especially about that real life example is that those students are old enough to legally make their own decisions. It's not about compulsion. Their respect and love for their parents motivates them to avoid things which would make their parents sad. Just, not enough to keep them out of trouble when their parents aren't around. Like most analogies, it breaks down. In my case, I never stayed in a college dorm. And, not everyone has good parents who portray selfless love. Even good parents make mistakes. To really drive this point home we'll need more. Since it is such and abstract concept to some, let's explore what it means to "love God" a little deeper.

I'll turn to the catholic website NewAdvent.org to further explain this commandment. The website is an online encyclopedia. I recommend it for questions on difficult or obscure subject matter, as they tackle such subject matter with wonderful skill and detail. It's not surprising. The Catholic Church is the oldest human organization still in existence. They pull from millennia of scholarly work when defining issues. That's a thing which is hard not to admire. That happens to be why I use this encyclopedia myself when finding better ways of putting points, or making points without error. Because this is possibly one of the most important theological issues which can be discussed, and I'll tread lightly to avoid raising any hackles. I'll be using their language here. These are the pages on New Advent I'm pulling the material from, in case you'd like to research them on our own: *Love (Theological Virtue)*, and *Christian and Religious Perfection*. Just search these pages in the search box and you should find them easily. On loving, God New Advent writes:

> The love of God is even more than a precept binding the human conscience; it is also, as Le Camus observes, "the principle and goal of moral perfection."

Brace yourself. Loving God is a precept that binds the human conscience. That's quite a statement. It goes by so fast. As a sentence you might miss it if you hadn't started this literary endeavor with reading Jefferson talking about precepts impressed on our hearts. As humans, it is the principle goal of our pursuits in moral perfection. It is established before the formation of conscience, separate from the conscience but acting upon it. This love provides direction for our conscience. The love of God provides a destination and a path on the road to morality. That's part of what the statement means that it would be the principle and goal of moral perfection. The answer is that it is both an avenue, and the end. Loving God in action is not only the way to achieve moral perfection. It is the goal of moral perfection. What, may you ask is moral perfection? For that I'll turn back to New Advent:

A thing is perfect in which nothing is wanting of its nature, purpose, or end.

And:

Christian perfection consists not only in the habit of charity, i.e. the possession of sanctifying grace and the constant will of preserving that grace, but also in the pursuit or practice of charity, which means the service of God and withdrawal of ourselves from those things which oppose or impede it.

That explanation is beautiful and succinct. It also introduces the concept of sanctifying grace. For those who don't recognize the term, sanctifying grace is a complex spiritual concept. It is a subject on which many books have been written and continue to be written. We won't try to tackle the whole of the subject matter, which we cannot do within the few pages of this literary work. We will confine our speaking on such grace to discussing those with a state of will which is, to a certain extent, observable through their conduct and which constantly seeks to do charity to others, while withdrawing from those things which impede living excellently. For everything else, we'll let the theologians to have their day. By limiting our discussion on loving God in terms of what is externally visible we can handle the subject without getting burned by the intensity of its heat. By attempting to write a book I'm already closer to Icarus that Daedalus. This way we can apply the subject directly to the intent of this literary work without getting distracted. In case you are wondering, in our lives this grace is described as something which produces a will in us to live out both laws of love. There is a drive and a push to live out both. When that invigorating action is absent, hidden by ignorance, or ignored due to willful ignorance such as is present in denial, the precept on the conscience is all that remains. To say this precept is pre-rational means it acts on us before we even start thinking about it. It's like being near someone cooking a meal that smells delicious when we haven't eaten for a while. You may not started with thinking about food, but your hunger and that great smell are working together somewhere deep inside to give you a whole new set of priorities. Without any rational consideration or effort being necessary, your priorities and what you apply your thoughts to will change from what you were working on a few minutes before your realized you were hungry. If you can't get the food you want, you may get upset, even grumpy. Thinking about how you want to fill your appetite didn't make you hungry. Being hungry led you to apply your mind, your emotions, and your strength to filling your appetite. You didn't require any cogitating to get to the point where your desires changed and you began planning to do some masticating.

This is a rich analogy, so let's take it further to better explain some of the material we've already covered. Either that or I like food. Both are true, really. We talked earlier about ignorance. Put fancy, deviation between the pre-rational drive and a full understanding causes a drift to occur. Desire without rational direction leads to courses of action which are driven by the strongest desires, rather than what is best for ourselves and society. So that's fancy, but it doesn't really grab everyone. Let's try to make it a little more relatable. You know how people get cravings for food? Yep, we're talking about hungry people again. We all get them, but pregnant women are possibly the most famous for their cravings. The weirdest combinations of food can sound incredibly delicious to women who are eating for themselves and baby. The child growing inside them needs nutrition that mom's normal diet may not provide. In feeding the baby, mom gets depleted of a vitamin or a mineral. Her body then starts going through its list of tastes associated with the vitamin or mineral it needs. Her body then tells her things you would never normally put together or snack on are absolutely appetizing because they are absolutely what she needs. Cravings can be a pre-rational desire that tell us how we should care for our health. Now, let's look at what happens when we don't understand our cravings, perhaps misinterpret them. There are food products that look and smell delicious. When we are hungry and craving food we may choose to eat them. But, these food products don't have the nutrients we need to satisfy our cravings. Rather than enjoying the pleasant satisfaction of a full stomach after a sumptuous meal that lasts until we need food again, we are left with a craving that persists or returns soon after. No amount of food can bring satisfaction if the food does not improve our health. The people who eat this type of food will eat and eat, gaining weight and only experiencing the fleeting satisfaction which comes from an expanding stomach. Eventually, they could suffer diabetes, malnutrition, or heart disease and eventually die, killed by improper use of food. That food may have originally come from good things which are intended for good uses. But, our misuse of it can diminish our quality of life, or even kill us. This is part of the peril of ignorance when it comes to things which drive us pre-rationally. We don't even need to recognize or acknowledge what's happening for acting in this kind of ignorance to kill us, quite the opposite, in fact. Of course, I'm talking about more than food at this point.

The first step to fixing a problem is recognizing and acknowledging the problem. And this is where many of us can get defensive. If you ask me about my weight I won't be very pleasant with you, or point you to the best restaurants. See what I mean? But we need to be willing to have an honest discussion about the problems we're facing in this nation if we want to fix them. In those predisposed toward the moral command to love God that Jesus described this means they are inclined to their own sense of perfection, and freedom from moral impediments in the pursuit their own happiness, and/or "cravings." This, right here, is precisely the point where society begins to degrade from the U. S. political right. Rather take in a balanced moral "diet," some people will misread their cravings out of ignorance or malice, to the neglect of the tenets which come from the other commandment. We're talking about the first commandment to love right now, but it happens both ways. In those inclined to the first law of love, their favorite "food" is to fulfill the moral requirements of the first commandment. They ignore "cravings" for upholding the second law of love, or try to fill those cravings with their favorite moral meal. The obligations which draw their moral foundation from the second law of love are ignored more and more as those on the right drift away from healthy morality. If you were to confront them they might quite confused by your accusation, or even offended. Remember, they have been eating moral food. If you accuse them of being immoral they might counter saying they are completely focused on morality. This may even be true, just not as full a morality as is needed to live a healthy life. That's like someone getting indignant when you ask them if they've been eating, and they respond that they keep a steady diet meat, but eat no fruit. Then they go on to claim scurvy is normal and healthy is abnormal. But, I'm getting ahead of myself.

This is where education on and commitment to a full and balanced moral life would act as a stabilizing force, in much the same way a healthy meal plan would affect us. We might not be inclined to eat certain foods, but we do eat them because they are the best way we know of for enjoying the benefits of good health. When it comes to morality these decisions affect the health individuals and of society as a whole. When ignorance and the desire to fill pre-rational cravings combine it is amazing what finds its way into our moral diets. Have you ever seen someone eating a food that repulses you just looking at it? The person enjoying their meal at one point was hungry enough, or willing to hold their nose long enough to get past their revulsion and make a meal out of that food. Eventually, they got used to eating it, maybe even learned how to like it. It's not all that consequential or important when discussing dinner, unless you have to eat sitting next to that person. Without the direction and clarity offered in both laws of love, all manner of actions harmful to society find their way into our sense of normalcy. A look at the highly educated doctors who worked in Auschwitz or the prominent and respected people who held slaves in the world will tell you this. We can learn, though. Auschwitz was liberated and slavery was abolished in advanced civilizations. The British have got a bit of a hard time so far, but they were allies in liberation and ahead of us on abolition.

Speaking of being able to learn, I feel my thoughts drawn to food again. Maybe I should stop sitting down to write so close to lunch…. I remember once I was out of the country for a couple weeks. During that time I ate nothing but fresh meats and vegetables. While I was gone I missed one of my favorite foods, pizza. A big, greasy pizza was what seemed normal to me, and I was missing it. I know some people are saying pizza doesn't have to be greasy, but that's how I ate it back then. The first thing I did when I got back on U. S. soil was have a pizza. I didn't even make it out of the airport. There was a pizza vendor in the airport, and I couldn't wait. That pizza was just like I remembered. It was so greasy the slices of pepperoni resembled little cups, curled up by the heat and filled to the brim with melted fatty oils. I ate so fast I could barely had time to taste what I was eating. Then, something surprised me. I was sick. After two weeks of the gentlest diet I had experienced in my lifetime I could feel that hunk of dough, meat, and cheese sitting in my stomach. Not only that, I could feel the oil, sopping the pizza like a wet sock and forming a protective barrier against all attempts at digestion. I eventually won the war, but that night I was definitely losing the battle. I was wrecked for two days after that experience. It was amazing that something that heavy and hard to digest seemed normal to me. Of course, I gradually adjusted back to the typical American fare I had eaten all my life, but with some changes. I use a little more sense now in choosing and preparing my meals. That night was a learning experience. It taught me something about what a person can come to think of as normal. I'm not extremely health conscious now. But, I did learn the need to not settle for what is considered normal when normal has the potential to hurt. In what we do and what we fail to do we help stabilize or destabilize our community. When we don't have a trustworthy guide in forming stability we can learn to accept many things we should never accept as normal.

The Ten Commandments include such imperatives as don't steal and don't murder. These are examples of good principles which feel right to a healthy conscience and begin to compose our concept of what is normal when common in a society. Because we are comfortable with rules like this it is easier for us to accept that through refraining from doing these things, even when the immediate results of such actions might seem favorable, we are ultimately advancing our own interests. A good person lives with the expectation that they are giving up these prohibited methods of advancing their own aims in return for something better. As such the commandments offer a more valuable selection rather than a limiting denial. They represent a better choice, to which our personal preferences might not otherwise lead. Actions such as those which are prohibited by moral law are actions we understand as ultimately harmful to the society in which we must live, all the time. Moral laws don't just protect the material. They also protect the less tangible, like our sense of trust. Other commandments, such as honoring a day of rest, contribute to our overall health and sense of wellbeing. This concept of a day without compulsion is another example of giving up our ideas for a better way. Honoring father and mother, another commandment, helps pass down traditions and provide care for the elderly. I use these examples because they describe how moral laws work. All laws are either moral or immoral in the effect they cause. That is to say, they either contribute to freedom and order in a society or contribute to loss of freedom and societal disorder. Laws which protect and contribute to freedom and order in society do so by upholding both laws of love in our lives, as articulated by Jesus.

The commandment to love God is personally compelling. It requires sacrifice, motivates us to embrace challenges, and make use of the gifts we are endowed with to their fullest. This kind of sacrifice required by the first law of love is a way of living which creates a better society through improving the people who populate that society. The giving up of our way for the way outlined as the way of Jesus creates an environment where even the smallest minority is encouraged to succeed. Living under the second law of love guarantees universal protection of interests. No matter how well someone does with what they've been given, the second law demands proper due be given to even the smallest interests of another person. Since both laws of love come from a place which is immutable they are enduring. The better a society does at creating balanced laws the more it creates an environment where all strata of the society find incentive to contribute. If you're having trouble conceptualizing the benefit of this effect, consider this sports analogy. Why do division one schools play at a higher level than division three schools? The difference is that the bigger schools have bigger talent pools to recruit players from. Living both laws of love leads to more citizens participating in the wellbeing of a society. These commandments demand a society guard our human dignity on every level. Even though something is being given up when people are constrained from violating moral laws against stealing and murdering, rather than having a curtailing effect, our interests expand. What about people who refuse to follow moral laws? Well, in the case of people who are only interested in stealing and murdering, they are forced to go on a diet because the junk food they are using to fill their cravings is infringing on other people's enjoyment of freedom and order.

We've talked about the first law of love. Let's talk some more about the second. The second law of love governs actions flowing from a life lived in pursuit of loving others. This one is easier to comprehend, but in some cases harder to convince some people to try. The concept of a God may be a hard to approach if it is a concept with which one is unfamiliar. Knowing how to love a being that needs nothing can provide more challenges. There's less confusion on the existence of other people. Walk the opposite direction as the oncoming foot traffic on a busy sidewalk and you'll be reminded of the existence of other people. Cheer loudly for the opposing team in the home section of a sporting event, or read a book in the stands when the score is tied, and you'll be reminded of the existence of other people. If you chew with your mouth wide open and blow your nose at the dinner table you will likely be reminded of the existence of other people. The real trick here is showing love to the people you run into who do all these things and more. That's the point where you will usually start hearing excuses. The first law is also a little harder see as a societal force since the effect is secondary, derived. I think conservatives take to the concept of trickle down economics so readily because they already know and practice trickle down morality. But, for those not so inclined, the concept of personal actions aggregating to form the basis for an equitable society requires a mental leap to accept. One can see why concepts like this would need explaining, and be gain popularity among those who enjoy working through mental abstracts. The love of we show one another, however, requires little explanation. It doesn't need to be practical, or even make sense for the efficacy to be self evident. Sometimes there is really no rational explanation for these actions other than charity itself. This is one of the ways charity exists as its own principle and goal.

Here's a fun example. Why do perfectly sensible people with no professional background in music take time to gather together and practice singing? Wait, I'm not done yet. Then, these otherwise reasonable people go out in freezing cold to sing in frigid air. It doesn't seem rational. Just breathing outside in low temperatures can be unpleasant, they're singing. And, why do people open their doors and happily listen to amateurs singing in the cold? It happens every year around the world at Christmas time. It's called caroling. The people who enjoy doing the singing don't regret the time spent in preparation, or the cold. Those who listen often smile and applaud these amateurs singing in conditions which only further challenge their performance. The math doesn't add up. Fun is hard to explain. The fun gained from acts of compassion is even harder. You can talk to me about psychological grounds and adaptive behaviors all you want. Basic survival doesn't explain it. The reason is compassion. Love is a means and an end in and of itself. We can strain to plumb its depths but will only find that compassion reaches beyond the limits of our reason. Even if it isn't always reasonable to us, charity obviously improves the world we live in. After all, wouldn't we prefer to live in a society with compassion? That is another defense for the second law of love.

The interpretation Jesus offered of the heart of Mosaic Law goes deep than anything I can find or put together. Jesus said the entirety of their system of law was based on these two commandments. And, so is ours. The moral structure undergirding our laws comes from a Judeo-Christian culture and heritage. With

71

that, we've found the understanding we've been looking for. We now know the "what, where, when, and how." With these we can uncover the "why." If that's the moral foundation their system was based on, and our moral system had its origins in their culture, it stands to reason that we can employ a solution from their time. The solution Jesus offered proved so powerful it thrived through persecution and ultimately conquered the Roman Empire when military force could not. And, it is readily available to us in our time as well. Their society traced its trajectory thousands of years ago in a vastly different period. The issues they considered relevant may have been different. But, even so their politics seemed to divide along the same lines in human nature as ours do today. It is astonishing, but that same trajectory seems to be working itself out in our culture. And, we may still have time to heed the wisdom of our recognized teacher before the time comes when our own divisions progress to the point of being sparked by either hardship or corruption. An extreme conservative is really just a modern day Pharisee. An extreme liberal is really just a modern day Sadducee. Can a superpower status nation in an age of jet planes and computers located half a world away have that much in common with a small Roman ruled nation in the first century? After all, these events took place in a time when the western world didn't even know the American continent existed. How does this even happen? The answer is human nature. It doesn't change. This is all happening because it's in our nature. Take a journey with me on the road to re-discovering our nature.

# THE ROAD TO DAMASCUS

You might be wondering what a dusty road that ran from first century Jerusalem to one of the oldest cities in the world has to do with today's U. S. politics. That's a fair question. Just to make things fun, I think we can even tease the question out a little further. We'll start by saying this chapter isn't about either city. The setting is the road. Back then it proceeded between the Israelite city of Jerusalem and the Syrian city of Damascus. We're interested in certain events which occurred on these roads. These events were significant enough that those in the past saw fit to record them in their most prized documents, and to pass them on. These events told the story of a person who was confronted with the reality of his convictions. When a person is confronted with the gap between what they believe and what they are actually achieving lives can move in a radically different direction. That place of confrontation and realization is often a focal point in the drama of our lives. The assumptions act on can take us far from where we would want to be if we only knew more. The decisions we make based on what we do know eventually lead us onto ground that is less familiar. Life happens through trial and error. Many times the less we know in our period of trial the worse the error which comes after. That's why when I start thinking highly of my accomplishments I remind myself the famous saying après moi le déluge applies to my own personal life. Regrets are often measured as the distance between what we've done and what we would have done if we only knew in our past what we've learned since. It may be fair to say that we rarely regret as fully as we should since we're always ignorant of some ramification. That thought is terrifying, but explains how ignorance is at the same time bliss and a danger. For a moment, this to Damascus was a place of revealing. Holding a starring role in our historical theater was someone who ardently believed himself in the right in his own eyes. His turn around moment happened when he was given a blinding glimpse of what his actions were actually accomplishing. These events have an allegorical quality for our own lives. We all have our own places in life, whether we consider them large or small, where we are blind to the consequences of our actions. When the proverbial blinders are removed we realize our blindness. We experience the terror of regretting actions which grossly violate our beliefs, and we can't take them back. When what had been believed reliable melted to reveal the real, that terrible place is where our star found fear is conquered through following. Hearts who witnessed this redemption were thrilled and emboldened by a message of peace. Lesser loves faded as true love was revealed and ascended in lives. It was on a dusty road, lost to time, that a man named Saul of Tarsus found truth so compelling he gained a new name. They called him Paul.

I'd like to introduce you to another historical figure. Paul, formerly known as Saul of Tarsus, was trained in the tradition of the best religious minds of his day. He was a Jew who was born into Roman citizenship. He was a rabbi (a teacher), and a Pharisee. Saul was known for his zeal. And, that zeal is what took him for a dark turn. While acting under the given name Saul, he hunted down those who followed Jesus. He was sure in the conviction that what he did was right. A man name Stephen was executed by being beaten to death with heavy rocks, and Saul played a part. Men and women were thrown into prison by him. Many were executed, tearing families apart over what they believed. Saul only expanded his efforts. With every breath he uttered threats against the followers of Jesus. Saul was described as being eager to kill these followers of Jesus who preached love and peace, I repeat, eager. One day, on a mission that would take him from Jerusalem to Damascus where he planned to place more men and women in chains, there was a major turning point. Saul was just on the outset of his mission. On that dusty road Saul came face to face with the realization that what he was doing was against everything he believed in and believed right. The message of Jesus outshone Saul's own aspirations and illuminated how blind he had been with a blinding brilliance. A while after he found a new way on that dusty road Saul began going by the name Paul. His methods and station which had fired his zeal were replaced with true, selfless love, and a name that meant humble. This humble man went on to write what would become the majority of the part of the Bible referred to as the New Testament.

Isn't that what we want for our country? In the eyes of his government, his party, and the authorities to which he answered, Paul was the right kind of man. It could be argued he started out with all the right reasons. His zeal, after all, was real. Paul's morals, as they existed, had informed him persecuting a group of people who believed differently than he did was a good thing. It wasn't until he was confronted with a fuller picture of morality that Paul understood what he had been doing and realized his error. This realization really affected him. It's hard to read what he wrote after and not feel that he deeply regretted his actions. Paul later wrote in a letter to a friend named Timothy that of all humanity he, Paul, was the worst. Paul also knew where this new way would lead him. He had been the reason mommies and daddies wouldn't be coming home anymore. He knew what his former bosses would do to him when they found out he had joined the people he was tasked to bring back in chains, oh how he knew. And, if his former bosses didn't finish him personally they would get the Romans to do to him what they did to Jesus. But, he was willing to live and eventually die as a rebel in civil disobedience because he had found something real. Paul had found hope. That hope Paul found brought about a dramatic change in his life.

We'll get back to Paul in a moment. But first, let's talk about the spirit of our people. The kind of threat Paul lived under may seem remote. But, there are still places on this earth where people daily face the prospect of dying for what they believe. Thankfully, the U. S. isn't one of those places.

But, it has been in the past. We live in security now because of the hard won freedom paid for by those who came before us. That courage hasn't died out, either. There are still those here willing to face personal sacrifice in the hope of preserving that which they believe. We also send people to other places in the world to aid in causes which help others even though the potential may exist for great personal cost. Recently, our news was filled with stories about a doctor who contracted Ebola because he believed in helping people suffering from it. That belief put him directly in harms way. It wasn't a normal, necessary risk for that doctor. We don't have outbreaks of Ebola in the U. S. Doctors and other medical staff members from the U. S. are willing to perform acts of service for those who are suffering from a horrible hemorrhagic disease, even if that means they might catch it too. We still have people who boldly go to offer their life in service of their fellow man, to do something greater. We still have that spirit. But, it has been a while since we've paid that last full measure of devotion as a cost of citizenship, rather than volunteering for it. Thankfully, the cost we pay to live out our freedom here today is less demanding than the cost paid by previous generations. We're merely paying the cost of maintenance.

 Sometimes we hear about heated rhetoric on shows, or read it in blogs, or messaging services. There are those in our time who see people with a different opinion as evil rather than just different, or even misguided. It is true that zealous pursuing of a misguided worldview can cause great evil. The story of Paul is a real example of what happens when zeal is misguided. Our goal, however, even in the face of real evil is to hate the evil, not the person. The potential every person has to turn their life around is amazing. The world might not be the same if Paul hadn't gone on to explain the teachings of Jesus in a way that caught on outside of first century Jewish culture. If you were to look at the monster breathing threats, and hate him instead of what he did, we would have never seen that zeal turned towards spreading a message of peace and love. We would have been blinded from seeing a man who changed so deeply that he gained a new name. We are stronger for every person we gain in the pursuit to craft a more perfect union. This is also true when it comes to the zealous. Even someone who separated families, dragging mothers and fathers down to death, can be redeemed. The possibility remains whether we are dealing with true evil or simply the zealous and misguided. We don't know the condition of their hearts. We don't know what ignorance now will melt into regret later. Practically speaking now, keep an open mind in the pages ahead when we talk about the other side. It is our role as citizens to be living examples, witnesses to the entirety of moral law. As we do this, those who want to do good things but are missing the big picture may one day see their error in our words and deeds, somehow, miraculously above all our mistakes. Then, they may apply themselves to bringing us together instead of polarizing our nation further. It is essential to our wellbeing that a non-violent message of love which tells the whole moral truth must be proclaimed, both with our words and our lives. So do be afraid, or give into the feeling that it's not worth the effort. Think of the hard cases in your life, the truly misguided. Think of that one person who upsets you more than anyone else. If they meet love on the road they travel, they could come out the other side with a new name. For that reason, and so many more, be the loving light others need to see.

After his life was illuminated, Paul went by a different name and led a radically different life. He proclaimed the message he had worked to stamp out. His education, experiences, and yes, zeal aided him greatly. He needed it all to walk the rest of the new road he had been set upon. In the course of sharing this newfound fullness of love with those he came into contact with on this earth, Paul was tortured, shipwrecked, rejected, and ultimately executed. Each time he experienced what he considered a setback, something we might think would be the precursor to a life of therapy if any one had happened to us, his zeal and hope combined to lead him to get back up again. Before he died Paul his body became a roadmap of the personal sacrifices he made so others could experience his revelation, too. On his path Paul would become the person theologians would later consider the greatest expositor of Jesus and his teachings. For those who aren't familiar with theological terms, this means Paul was truly great at explaining the teaching and life of Jesus.

This, and the example he gave us, is largely why we're including him in our discussion. Paul paid a cost in personal experience I wouldn't wish on an enemy. He had the deaths of untold innocent people on his conscience before he changed. He learned only after his mistakes were already made that he was wasn't living as excellently as we humans are capable of living. Experience is such a costly teacher. You've got to wonder how many faces he saw when he closed his eyes to sleep at night. The community that welcomed him was the community he had been persecuting. He was being shown love and acceptance from friends and family of the people who he had taken away from that community.

Looking back through history will tell you that things can get out of control quickly, and sometimes people will go about doing what is right in their own eyes. What has happened many, many times in history can certainly happen again. Human nature doesn't change. That means all the human elements that made the worst disasters in history can still be there. Learning from Paul's experience and what he had to teach is certainly preferable to repeating bad experiences. While the merit of this statement is readily apparent, Paul's may seem to be an extreme comparison. Please remember that we are in the early stages of polarization. We're only experiencing the first effects of a polarized culture, and without pressing urgency demanding action. Any solutions coming from either side in this cultural climate will too often be charged and opposed to the other side. When one side tries to implement their solution forcefully, maybe citing because of an emergency, the other side will push back forcefully. A few times of this back and forth and what happens to our patience with our political process? Polarization is a thing which accelerates the longer it continues to break apart. You see, over time the offenses grow greater and harder to overcome. What happens when civil boundaries start breaking down at a faster rate? If the thought of repeating an experience like Paul's seems unlikely to you, consider the wars and atrocities polarization has led to in the past. Paul was a symptom of a polarized era. He was groomed into his positions. What he did as Saul was led by the powers in his local government. We have reason to believe he did what he thought a good citizen should do. It is reasonable to assume that not everyone in Paul's life pushed him to do harm. Gamaliel, who had a good reputation that has lasted to this day, was one of Paul's teachers. But, it was a dark time. Some have argued that overall it was possibly the darkest in human history. There is hope, though. Like a disease, polarization has pathology. The extremity of Paul's situation creates a clear example of what works in even the worst situations. It may even have been an example of the worst a society can become and still be considered functioning. In one sense, it hurts to even think about. In another sense, if we can take a step back and see it, that's a robust testing ground from which to learn.

 Rather than count degrees between where we are and something worse, it makes sense that we should work to improve our current situation. Maybe through vigilance and forethought we can even prevent future tragedies. Let's learn from Paul, rather than repeating his mistakes in any degree. For that purpose, let's examine him in his own words as he explains more fully the answers we've found. Paul would often communicate with other followers of Jesus via letters. Because they didn't have email back then, letters were often intended to circulate. You couldn't just include everyone in an email address list and hit forward, or make a posting out of a letter for everyone to see on a share site. Rather than write several letters, Paul would write one letter to be read by everyone who was interested in a town or city. The letter would circulate between readers, or more commonly would be read to others at gatherings. It would then be kept safe until it was pulled out for someone who wanted to go over it again. This means such letters were written to apply to as many listeners as possible, and with the intention in mind that they would be kept for future reading. In that way letters were passed on to everyone in the community who wanted to hear from Paul. Paul traveled often, and was imprisoned later in life. Letters were his only option to stay in touch with all the people he met on his journeys. When he couldn't come to loved ones in person Paul poured all he felt, and all he knew that could guide protect his loved ones into his writings. Sometimes they teach, and sometimes it feels like you're reading someone's friendship when reading these letters. Given the richness of training and experiences that Paul possessed, these letters were very valuable. Where they specifically impact our discussion on human nature and polarization is in a letter Paul wrote to those following the way of Jesus in Rome. The contents of this letter marked it as one the followers in Rome would consider important enough to preserved and hand down, not just in their time, but down through time. Within this letter written to Romans of that time is included arguably the best explanation of the moral understanding behind the Law every written by a follower of Jesus. This letter became one of the missives recorded in the Bible under the name Romans.

You've got to love the simplicity of the lexicon for naming books in the Bible. This book of the Bible was a letter. It was written by one person to group of people in another city. Once you include it in a collection of works, how do you reference it? It's not like it came with a name. Do you name your letters? Subject lines in emails don't count. So, it didn't come with a title as we understand a title. But, as part of a collection in a larger collection of books, it helps to have a recognizable title so other people will know what you're talking about. We've got a letter written to people living in Rome so... Romans. I'm just glad the letter wasn't written to a Flushing or a Poughkeepsie, no offense to people living in those cities. It just wouldn't have had the same flow, pardon the pun. We'll now look at the passage contained here where we find a piece of the understanding we seek to cure our national ills. In Romans chapter two, verses fourteen and fifteen, Paul says those who do not have the moral understanding provided by the tradition of Jewish Law, referred to here generally as gentiles, follow parts of the Law because it is in their nature, referred to here as the conscience. Does that remind you of anything? It does bear a certain similitude to the Jefferson quote which graces the beginning of this book. There's more than similarity between these two statements. They are making the same assertion. Two figures, approved by history as experts in the moral understanding on which the government of our nation was founded, Thomas Jefferson and Paul, are agreeing. To put it mildly, that might mean something. We should explore this further.

I'm not the best at explaining things. I mean, I'm ok. I'm not terrible at it. I'm just not the best. The point being, when something is really important it would be nice, at least, to hear it from the best. So, I'll turn to a modern day theologian who is considered one of the very best, if not the best at explaining things. Turning to a more modern theologian is great because you skip many of the explanations necessary to understand their use of language. For those of you complaining about the inclusion of yet another figure from among the practice of religion, remember, religion opened the door of how humanity understands of human nature. They've been studying us, and relationships like how we treat each other ever since. They may be trying to win your support. But, unlike politicians these days, they can't pass a law to tax you. That difference in motivation leads the fruits of their study on us to vastly more accessible. It follows that one of their ranks would be worth quoting on the subject of moral law, especially on a figure like Paul. One of the best theologians of our time was George Eldon Ladd, which is why we're using his work. On page four hundred forty-four of his book titled "A Theology of the New Testament" Ladd writes,

"Paul does not mean to say that conscience is an infallible guide in all questions or that conscience is a guide equal to the Law. He only means to say that all people have conscience, which gives them a sense of moral values...."

What Ladd tells us here is that according to Paul, without prior instruction we exist with a sense of moral values. And, that this sense of moral values which we grasp is incomplete. We each have our own pieces of the morality big picture. At this point I'd like to point out that we have Ladd expounding on Paul, expounding on Jesus, expounding on Moses. Yep, that's how scholarly types work. The point of going through all is to unearth what we have finally exposed, that there are two moral laws undergirding the values which shape our law and politics, and that we each start with a piece of the moral big picture. I could have said that in a few sentences. But, this is like math. It's not always enough to have the right answer. You've got to show your work if you want others to be able to recognize what you're doing and play along. Like I stated earlier, we need every person possible playing along to really prosper. And, it wouldn't be much of a book if I wrapped it up in twenty-five pages. That's an inside joke for my editor.

 We act on what we know. If we act against what we know, morally speaking, we suffer the pangs of something called cognitive dissonance. Rather than get into the subject too deeply here I'll assign some more homework. I recommend those who are interested to look up Leon Festinger's 1957 Theory of Cognitive Dissonance. That work goes into much more detail, but I'll try to sum it up for the casual reader. This is the short form of how I explain it. Life forces us to make choices. Living with some choices hurts more than others, depending on the beliefs we hold. We have to change something as pains compile and compete for the direction our lives take. Think of a person who steals to feed his or her family. That person might have said stealing is wrong before being put into that situation. But, if you asked them in that moment they would likely say they're not stealing they're feeding their family. And, they make themselves believe it. Or, they would say they no longer have a problem with stealing. Or, they might work to find a way to stop stealing to feed their family. Of course, we all have a responsibility to create a society where that situation doesn't happen. When someone is left no other options and is forced to choose between starvation and thievery, we've failed them as much as they've failed us. As an extreme example, however, it illustrates the moral choices people make every day and how they want their actions to match up with their beliefs. We may be starting to better understand the linkage between political practices in a society and what Jefferson was talking about when he referred to moral precepts. It will get even clearer as we go. Our choices, when repeated over time and put through the process of attempting to gain what Festinger referred to as cognitive consistency, over time play an important role in conscience formation. Some of the moral beliefs we hold are harder to act contrary to than others. The beliefs we believe in deeply tend to be more resilient against rationalization or change. These parts of our conscience continue to influence our process of making decisions over the course of our lives. Our most deeply held beliefs are important to us, and we will make sacrifices to preserve them. That includes when we are placed in situations which require weighing the assumptions we've made based on one belief against another. The less we understand morality, the more we can be made to believe that the beliefs we care less for can be opposed to and must be sacrificed to preserve the beliefs we hold most dear. That makes sense in light of Paul and Ladd if you naturally have a bigger part of the full morality picture in one area than another. It also makes sense that if you know more about one area than another you'll endeavor act in accordance with what you know. We want to preserve our sense of normalcy as well as avoid the anguish and internal conflict caused by cognitive dissonance. We'll live in such a way that we believe will lead to the most satisfaction and least cognitive dissonance possible.

 Without guidance in the areas of morality we're left to act through trial and error. That process incurs all the anguish associated with erring in areas about which we care deeply. Over time, a person would be likely to develop the parts of the moral big picture they are more naturally attracted to over other areas. People are generally willing to suffer the downside of learning through experience while they are pursuing or opposing the things about which they feel are important. That willingness evaporates like water in the New Mexico sun when they suffer for things they do not find even mildly concerning. Of course, if we get too close to what matters to us most deeply and we don't know how to approach them we can shy away, or become belligerent. I think many of us have known parent and their adult child who escalate their conflicts explosively because the have so much in common. The parent sees the parts of themselves which affect them most deeply in their children. It can be an unnerving experience. The same thing happens in politics when the issues we care most about come up. This avoidance of the sensitive and apathy on the other side bound the band of where we deliberate and make our daily decisions. Within this band we develop ideas and explore new ones. When you plot the bands of the politically active on either side of the ideological divide it creates a bell curve defining the area where we are willing to function daily, the areas we care most about, and in the middle is the line of balance. Just off this line on either side is where the wedge issues reside. We'll talk more about those later. You can see the chart laid on the following page.

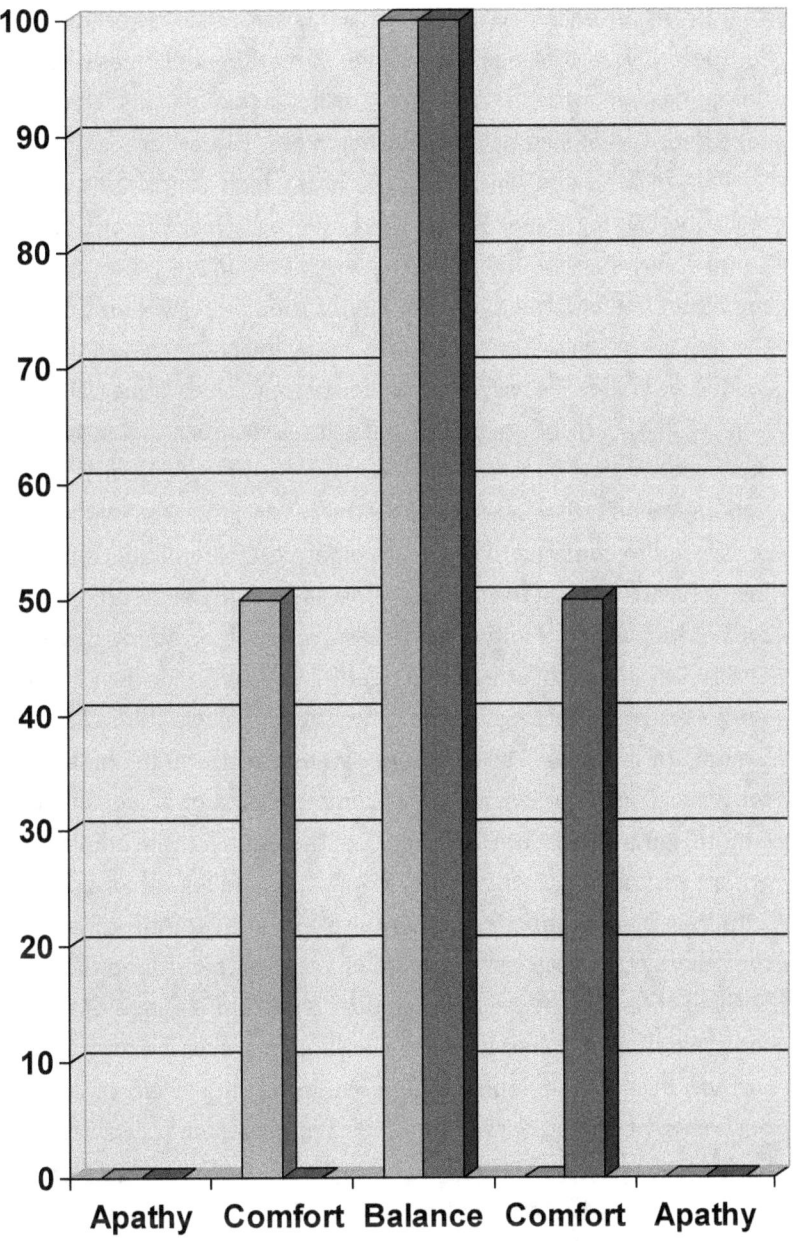

Some topics and actions are avoided because making mistakes in those moral areas would hurt too much for us to bear. Other areas are avoided because we really don't care about them. Somewhere in the middle we gain the experience necessary to make wise decisions and function competently. At that point ignorance of morality becomes a self-defeating cage into which we humans get lock ourselves. The key to our cage becomes locked beyond our reach because we are our own jailors. It is our own decisions which form the bars which imprison us within the bell curve. Our ignorance makes us blind to even seeing the cage, let alone how we are building it with every decision we make. The greater our ignorance and willingness to ignore the things we don't want grows the larger our blindness grows with it. A blind spot that might have once hidden a small crack will grow over time and generations to hide an entire house full of corruption. Even a once great society can develop massive blind spots where their society begins to crumble. Segments of the population on either side won't do the hard but necessary things for prosperity to continue in the areas where they are blind. Our morality is the resource we pull from to craft the values we use to prosper in every area of life, whether in the home or at work. Think about a good work ethic which leads to a clean and healthy bathroom, or the company values which protect against harassment. Where do things like this come from if not morality? What happens when the moral understanding that protects against harassment, for example, is lost to an advancing tide of cultural ignorance? Entire groups become prey in the workplace. Other groups become predators. Both groups become less productive or withdraw from productive activity altogether. Everyone is distracted from their work by the sad human drama happening all around them. But, nothing gets done because not enough people are aware of the severity the problem poses, and of those who are aware, some just think that's the way it is. Some people won't even engage in the workplace for fear of becoming victims of harassment. I picked harassment as an example because everyone with a modicum of sense agrees that all kinds of harassment are harmful, but society didn't always police harassment as well as we do today. If you compare the culture depicted in my example side by side with a moral culture where rights are universally protected and everyone is free to participate then the moral culture wins in productivity, in addition to enjoying the superior ingenuity which comes in part from having a larger talent pool of engaged individuals. When you consider this example playing out across the fabric of our nation in every social group you gain a better understanding of how morality affects every area of life. A culture does not even need to be immoral to experience decay. A culture need only be sufficiently ignorant of morality throughout their population to bring the business of governing that society to an eventual impasse between groups operating on opposing ends of the morality bell curve. You see, half of that bell curve representing the moral comfort zone of society as a whole is red, and the other half of that curve is blue.

Enlightenment is a lofty goal, but we are also seeing how it is an inevitable necessity. Each new generation is born without the benefit of the prior generation's learning unless they encounter it. The cycle of life continues and new generations are born and follow their predecessors through the stages of life. Rather than lose understanding to the advance of time, leaving our posterity facing a costly mortgage to claim knowledge we have lost, we have in our time a responsibility to provide the possibility of a better future for those who come after us. Moral understanding can be passed down through the generations in a number of ways. One of the ways societies have learned to pass on a roadmap of our beliefs is through traditions, passed from an older more experienced generation to a younger generation. Traditions can pass down moral knowledge, revealing more of the big picture than a member of the younger generation might initially start with. That means they will more clearly recognize and understand their own beliefs and the causes of cognitive dissonance in themselves and in others. The hope is that the younger generation won't have to learn the hard way, and the older generation won't have to be part of a society which is impoverished from paying the high cost of education with each new generation. A more formal means of passing on might be what we refer to as education. Education is a process we're all familiar with, since school is a legal imperative, and there are schools in all levels of education which provide excellent moral information. Without enlightening forces like education, first hand experience, or the cultural push for adherence provided by tradition, people tend to make decisions on whatever combination of desires and beliefs is strongest within them. They learn by trial and error, changing their actions, their perception of their actions, or their beliefs as they go. People move forward by mentally marking the lines which cause the pain of cognitive dissonance, all too often after they have crossed those lines and suffered anguish. If it sounds like a messy way to live life, that's because it is. All it takes to live with pain is to believe in a moral value, and act contrary to that belief. A person in that situation will have some things to figure out. They can get so wrapped up in that painful process, depending on how their actions affect them, that they don't enjoy the richness and satisfaction of life. It is easy to understand how that hurts. It's a messy way to learn. We're not perfect, and we will always make mistakes. But, shouldn't we mitigate the impact of mistakes as much as possible in society through offering education and training in ways to live life that don't hurt? Shouldn't we venerate that message and way of living? If we pay the high cost of experiential education over and over again with each passing generation it will bankrupt our society in tangible ways. Paul explained there are beliefs in morality we posses naturally as well as a larger understanding we have to embrace through experience. Specifically, Paul points to embracing the fuller conception of morality contained in the Law, even if we cannot hope to achieve moral perfection on our own. There is a purpose in life for coming to the place where we personally agree, at the level of our most deeply held convictions, that living morally is good. The premise here is that the fuller our shared moral image becomes, the happier a society will be. Of course, Paul argues that even if we know what to do, we need help living it. There's plenty of room for grace here. But, exploring that dynamic would take us down the path of a religious apologetic. This is a book on polarization and human nature. I encourage you to read the rest of Paul's letter to the Romans if you are interested in the theological argument concerning the disparity between what we know and what we do. The book you are currently reading is targeted to increase what we know. What we do from there will be, at least in part, up to you.

Picking up where we left off, were talking about principles which may have previously seemed ethereal, but, when discussed and applied to reason make sense. It's about what matters to us. We create laws based on what matters to us. Where does what matters to us come from? That's where morality comes into play. There is a step that comes before what is covered in modern behavioral science, such as what is used to create cognitive and personality inventories. That science studies the building blocks of personality which come from a natural place. But, this understanding morality could be even more basic. This comparison is the difference between talking about electrons and quarks. The concept we're discussing comes before the formation of the conscience. Values are then informed by the interaction between the conscience and our experience. If we are to believe Jefferson, Paul, and Ladd, our initial moral understanding and primary moral focus is something that happens before we have noteworthy experiences. It is something every human being is born with in some way or another, and is resistant to change from there. We're talking a pre-rational, pre-experiential, resilient influence on our belief structure. It is a predisposition. Upon this predisposition, as adults, we build our sense of what matters enough to be enforced through the power of government. Before tradition or other forms of conscience formation, our very nature informs our values. As to whether one should endeavor to fill the gaps in their moral understanding, Paul and Ladd agree on the need to inform the conscience beyond its original state. Every person has their own piece of the moral puzzle that they can learn to be the best at living. We learn from example. The best hope we have for our society is ourselves and our neighbors living a rich and satisfying life that comes from living out the good values that we hold dear, and learning from the good examples we see around us. Any obstacle which creates division among people of good conscience is an obstacle to fulfillment, the health the greater society, and our own happy ending.

# THE FRIED CHICKEN CLAUSE

Why do we have politicians? And why on earth do we let them organize? There has to be a compelling reason, because I can't imagine any sane person who would allow them otherwise. Given, there must be a system by which the basic functions of government are directed. To get big things done there has to be consensus, or at least a plurality that everyone agrees to live with. To achieve that agreement there have to be people who can come up with the terms of what we're agreeing to do. One person can't just run things for everyone else. That method has been tried many times throughout history and it always ends badly, given enough time. Doing things differently requires a way of getting as many stakeholders informed and involved in the decisions being made as possible. Organization will be necessary at some level to make this happen. People can't be leaving their jobs all the time to answer every little question of how to organize a nation or nothing would get done. That means representation would have to be a part of the organizing at some point. I'm still waiting for the next Jefferson who will figure out how to skip the involving politicians altogether. For now, they seem necessary unless you'd like to spend all your time on Capitol Hill handling the work of organizing a nation, along with roughly three hundred million of your closest friends. I can only imagine the traffic jams. I think I'd much rather pass on that way of government. It is still a reality, however, that we do need at least the spirit of consensus. How do we build consensus? How do we create harmony and protects rights while getting things done without our system of government spiraling out of control? I think that's something which comes in several stages.

All the stakeholders concerns need to be identified and addressed. That means everyone of voting age who is motivated enough to express their political will through a ballot. To accomplish this, representatives need to be elected. To keep their jobs, they will need to get reelected. That way they have an incentive to know what matters to us and how the people who will be voting for them are thinking. The system has to represent each group of voters fairly compared to other groups of voters. Otherwise, the unfairly treated groups won't support decisions and there will be no consensus. That means there have to be limits on how many representatives are elected. Limits mean the potential for more candidates than there are open positions as our representative. We will want the best person for the job, so that means the candidates will have to compete. They will have to address issues that motivate their voters in order to rally support. So then, what kind of behavior do we reward with the investiture of our combined political power? Some politicians merely pay lip service to whatever will get them elected. Others actually have specific goals they plan to accomplish while in office. We don't always pay attention to the ramifications of the actions the take with the intention of staying in office while maintaining power as a group. We pay attention to our lives, our dreams, our aspirations. Meanwhile, they pay attention to us. They watch us, even when we're not paying attention. When we hold them accountable for their actions, under the threat of losing their job, they usually stay focused on the good work of running a nation. Either that or we fire them by voting for a challenger who will do good work. Usually, electing challengers in primary elections who don't have the same political connections previous office holder will send the clearest message of dissatisfaction. But, to even know who is running in a primary we have to be paying attention to them. When we become distracted, that is the point where focus starts to shift. It began with us sending them to do what we want. That's the way our government is meant to work. We determine the work that they do for us as our representatives. But, under this system when we stop paying attention we are left with politicians in power who are still experts at finding what motivates us. If we're not actively directing them and providing oversight for how they use their acumen there's nothing to determine how they use their ability to motivate us but their own beliefs and ambitions. Our mighty juggernaut of a nation, which has survived hardship and international competition to rise to the status of superpower, hangs on a fragile reality. Our attentiveness is all that protects our rights and assures our liberty will not turn into tyranny.

That may seem like a bit of a leap to some. But, consider the political parties. The very concept of political parties rests on the effectiveness of the party's concerted effort to divide large numbers of the population into groups of people who will vote along party lines. If that dynamic were not in effect there wouldn't be political parties. That says something by itself. When our focus is on politicians the division that occurs is about dividing problems into more manageable portions. Diverse voices are included in offering solutions because the politicians are held accountable for producing the best possible solutions. Politics works well for the people when division is an organizational strategy employed to prioritize issues and methods. We direct the focus of politicians toward dividing and conquering what we define as the problems facing the nation. While we are paying attention there is little room for them to herd us. They may know what we find motivating, but if they don't use that information to our approval we find representatives who will. People don't generally like being used or manipulated, so when they notice politicians trying to use the people's concerted will for their own gain there are usually consequences. When politicians try to take us in a direction we don't want to go, an informed nation will call them on it. At that point the politicians can either stop offending or get voted out the next election. But, when we stop paying attention, the politicians are allowed room to shift their focus from the priorities we define to the problems they face, namely getting reelected. These experts at dividing and conquering turn their motivational skills toward dividing us. That's when we begin living like a conquered people. When we complain, they give us excuses. If we aren't up to speed we don't know whether to take the excuses seriously, or use them as grounds for dismissing an undesirable politician. When there are enough people who don't know how to recognize a lousy excuse the people taking lousy seriously begin to drown out the people who know better. Then you start getting interests groups which exist to capitalize on the political power embodied in amassing the will of the politically ignorant. These groups argue as people who know better but like what the lousy politicians are doing. Some people make money off the arguing because they just like arguing. And, eventually you get people who don't like arguing, who get upset at all arguing, and then begin to argue against the people doing the arguing. Why do we let politicians organize again...?

Ok, let's try to ask a more productive question by introducing a new term and changing our approach. How does cognitive dissonance factor into this? Politicians like to separate us into groups of those who will vote for them and won't vote for their opponents. They don't need to get everybody. They just need to separate out a large enough groups to get elected, and then defend that political turf. That kind of division is what they would call good for party business. The policies that members of political parties espouse and defend are their main tool for doing this kind of dividing. They use stances on the issues you care about to maintain support from those groups of voters which make up their political base. The policies they put out are worked so that if the people in their base do not agree with and support them they are going to have to live with cognitive dissonance. Then, they spend the rest of their time framing themselves as the champions of these issues. So, why doesn't the other side just steal these issues if they can garner such a following? The parties think of that too. They pick issues to champion which are simultaneously motivating to their base and distasteful to the other side. They then invest a great amount of their time and effort into filling out these narratives. Meanwhile, the party on the other side is busy doing the same thing. Each side then points at the other as the source of our nation's pain when it gets close to voting time. That's called campaign season. We get bombarded with divisive messages on the issues that we find most motivating. Because we're reacting from a deep, inward place we are roused just enough to make it to the polls and vote for our side. Campaigns targeting those on the other side either fail to rouse us from our inattentiveness or have wounded by stepping on values in clumsy ways. Under these circumstances those on the other side are not going to uphold the merit of your side no matter how persuasive your argument gets. And, that works to the politicians benefit. In that kind of situation they don't have to be clever, or even honest. They don't have to compete for power, they just consolidate. While centralizing power they point to the other side and say, they'll make you live contrary to the things you care about most. If we recognized what they were doing, and how easily they were manipulating us, we would take offense. If we were paying attention we would see what they are doing. Reasonable people from either side of the political divide would have a good chance of gaining popular support from everyone based on the quality of their ideas and competency. But, when each side is only interested in relieving their own cognitive dissonance, while they do things in their policies that cause cognitive dissonance in the other side, the talent pool of people with solutions begins to shrink. What's worse, the agreement needed for national productivity and political oversight is going to evaporate.

The ability of political parties to divide the country on ideological lines has unfortunately taken on a new, more expansive role in today's politics. Politicians have learned an ideological argument which creates a false "vote for us or lose all you care about" scenario can also take scrutiny off the actions of those in government. Once we've stopped paying attention, they can use these arguments to make it even harder for us to start looking in the right areas again. Politicians have learned these issues can blind us to all but the most basic reactions. This is a tactic that works broadly. But, it is most effective among groups of people who don't want to bother getting educated on their politics to begin with. These are people who want certain political results but don't want to be bothered with details. Like anyone else, these people wish to live in a society that reflects their desires. But, they are not typically motivated to enact political change unless someone first motivates them. This provides the opportunity for a designer base of voters supporting whoever is willing to properly motivate them. I say properly because they're not going to go out and vote something that doesn't at least appear to align with what they support. Some people want to be rallied for any reason. Most of us want to see a particular return for our effort, however. When we take the effort to go out and support a candidate, or tell the people we know about a political issue, it stands to reason that we do so with expectations. Getting pitted against each other in blind support of a political brand name at the expense of seeing improvement in the welfare of our communities is not the return we're seeking. Granted, more and more people are letting envy invade their decision making. But, when we think in terms of the things that matter most I think most of us would not want to trade what we value most for being caught up in a vacuous political game. The best defense to avoid getting pitted against each other by politicians who are playing us is to learn the way things are supposed to work.

I liken an education in politics to eating a proper diet. If you can't tell by now, I like food. I hope you have a full stomach and aren't hungry, because you're going to be hearing about food a lot. Eating balanced meals can take effort and planning where people may not feel they have time. A balanced meal plan is not necessarily something everyone wants, or even enjoys. But, no one likes getting scurvy, rickets, or other consequences of malnutrition either. It can happen when you don't eat enough good nutrition. And, scurvy is certainly not attractive. An uninformed populace will also begin to see their society develop in unattractive and undesirable ways. Getting someone to prioritize the time and effort spent in consuming political education can be challenging. Education of this kind not always considered appetizing, especially when there's so much political junk food out there. Taking on this kind of self education often requires a support structure, and self-motivation to withstand the counter motivation mounted by politicians who are trying to protect their turf. Just remember that they consider you their turf. I find that helps raise my own personal level of motivation. Speaking of things politicians are doing that helps you motivate yourself, I also find that when I am looking for motivation few things animate like learning what politicians are actually doing to us, in our name. We'll take advantage of that realization as we delve into the way politics seem to be working currently. For those of us who dislike politics, I'm sorry to say that events in our history have placed you in an unfortunate position. You'll likely need to pitch in before we finally get our nation, and you, back out of the position it is in. I'm going to have to ask you to hold your nose and take one for the team here. It's "all hands on deck" in the nation today. For those of you who enjoy politics, I hope you are enjoying yourselves thoroughly. Everyone, please tell all your friends what a great book you are reading so maybe we can get them active too.

 When divisive attacks get leveled along ideological lines, each side is afraid their ideology won't be upheld. Values run deep. Merely looking at where our values come from can cause discomfort and pain. It's like looking directly at the sun. You know it's going to hurt, you avoid it if at all possible, and you're concerned about the long term consequences if you look too long. We're going deep, to the level of that part of us which informs our values. Where values come from runs even deeper than our values. We remember from what we've previously discussed that there are two laws of love on which morality hinges. How does this reality factor into our discussion about politicians? The people who are politically active or can be motivated to become politically active lean toward either moral law, and are generally consumed with their own lives. Their leaning plays out fairly clearly through their actions on voting day and in the support of the issues for which they care most. The most active group in the field of politics is called likely voters. These are people whose actions as a group have been tracked and recorded from election to election for years. These are the people deemed most likely to cast their vote each election. These voters can be shocked into political action in the voting booth when they are told from a source they deem credible that the principles which come from their very core will be ignored, or even violated by the other side. My assertion, which I think has been borne out in likely voting trends over the past dozen years or so, is that roughly forty percent of today's voting population naturally favors the first law of love. Another forty percent naturally favors the second law of love. These groups constitute the main voting base of each party. The remaining twenty percent may lean toward one law or the other, but do not want to be identified either way. Whether it was inherent, or through life circumstances, they have decided to declare themselves as politically separate. Those twenty percent are either not as strongly oriented to one side, simply do not want to declare for any one side, or are more mixed through their experiences. As a group they are not as easily motivated by broad arguments, are resistant to external motivation, or just think it is cool to resist a label. This resistance to association can continue even though they may very well vote with one side consistently. In the past, they have been viewed as those not caught in the wide ranging nets political parties cast when amassing their base. When referred to as a unit, the members of this third group are called Independent.

Going after the Independents is a bit like dating. If they see you run right after them they either scatter, or only keep you around long enough to rouse the jealousy of the person in whom they are actually interested. Generally, the disdain for association they posses means they want a politician who is also not overly associated with either party. Electrify and engage your base in ways that create excitement and the Independents will respond differently. The ones who just want to be contrarian aren't likely to be won by someone who's carries majority support anyway. If a politician continues to pursue this voting group after they shy away, they may ultimately gain their support, but they'll run the risk of losing support from their base in the process. In my opinion, the best way to attract independents is the same way a charming young man might attract a girl. When she sees the caring, respectful, and lovingly affectionate way he interacts with his sisters and his mother she may think that's a pretty good deal to sign up for. If a politician treats his or her base this in a way while incorporating the tenets of the laws of love, they'll motivate their own base while attracting the other side's base in ways so that they don't feel neglected or rejected. That's the making of a landslide election. But, we'll get into that more later on. If there are some who feel a little left out by my hypothetical, I'm a traditional guy with no experience dating men. You'll have to forgive me for not writing from that perspective. Hopefully, sharing my own personal experiences has helped clear up the cloudy issue of the independents. It may not seem that important, but Independents are the subject of much discussion each election cycle. Some may find this hard to believe, but both parties actually pay campaign consultants obscene amounts of money to tell them how to get the independents. I guess running candidates who often haven't dated socially in over a decade also risks running people who have forgotten the rules of dating. Regardless, that's how the likely voting groups balkanize.

 Some may say I just gave away the proverbial keys to the kingdom by explaining how the laws of love motivate us to define the way major voting blocs function, and I did. But, there's a nasty surprise waiting for anyone who doesn't follow through on campaign promises that people really care about. When you mess with the sort of things people have a hard time even looking at, you're messing with the source that powers every third rail in politics. If someone raises expectations by exciting people on what matters most to them in order to get elected, that same excitement will run against you in the form of upset voters when they figure that candidate either can't, or won't deliver on their promises. Or, someone who runs on extreme motivation will be forced to remain extreme in governing to avoid angering their base. That's why each year the establishment of both parties tries to keep expectations as low as possible while still getting enough people to the polling booths to win. How, you may ask, does a politician get people out to vote without raising expectations? Of course, there's always doing something historic and then being as intentionally vague as possible to get elected. But, if a candidate can't find something once in a lifetime about themselves that gets people to come out, they've got to find another way.

 People are so aligned to the two laws of love that a voter's natural orientation towards one of the laws of love predicts voting behavior when considered in sufficient numbers to create a voting majority. So how did the political parties figure out a way to tap into the power of the sun without frying themselves? Because our moral orientation defines the core values from voting constituents vote, the political parties who have so very much to gain in understanding them on an experiential level. They sounded out the dimensions of these laws within our heats by observation of the impact the values they inform have on voting habits through past elections. Remember, I mentioned they've been keeping track of how likely voters vote? These dimensions have been organized to form the length and width of party political platforms. These platforms are the list of things for which the parties claim to stand. Many say these platforms have become an outdated joke because in too many instances the parties do not uphold these claims well or with any regularity. But the people who hold this sentiment don't understand the use of party platforms in the modern age. They don't exist primarily as a list of what can be that excites people to voter. Party platforms exist now as a list of what will be lost if the party loses power. They are primarily a list that can be used to primarily to threaten the base if they stay home or let the other party get their way. It's frightening how effective this tactic is when we aren't paying attention, aren't checking to see if the values politicians claim to uphold are actually guiding their hands. Under these conditions, even when mere lip service is paid to these platforms they still hold great power to motivate voters.

It is important to note here that values are what a person votes from, not merely nature. Nature cannot be changed. Experience and learning can, however, inform and change values. Studying nature and perfecting our values can enrich us very much. This education, and the character expansion which follows from applying ourselves to what we learn, allows us greater ability to do good things which may not be our taste, but we know to be the best choice. With understanding we can learn how to act in ways that bring about what is best for both sides, without fear of acting contrary our nature. The pursuit of forming more perfect values is the process of molding our values to embrace both laws of love. This may sound controversial to some, as our culture hasn't really popularized sublime pursuits of late. We, as a nation, have settled into base reactions. It's sad but true. Oh, no, don't be sad. It's not the end yet. We just have to understand what's going on so we know what needs to be fixed. Sure, there are still innovators and those with aspirations among us. But, envy has become the new American past time. It's right up there next to baseball and orange construction barrels. Those who publicly enjoy success under any definition are often reviled in our culture. Many of us want to believe we live in an idyllic America. But, voting habits cannot remain untouched by culture, and the way our government is operated follows voting. The U. S. voter, by and large, has turned to voting in support of the candidate or party least likely to challenge their individually held inclinations, formed along the lines of one of the two laws of love. This creates a situation where indiscretions, failures to act, even lawless behavior is excused. That's because the primary reason to get out and vote isn't what the voter's party will do in power, it's what the other side's party might do. Candidates and parties perceived as oppositional to the voter's core ideology serve as motivation to not allow the other side a chance to act in power. Notice my emphasis on core ideology. As long as each side's political agents uphold their side's core values without transgressing them, then there is a great deal which will be left out of public scrutiny or tolerated. Politicians in this environment get to keep playing at their sport so long as they can keep you believing the other guy is going to act against your nature more than they. When the established power structure of both major political parties plays this game, you can be reasonably sure little that is good, useful, or universally agreeable is going to get accomplished. They don't have to do anything productive. They just have to build up fears in voters of how the other side will behave. There are little to no expectations being developed. If one side fails to replace these methods with something equal in ability to get us into the voting both, without raising our expectations to the point that we demand results later, the other side starts winning. Even that can be acceptable in their eyes, however, as long as the only place a person can go for influence and power is one of the two major parties. It's a mess.

That's why combining a disinterested voting population with politicians who are constantly studying us ends in a bad national direction. They inevitably begin the political equivalent of triangulation to figure out exactly what they can get away with, which leads to a corrupt government. Corruption is allowed to grow when we fail to respond punitively to actions which are not morally balanced, and fail to reward those who reliably serve the national interest. The best way I've heard to describe how corruption of this nature begins and consequently progresses is called "The Christmas Tree Effect." As dysfunction from actions which are not in the national interest grows, the government tries very hard to maintain the kind of appearances which will lead you to believe everything is ok. An example of this effort to keep up the appearance of stability which readily comes to mind is the unemployment rate which is emphasized by the administration in power. An economy where more people can find career level jobs makes for a nation with greater wealth and more possibilities for its citizens. That's why a higher rate of unemployment is a bad thing. When unemployment gets bad a lot of people can't find jobs. Eventually, after trying unsuccessfully to find employment again and again, unemployed workers realize they have been left without the possibility of returning to gainful employment. They then quit looking for what they have come to believe through repeated experience isn't there. Instead of our government reporting honestly with an emphasis on the total number of jobs being down from where it needs to be for real opportunity to flourish and these unemployed workers to find good jobs, the government instead cites some abstract number that doesn't count the long term unemployed. Louis Effron wrote an article on August twentieth of year two thousand fourteen for Forbes.com titled "Tackling The Real Unemployment Rate: 12.6%." In this article he explains how the real unemployment rate was twelve point six percent, while the government reported a number that sparked much less outrage in voters, six point two percent. That's the sort of thing that should upset voters. When they hear their government is deliberately misleading them as to the health of the economy, people who are paying attention react strongly. Some people want to be lied to, but well get to them later. Those who aren't paying attention when competing unemployment figure get laid out in front of them may remember the aversion they had to percents and fractions in math class. If you find yourself interested in an explanation of how this slick trick in unemployment reporting and, as well as what unemployment and underemployment do to a nation, you may want to read the article.

Why does this deception matter? That question can be answered by another question. How can you properly and proactively work to fix a problem you don't even know exists? Why do politicians tell you things are fine when they are falling apart? Politicians don't usually want you trying to fix problems in government because your idea of functioning government may conflict with the interests of the political class. That's why politicians try very hard to convince us to pay less attention as soon as possible in between their campaigns to get re-elected. Every press conference held by the party in power in between elections seems to be an effort to portray our future as lush and green. If you think the situation is normal they believe from experience that you'll go back to your daily affairs, leaving them to their machinations. If you think the government isn't going as well as it should you'll start paying attention to their business. That hampers their ability to do business in a way that benefits them most. Time and association between those with control of resources creates interests in any group, as well as attracting interest from outside groups. A group with control of resources attracts the attention of those who desire or need those resources. But, we want the politicians we elect to serve our interest, which comprise the general welfare of the country, rather than their own or those of other groups, also known as interest groups. If we the people start fixing things by voting the political office holders out who don't serve our interests we'll disrupt the time and association necessary to maintain the interests of the established political structure. They don't want that. If things are bad for long enough, that's exactly what will begin to happen. You'll start voting people out of office to give someone else a try at fixing our problems. They figure rightly that you'll be less inclined to vote them out if you don't know there is a problem that needs fixed. Because they don't want voted out, they'll keep you in the dark for as long as possible and as often as the ability to maintain their interests is threatened. Some people don't want to believe their government would lie to them. But, if you find that you don't think politicians have managed to keep us in the dark try asking the people you know what the unemployment rate is. Some problems go untreated because the solutions aren't good for business from the political establishment perspective, and because those of us who would make fixing the problems a priority don't even know they exist. More and more money and resources are spent on bail outs, slush funds, and throwing good money after bad. After a while, there is nothing left to use on keeping up appearances. The Christmas tree is no longer green. Even the most stubborn or sophisticated ideological sophists are unable to maintain the ruse any longer. Denial and inattentiveness no longer works for the rest of us, since the problems afflicting us have by then become unavoidable. What was easily correctable before now brings realities that are life changing. The tree is dead, its color has faded, and needles once vibrant with life have become brittle and fallen to the floor. The tree died long ago, when it was separated from its roots. The tree continued to drink the resource of water, keeping up its appearance, until even the appearance of life could no longer be maintained. The tree is now fully dead, leaving nothing left to be done at that point but to throw the tree out and start over next year. The key to life is to stay attached to our roots. Fortunately for us, when it comes to politics, our roots are something we can rediscover.

This dynamic of what motivates many people to vote now is very important, so I'll take a moment to restate it. Primarily we're not voting to make something happen. Too many of us are voting to keep something from happening. That leaves a lot of room open for what can happen as a result. This practice has allowed politicians to act in ways contrary to the public interest. The use of their political power was not defined in the mind of the populace before they took office. They didn't want to define it either, because some potential voters might not like their definition, using it as a reason not to vote for them. This lack of defining what they would stand for is allowed by us because we have taken to voting against an intangible, rather than voting for a clearly defined tangible. Politicians are largely not being judged for what they are doing. Politicians today are primarily rewarded with power for what they claim to prevent oppositional agents in the other party, and sometimes in the primaries within their own parties, from doing. And, because we're not following up on their record between campaign seasons the key word here is "claim." Politicians in the past seemed to walk a fine line between what they can get you to believe, and claims that would incur incredulity. Now, politicians who run in polarized districts can get away with saying highly incredulous things as long as they don't step on values which comprise their side's orthodoxy. You can almost measure a state's degree of polarization by the number of inane comments coming out of their political leaders. That's a terrifying thought at the moment, isn't it? If there is anyone out there reading this that is clever, honest, and amenable, I would love to see a map of the U. S. laid out like a periodic table which shows electronegativity. But, instead of the magnitude of attractiveness in relation to electrons it would show the magnitude of political polarization. In addition to the educational benefit, there may be some humor in there as well if weighted by number of regrettable comments.

 In too many cases these days it is not about how well or how poorly elected officials do their job. The main reason politicians are elected to office is because the voters have been convinced that the values they hold dear will not he upheld if the other side gets in office. Sometimes, when both sides run are highly polarized, those fears are valid. But, that's not a reason to skip looking for better candidates, which is what we did for too long. It's reactive. It's an ugly way to run a country. It pushes the worst to the top as their aggression is judged most likely to rebuff the other party. And, it's where we are. The only area in which politicians seem to take credit for any kind of results or proactive measures would when there is good news in the economy. That's like taking credit for the weather. One night, while I was writing this book, the weather forecast called for three to six inches of snow. That night there was an obvious lack of snow. We are all familiar with the fact that even after years of education and professional experience meteorologists can't reliably tell us exactly what the high temperature will be for a day, let alone where snow will land. Like meteorologists, politicians can only dream of raising the GDP, or unemployment a point or two to meet their prognostications.

They can hurt those numbers if they make a concerted effort, but that's a different story. Again, just like a meteorologist on a beautiful and sunny day, politicians line up to bring us good economic news. I personally find it the height of irony that the major parties find the nerve to even talk about the economy these days. I think we all know major political parties are a drag on the overall economy these days. And, just like our environment, we need to be good stewards of our economy. It has laws we can't alter which govern the health of our economy. We'll be the ones who suffer if we go about acting contrary to the laws of economics because we'll be the ones who have to make a living in our economy after trashing it. We know so far that politicians are using divisive tactics to separate the population into the widest possible collection of voting blocks. How is that hurting our economy? The way politicians are using division is creating economic headwinds and ignoring economic laws. The best way I've found to describe what is happening in Washington D. C. is to draw a contrast with something we do understand. And, I imagine this would all be more entertaining if I explained it using a food context. How fortunate for us that a good contrast exists between business as usual in federal government and the way Kentucky Fried Chicken franchising began. In case anyone is wondering, I'm an extra crispy man myself.

It started in the time when Colonel Harland Sanders was in the foodservice business. Here's the story as I understand it. The Colonel had found a great product in his fried chicken, which he sold from a location in Corbin Kentucky. It was a nice location. There was decent traffic. Hungry travelers stopped in off the highway that ran by the restaurant to enjoy their hospitality. The traffic that ran by provided a steady stream of business and everything was going well. Then, things started to change. A newer highway was planned, and eventually ran through the area. This new highway was something different. It was an interstate highway, and it connected more people over a greater distances. Because of how it was built, Interstate 75 was able to move more traffic more efficiently than the old roads, like the one that ran by the Colonel's restaurant. The new highway was fantastic for all the weary travelers who wanted to get down the road faster and with less hassle. It met a public need and everyone seemed to be on the new highway.

The new thoroughfare presented a problem for the Colonel, however. His nice restaurant wasn't on the new interstate. It was on the old road. His business model wasn't built to do well on the decreased traffic now that people were driving on the new highway. It was based on the traffic pattern when those people had to drive by his restaurant. The travelers, who used to find stopping in for food convenient on their way to where they were going, now had to go out of their way to find his fine fare. As traffic around the Colonel's restaurant decreased, so did his business. Seeing the direction where the trend was pointing, and not wanting to be left in the past, he sold his interest in the restaurant. It was time for a change. The Colonel used his experience and ingenuity to see the opportunity provided by an improvement in infrastructure. While the interstate had pulled traffic from his area, it also rerouted traffic from other areas as well, consolidating traffic along one route. This accessible improvement in the lives of the populace had attracted many travelers. Because of his experience serving travelers, the Colonel was able to recognize that the interstate had created a collection of people with the same needs. It had created a market. All those people traveling the new interstate created a new demand specific to that route. Colonel Sanders realized he knew how to meet that demand. He began tailoring his efforts to the specific needs of hungry highway travelers. A big part of this tailoring was redirecting efforts into starting franchises targeted to major traffic arteries. In a short time business was booming. The Colonel was making more money than he knew what to do with. The invention that redirected business traffic, and drove him out of his business, also provided the opportunity to begin again. This opportunity rewarded his ingenuity, work ethic, and experience. He was able to combine all these assets, along with the resources at his disposal, to capitalize on opportunity.

That's the influence innovation has on the marketplace. Inventions create change. Business traffic redirects to align with the new innovations. Some businesses and markets are left behind. But, new opportunities created by inventions also allow people to ply their experience in new markets where there is even greater opportunity. The end result, just as with Colonel Sanders, is more net opportunities and amenities. I'm not implying that the nice people at a certain chicken serving establishment agree with anything I have to say. I just think the Colonel's story provides a real life example of the path that innovation takes. The rest is all my opinion on the difference that makes. Whether they love me or hate me for including them in my musings, I'll still love their crispy chicken.

I bet you're wondering where politics fits into all of this talk about economic development. To see the where politics and economics mesh one must take a step back and look at the big picture. From there you begin to see the all the different transactions as they take place. Watching markets respond as forces exert themselves them is like watching a flock of birds taking off, changing direction in flight, and landing again. All those little birds are independently making their own decisions. But, they move in a coordinated way through a series of intricate interactions as they go about their hunt for food and other things that interest them. The way they move through the sky looks from a distance like one creature moving, as long as they don't feel threatened. When the neighbor's dog comes bounding through they take off in all directions for somewhere safe to sit it out until the rambunctious puppy leaves. That actually reminds me of a story about a red tailed hawk and a toy poodle, but we won't tell that story here. Suffice to say; sometimes the market turns on the people who try to control it, laws of economics and laws of nature being what they are. Anyway, the analogy of a flock of birds following their interests that eventually gets interrupted by a curious canine is useful because it describes a market operating under normal circumstances, as well as what happens when the market panics. This is important to know because new inventions aren't the only thing with the power to redirect business traffic on a large scale. The government can exert influence on the market as well. Government can easily force a change in a market by taxing products and services, heavily regulating them, or making them entirely illegal. Government can punish the people who continue doing business using those products or services. The force applied in such a sweeping way does not always achieve the goal for which it was intended. But, the market is certainly distorted. Whether this action destroys demand for the goods and services, or raises demand in the case of prohibition, the end result is rarely positive for the customer. Sometimes the elected representatives or the party that caused these distortions in the lives of intended prey find themselves playing the poodle as public sentiment turns on them. But that's what is possible when some people operate under the expectation that they can create an environment where other people will against their nature.

There are some exceptions where government intervention in the marketplace is almost always welcomed. Hard drugs like cocaine can make someone a lifelong addict in one dose. Pernicious substances have a reputation for ruining lives and stealing dreams. Perhaps the worst thing about some substances is that they take whatever you desire and replace those priorities with them as your highest priority. Even drugs considered to be benign on the body are known to have a wasting effect on our aspirations. Because they take away from the possibly the most unique aspects of every person and replace this beauty with a merciless need for themselves they have been reviled by society. The government has outlawed such obviously harmful products. And, the majority of society doesn't have a problem with this use of government force to constrain a market. I think therein lies the key. Government has to act within the boundaries of where society has already formed a consensus to avoid going from puppy to poodle. The more a society realizes their strength, the more that people recognize and values their rights, the more their government has to stay within acceptable boundaries. That recognition is a key factor in what makes government actions helpful and successful in the long term. It is worthwhile to note here that our government works on the factual premise that power flows from the consent of the governed. There is recognition here that "We the People" not only create the boundaries for decision making, we are responsible for upholding decisions.

What happens when the use of government force is not limited to within the boundaries a society has set? What if government force is used to outlaw something innocuous and desirable? What if something is legalized that the people believe should be outlawed, or existing laws with public support are ignored? What if government force is used for reasons other than the public welfare? Given the power government has to change spending habits, these questions should be asked. These questions condense to one single, simple question. Does the government exist to serve us, or do we exist to serve those in government? The resources our government relies on to function come from the people. If the government begins making decisions which do not represent the people, using their resources to do so, it's a bit like a rebellious teenager. The car is borrowed without permission, there are constant parties paid for at your expense, the house gets trashed. The poor parents who have refused to take control of their house are waiting for the day when they go broke, lose the kid to dangerous life choices, or lose the house because the police found something that illegal on a complaint call from a neighbor. In a scenario where the government is acting like an out of control teenager and the people do nothing to stop it they are then in service to the government. If the parents make good choices they can correct the situation early in a way that leads everyone to enjoy healthy, adaptive choices. If they let an out of control situation get worse relationships will shatter and someone could be going to jail. The most compassionate thing for everyone in this scenario is to address the situation early.

If you pay someone to do a service you desire and they do it, they are serving you. If someone takes the fruit of your labor without compensating you, using it for their own purposes, that's something totally different. If a person or an entity takes your resources to act against your interests, even in part, that creates a moral quandary. In our system of governance I've noticed the major political parties have found a way of serving and even advancing their own interests. This appears to have been done among the established among the parties by turning the business of running the government, at least in part, into their own private business. Interest groups and others lobby member of congress. Legislation gets passed. Grants are given. People and groups who have the ability to influence the government make deals with willing parties. The result of these deals is to create favorable conditions in the market for select groups and individuals to make more money. These decisions lack the spark of invention which creates new opportunity. These deals, enforced by our government, divert the flow of business traffic. As a result, this use of legal force hurts the market and jobs without creating new ways to succeed. Have you ever wondered why the tax code is so convoluted and hasn't been reformed? I can't help but notice that an arcane tax system makes lobbing for special exceptions all the more tempting. If the tax code were to be simplified and reformed there would be less advantage available to those who would manipulate it. That would mean less power in the hands of the government over our daily affairs. At the very least a more transparent tax code would mean that when someone lobbies for and gets a sweet tax advantage over their competitors from the government it would be clear to the average voter what was transpiring. But that's just one example. The ways power can be exerted are manifold, and reform is needed across government. We haven't even touched on the effect regulations can have on an economy.

 Parties in power merely need to divert the existing flow of business traffic past their associates, placed along the new revenue path. Colonel Sanders knew placing business along the exits to major thoroughfares would place him in position to create an empire in the food service industry. What does a change in roads have to do with fried chicken? To him, the answer was everything, and he did it the right way. These people lobbying for changes in laws, tax policy, regulations, etc. reap the rewards of being strategically placed along the new path forced by changes coming from the government. These newly enriched associates then use those rewards to do things, like making large campaign contributions to the politicians who accommodated them or inflating their assets. Fox News has done a significant amount of reporting on schemes like this, referring to them under the title Crime Inc. I'm citing sources from all over so I would almost be remiss if I did not include Fox News on this topic. In an article dated May fourteenth of two thousand ten titled "Crime Inc.: What the 'Greening of America' Really Means" on FoxNews.com they explain how this works in practice. This one was actually prevented, in my opinion because it was a bit too audacious, but that's what makes it such a clear example. What's especially chilling is how things like these are crafted to appear worthy of public support from a distance. They'll go through congress under bills with names like the, "Save the World Now By Voting For This Bill and if You Don't You Hate Children and the World Will End Tomorrow and It Will Be All Your Fault," bill. It's the people who are willing to pay close attention who catch the game being played against them. The people do pay attention end up facing resistance from other people who are also being taken advantage. Reactive people who stand to be impoverished by the success of bad legislation can act out of ignorance against the people very trying to protect them because they buy into seductive marketing. It is important to understand how industries we rely are forced to change by our government, so I'll explain using an example of a product nearly everyone is familiar with.

Recently, the most commonly used existing styles of the incandescent light bulb were made illegal to be produced in the U. S. by legislation. You read right. They made it against the law to manufacture or import traditional light bulbs. In "The Energy Independence and Security Act (P.L. 110-140, H.R. 6)" the way in which they went about banning the incandescent bulb is explained. Rather than bore you with the details of how they went about demanding that a perfectly functioning bulb do things it can't do or face punishment, I'll go straight to what impacts you. The old bulb could be measured in cents. The new bulbs cost dollars, multiple dollars. That extra cost is paid by you. What caused the need for an inexpensive product that most people liked to be replaced with a more expensive product in the market? I bet you never knew the terror that lurked in your lamp. Wait, no, there was never actually any terror. Lot's of hype, but no terror. Some claimed that the old bulbs used too much energy, and were therefore bad for the environment. But, the halogen replacements burn hotter. That heat represents lost energy compared to competitors like the L.E.D. or compact fluorescent bulbs. Oh, and touching it with your fingers can do anything from causing the bulb to explode in some models to shortening its life span. L.E.D. lights just aren't there yet. They don't do as well at higher wattages we're used to, and it is hard to get them to shine in more that one direction. Think flashlight, although improvements are constantly being made, and expect to pay for improvements. Compact fluorescent bulbs are said to consume less coal fired power, leading to less mercury in the environment. But, CFL's have mercury in them that you bring into your home when you buy one for your reading lamp. All the substitutes for the classic bulb I've seen have cost the consumer considerably more. If you know a better choice that costs less, please, surprise me. Otherwise, I'll be buying my sixty watts from somewhere like Mexico or buying specialty incandescent bulbs that as long as they are legal. So far I'm not seeing an appreciable improvement, environmentally or economically. And, we haven't even considered the important personal cost. Have you ever burned yourself on a light bulb? I know I have. You learn not to touch the things after they've been on for a minute or two. But, accidents still happen. These accidents hurt for a moment, but then you moved on. Well, as we've already stated the halogen replacements are hotter. Enjoy looking forward to making that memory. The next time Murphy's Law proves itself try to remember why you paid several dollars more for the pleasure of burning yourself on a hotter bulb.

With such an obviously inferior selection of alternatives, where will the smart money go from this change in buying habits? The easy way to determine this, where legislation is concerned, is to follow the loudest sales pitch. Politicians claimed that new and efficient fluorescent bulbs would be better for the environment. Well, that's a good candidate. When politicians invoke the environment it is about as close to invoking the name of the deity as you'll get from secularists. If you are fan of conservation it is especially frustrating. Practically speaking, when they use the name of the environment too many times if just feels like grease for what's about to happen. Does the sales pitch surrounding getting rid of the incandescent bulb sound too good to be true? Here's the biggest problem. As was already stated, the new CFL bulbs contain mercury. For those who don't know, that's toxic in the vapor form found inside CFL bulbs. According to MarchofDimes.org, pregnant women especially should beware. If you break one of these compact bulbs, and who hasn't broken a light bulb, you've now poisoned the environment. More to the point, you've just poisoned your environment. Some people say those bulbs are harder to break. Those people have no respect for Murphy. Now, for a little morbid fun, let's go over some of the EPA's recommended steps for when a compact fluorescent bulb breaks.

## CLEANUP AND DISPOSAL OVERVIEW

The most important steps to reduce exposure to mercury vapor from a broken bulb are:

### 1. Before cleanup

a. Have people and pets leave the room.

b. Air out the room for 5-10 minutes by opening a window or door to the outdoor

environment.

c. Shut off the central forced air heating/air-conditioning system, if you have one.

d. Collect materials needed to clean up broken bulb:

☐ stiff paper or cardboard;

☐ sticky tape;

☐ damp paper towels or disposable wet wipes (for hard surfaces); and

☐ a glass jar with a metal lid or a sealable plastic bag.

### 2. During cleanup

a. DO NOT VACUUM. Vacuuming is not recommended unless broken glass remains after all

other cleanup steps have been taken. Vacuuming could spread mercury-containing powder

or mercury vapor.

b. Be thorough in collecting broken glass and visible powder.

c. Place cleanup materials in a sealable container.

### 3. After cleanup

a. Promptly place all bulb debris and cleanup materials outdoors in a trash container or

protected area until materials can be disposed of. Avoid leaving any bulb fragments or

cleanup materials indoors.

b. Next, check with your local government about disposal requirements in your area, because

some localities require fluorescent bulbs (broken or unbroken) be taken to a local recycling

center. If there is no such requirement in your area, you can dispose of the materials with

your household trash.

c. If practical, continue to air out the room where the bulb was broken and leave the

heating/air conditioning system shut off for several hours.

Step 1 a is my favorite with step 1 c as a close runner up. Both seem important but the sequence of events seems like it might be a little difficult to manage in a real world situation. How long do does a person have before they need to complete 1 c? What happens if I don't get 1 c done soon enough because the dog wanted to check out the mess, the kids wanted to help clean up the bulb, and the old windows kept sliding shut after I opened them? Someone's got to keep everyone else out of the toxic heavy metal fumes while all this is going on. Will I end up a cautionary tale for future fluorescent bulb owner if I don't get to 1 c soon enough?

When was the last time you had to rush everyone out of the room after breaking an incandescent bulb? At most, you made sure someone didn't step in the mess. But, that falls into the category of common sense, and does not rise to the level of a hazmat incident. Why is all this important? Because if a truly desirable market invention had taken place here, history tells us a law would not have been required. You would have run to the innovation, because you're smart. In competition with a better bulb which provided markedly better light and cost you less when it came time to pay your electricity bill, the incandescent bulb would have failed on its own. People who know the light bulb business would have made it their business to put competitors still selling the inferior incandescent out of business through providing you with that better bulb. It will happen eventually anyway. A reasonable person would expect that someday someone will make a better bulb. So, why did politicians pass the legislation that forced market change now?

This is a point many people have perhaps heard before, and dismissed. There is such a thing as trusts, monopolies, and death dated products. It can be hard to look past dirty tricks and abuses in the market to see advances which have improved society. So, I'll put it a little differently. Think about the last time you had a day to day need for barrels, or a cooper. Whisky and wine are still held in barrels. Barrels are used occasionally for aesthetics. But barrels are no longer household storage items. A barrel is not an item that sees widespread demand in our era.

They're heavy and not the sort of thing you'd want to keep around the house for extra storage. Better materials and products have taken their place. The new products are popular. Entire merchandising chains have been created, opening stores to serve the public need for the better products and materials. These stores sell strong, lightweight containers of all shapes and sizes to happy customers who fell in love with something they absolutely demanded come home with them.

Not surprisingly, no law was needed to change buying behavior. Votes in the form of money supported new means of hefting your storable stuff. People today buy recyclable plastic totes over heavy wood barrels on their own without coercion. The freedom of the marketplace, with all its flaws and shortcomings, inaugurated a new top product with an election that is held every day in stores around the world. Innovation met buyer's necessity in a way which allowed all to expend less effort, whether they are hard working or hardly working. Regardless of who got rich off it, improvement in our standard of living caused this change. The flow of business traffic responded to useful innovation. It reminds me of when I was standing in a retail store during the post-Christmas rush. I was waiting in the cashier lane. Lines are always long that time of year, but this was different. The line wasn't moving at all. People in line were starting to talk. The worst part was, I was only there because we had a special discount. I had been frustrated by this retailer before. I've been going back to that brand less and less. I don't think I'll be going back there again any time soon. But that's the wonder of a free system. That brand has very little power over my choices. Because they can't restrict my actions, they are left with enticement as their only option of getting me into their store. When they fail to entice you to spend money in their store competitors are left an opening, an opportunity where they can compete for your business. The government doesn't need to entice you. To put it bluntly, they pay people who carry guns. It may not be pretty, but some things in a nation require force to continue functioning. The problem is, when we fail to apply the power of a nation correctly its not like retail. You can't just switch to the next competitor. The closes you'll come to that kind of change within the national borders is an election.

That's why the question of how we use government force matters. It is the very question which contributed to forming our government.

Let's look at how the force of law can also be used to reroute business traffic. The availability of products on the open market can bend to government will just as surely as it does to the will of the people. Remember, government is nothing more than the condensed will of the people, coalesced and detached to bring force to bear by those who wield it. The market and the government both function off the same public will. The difference between government and the marketplace is the amount of distance and time between actions and consequences. Government puts distance between the actions taken using the force of a people's will and their consequences. It allows some consequences to be shifted to other groups. Those who escape consequences borne by others do not benefit from the kind of personal experience that educates. Others pay that high cost. The lessons that experience would teach must be carried on in the culture. I think now would be a good time to provide an example.

Think of our soldiers. They volunteer to pay the price of our continued freedom. They can come back broken, both in body and spirit for their service. Sometimes, they pay the ultimate price. On days like Memorial Day and Independence Day we reflect on the cost they paid for us so that we might be free. This reflection impacts our decisions in a positive way. We take our freedom more seriously, guarding it a little better, because we know it doesn't come cheaply. The gravity of the right to freedom of speech at home is better understood when we see it in the light of those who died somewhere else in service of that right. Because we value their service and what it means to us, we are outraged when our soldiers are not cared for properly. But, if we did not reflect on their sacrifice, or value the freedoms they fight for, would we even know the importance of supplying their needs? Would we act on their behalf? Would we care to know their circumstances? Diverting consequences can be disastrous when the lessons taught by nature don't make it across the cultural spectrum. People get used and institutions which safeguard our future rot from neglect and abuse. If we didn't support our troops, when our defenses are tested with a Pearl Harbor like incident, our failure to respect the cost others pay would result in tragedy. Eventually, we could all pay the high cost of education.

It sounds odd, but strong are our traditions which carry on this knowledge? Some traditions are strong. Others aren't. Without cheating, name the third president of the United States of America. Why are patents important, and how easy or costly should it be to obtain a patent? The way to supplement traditions and minimize the cost of personal experience is to make sure the people making the laws experience the consequences of their choices as soon and fully as possible. In the marketplace, money wasted costs you. You have an incentive to find out what products are good and what products are bad. There's not generally a buffer between the person spending the money and the consequences of bad choices. That's not the case in government. Government necessarily spends other people's resources. That means anything relegated to government relies on the traditions and disposition of the culture for maintaining the oversight necessary to avert tragedy. The cumulative will of the people is a powerful thing. A nation of our size and affluence, well, there's a reason we're described in international terms as a superpower. When the public is inattentive, and politicians are allowed to fight over the purse strings and power, it's like letting a drunk driver drive you, your friends, and your family home. The possibility for heartbreak is staggering.

Some detest strong statements. They don't like it when language is used which can be jarring, even if the heart of the matter is troubling by nature. Others are more comfortable understanding material when put a different way. I can't tell you how many times I asked teachers to repeat what they had just said from a different perspective over the years. For the kindred spirits and gentle souls who hold this work I will rephrase the content in a different analogy on a smaller scale. American football is a fun sport. It is an exhibition which displays dedication, teamwork, and personal achievement. Like any sport, there are rules. The rules are the way we know whether the teams are working together, and achieving. They are the measure by which it can be determined the game is being played in a fair way which endeavors to protect general wellbeing. When the referees, whose are charged with enforcing the rules, fail to call infractions the game changes.

Any sports fan has seen it. Someone tries an illegal move. If they get away with it they'll try again. If one side, either side, keeps getting away with it an unfair advantage is gained. The other side either tries to gain their own advantage, or neutralize the other side's advantage through their own cheating. The risky behavior escalates until players are doing things that are absolutely dangerous. The battle for advantage is a natural part of the game called competition. Both sides are sent out onto the field with one ultimate goal, winning. But, without the protection of well crafted rules, which are enforced fairly, strictly, and uniformly, the game can turn ugly. Everyone who has played in these lawless circumstances or watched a game like this knows the likely question is how many players will be carried off the field? A game without rules becomes blood sport. It is likely to cost someone their health, perhaps even their sporting career. What everyone doesn't always understand among us in the voting population is that we are the referees in the game called politics. We are charged by the U. S. Constitution with enforcing the rules. Like many analogies, this one carries only so far. When sports players cheat they injure each other. When politicians cheat, and we don't call them on it, politicians have figured out how to make sure we suffer the consequences. Why do we let them organize again...?

When a government forces a change on the marketplace, it is done with all the downsides market change can bring and rarely any of the positive or useful effects. The only predictable effect is that the parties who are profiting off the flow of your money change. Many times, hard working businesses built on providing a better product to you are bumped from the table to open up a seat for a company with connections to a campaign donor, or a company with a better lobbying arm. Someone out there is making money selling you more expensive light bulbs because a few politicians waved their pens.

At the risk of redundancy we will revisit the question of how government action creates net expense. When the government makes a change in a market it is the same as when your preferred telephone service or lawn care company are bought out. If the competitor who buys them provides worse service at higher costs you can't go back to your preferred company. The difference is that when the government making changes you can't drop your service and buy from a competitor. You have to absorb the cost of any failings. Every business counts on a number processes. Each one affects the cost of keeping the doors open. All this costs money. When companies are negatively impacted by changes imposed by the government they absorb what they can to stay competitive, and pass on whatever cost they can't absorb to you in the form of higher prices. Disruptions like these affect the revenue stream by raising the cost of doing business. Because the economy is interconnected, much like the environment, changes made in one part of the economy effect other parts. A rise in the price of corn, for example, can raise the price of products in the grocery store and the price of gasoline. It's like polluting a river in an economic sense. Everyone downstream suffers. Since government actions re generally constructed in a universal manner they can raise the cost of doing business across an entire market.

Raising the cost of doing business can lead to some entities which provide a product or service to consumers to close down. This reduces competition. When a variety of companies are all competing to win your business it becomes necessary for their survival to find out what you are willing to pay for. Then, they have to work a little harder than their competitors to please you if they want to keep your business. When a company is able to beat out the competition using the government to get your money it changes the dynamic. The game turns ugly. Now it is in their best interests to keep the regulators and legislators in Washington happy, not so much you. A company in that situation will spend its resources on appealing to the bureaucrat's interests above yours. That drives the cost to the consumer up even further. You've got to pay the added cost of keeping the bureaucrats happy. These, and other factors, pass the cost of redirecting a revenue stream on to you, the consumer. This rise in cost is generally accompanied by no improvement in the product or service being offered for your money. This explains how you bear the cost of their mistakes, or license.

In effect, the person who bears the cost of politicians moving money to the political friends who they are in business with is you. Many of the accidents are the same as invention. The end result of the business of politically redirecting revenue streams, however, is a net loss for the economy. The redirection of revenue under cover of political reasons, by government force, has become big business. From here we could go into how current tax law is so arcane it requires large amounts of money to be spent on cadres of tax attorneys. Or, we could explore how companies who don't spend money on lobbyists are significantly disadvantaged against companies who do have lobbyists in Washington. These are solid cases where the business of government gets in the way of the business of the people. Other examples can be pulled out of the headlines. But, we've made some good headway into the role of innovation, so let's allow that topic to play out further.

Invention creates opportunities. Job loss due to obsolescence is allayed in the case of invention because it lowers the cost of living, and creates access to opportunities which are favorable to the creation of new jobs. Politically motivated change typically has none of these effects. The government can bring about great and positive changes in the areas for which it is best suited, such as national defense and infrastructure. Filling potholes will never be a net gain on the books, but we all need good roads. Anyone who has lost a tire to a big one knows this personally. It is an expense which we all pay to mitigate greater costs. When government forgets its scope, and the force of the public will is applied to achieve private ends, positive change gets lost. This is because the political redirection of business traffic for private, selective reasons works almost exclusively with opportunity that already exists. Winning your patronage carries with it your demand for service worthy of the sacrifice you made while earning your means of payment. If that demand is not fulfilled, in a market with alternative competitors you may give your dollars to someone else who will serve you better.

Redirecting the flow of your dollars without giving you a good return for your sacrifice can require tricking you or lying to you. People don't typically like being taken advantage of, and generally resist it wherever possible. But, when you, the refs, don't call them on their lies and tricks, it creates an advantage in the halls of government power for those who are willing to cheat. This kind of untoward behavior is specifically incentivized when you're not calling them on the fouls because campaign coffers fill with ill gotten gains. When is no longer a downside in trying to part you from that which many have worked so hard to attain, the people who don't cheat become vulnerable. The game changes. People now get into office based on their ability to make money using every means possible without attracting your attention. It is no longer a matter of their ability to communicate with you and then express your will in government. That has died. You can put aside from the dampening effect these choices place on the economy and still see this is a bad convention. Even if for no other reason, this reason stands on its own. When the voters, you, aren't paying attention as much as they should, name recognition wins in a lot of elections.

People are confronted with how unfamiliar they politicians when they are standing in a voting booth, looking a list of names they know nothing about. In those moments a lot of people will pick out the name they recognize out and vote for that candidate. Don't get me wrong, I'm not throwing any stones on this one. I would say enough people have done it that hardly anyone could judge you if you've done it too. Think back to your voting experience. Have you ever picked a name out that belonged to someone you've never seen before just because somewhere in the back of your head their name struck you as familiar. That's what voting on name recognition is all about. And, that's why politicians who are running in elections spend more money than many of us will ever see getting their name in front of you. If you're not paying attention, you'll pay through the wallet. When's the last time how your representatives votes impact the campaign donations of players in the marketplace? You could be voting against your standard of living. Again, I'm not placing blame. It just time to change, that's all. These reasons explain why politically motivated change in the market typically creates a net loss, rather than gain. Politics shouldn't be allowed to become big business. It hurts us all. When politics become a business the incentives are no longer there for politicians to do the right thing for the country. The question becomes, is this good for business, like in any other business. We can't keep voting like we have been because, for some, capitalizing on our political ignorance at our expense has become big business.

We're nearing the end of a chapter again, so let's summarize. Here's my opinion on how government big business operates at a macro level:

- Members of our government, usually in influential committee positions, find or are approached by people and groups placed in a position where they can benefit from redirecting the normal flow of money.
- A way is found for the politicians to benefit from redirecting the flow of revenue into the hands of the complicit party.
- No new innovation helps the economy.
- Capital is lost and cost of living can increase for everyone.
- A select few and their friends benefit from the consent of our collected political power.

The chaff politicians throw up to hide their big business is the most galling part. I've heard it said the best lies have an element of truth. That is a horrible thing to do with the truth, pairing it with a lie to make it sell better. But, if one should cross over a moral line enough times it makes a habit. People don't tend to give their habits much thought. When people do think about them, these nasty habits, they tend to engender more lies. These lies are told by the liars for themselves. They rationalize their forays into the unscrupulous. These are some of the most believable lies, because the liars who tell these lies desperately want to believe they are true. Lust for power and greed always seem to be sold to the public as some great humanitarian pursuit. They told you your consent was being used to save the planet. Political power was accrued. Your favor was coalesced into force. The market bowed to your will, wielded by the winners of a ballot from a voting booth. This is the same voting booth where a frightening number every election have stood in bewilderment, and voted for a party because they've always voted for it, or pick the name that seems most familiar. Some claimed they were saving the world. Nope, they're worried about a different kind of warming on this one. They're trying to keep enough voters in the dark to avoid *political* heat. But that's the trick. You've got demanding lives. It's in our nature to strive for greater challenges. Between our loves and our aspirations only our disciplines remain. And politicians know a person can only consider so many things at once.

 They've got to keep you looking somewhere else for their song to continue. All the money and power of a nation opens before them. If only they can play well enough. The politicians need you to stay distracted if they are to continue the standard of living to which they have grown accustomed. They enjoy their vaunted positions. If you notice the tune they've been playing, notice what they're up to, you'll take exception and put a stop to it. So they give you a merry tune to distract. And they play, with sufficient fervor to turn your gaze. Savvy orators use skills gathered from years of tradition and experience, honed for the purpose of galvanizing the public. Sometimes, even with these skills conventional weapons of distraction fail. The stakes are perhaps higher now than any time we can remember in our lifetime. There's plenty of reason for all of us to pay attention. But, more people are dancing and less point out the charade. Unrepressed desire in the halls of power has crafted a tool for dark design. When distraction fails and we resist their tune, they play a different song inspired by their avarice and desperation. This tune takes the boogeyman out of the closet in our childhood, and moves the monster to the next house over, where our neighbors live. This tool is polarization, equivalent of nuclear proliferation in a culture.

Each side of the political divide arms up by pushing more and more polarizing arguments. They teach us to hate each other and the issues for which the other side stands. As polarization takes its course the culture becomes strained. Polarization, like a nuclear bomb, is believed to be a weapon so deadly the only effective deterrent to an aggressor who wants to use one on you is having one yourself. Of course, if you were to punish those who polarize in elections neither side would seek to acquire this weapon of mass distraction. But, that's not where we are now, and I'm not sure those who vote in our culture truly understand where to begin enforcing this non-proliferation yet. The national fabricate begins to tear. The cold war of resentment will flare into naked conflict as the political battle becomes pitched. Boom, we feel the seismic shift of one side finally achieving dominance as the flag tears down the middle. We no longer see the image of God in our neighbor who we are responsible for loving. Instead of seeing them, we see only the images we have been told see and to hate. In history this is the point where the worst things in human experience take off the mask they have been hiding behind and walk freely for a time.

It all starts so simply. Rather than repay moral violators with the enforcement of proper boundaries, evil is allowed to prosper. Watching this happen is perhaps most painful when the politicians play their tune only considering their desire, and people dance to that tune out of ignorance. They catch us unawares in the hopes that if we're attacking each other we'll never organize enough to question political leadership. We drastically outnumber the small groups willing to sacrifice all for personal gain. That's why they have to divide us to conquer us. And it lasts for a while, before the end. Political parties play their tune to as they turn the people's work into big business. Pundits keep score. The news outlets cannot fight the song and begin cheerleading. As the fight song plays the crowd rises in their seats to dance in the stands. The crowd goes wild when their side makes a polarizing point, not realizing they are cheering the hastening of their own demise. It's hard to watch. If you say something you realize that in the land of the blind, the one eyed man gets burned as a heretic. But, that's not an excuse for keeping the truth to your self. If you're reading this book and you're getting it, ignorance is no longer your excuse. Heavy stuff, huh? I think it is important to engage what they are up to before getting into how they are doing it. How they are doing it is can offend and cut deeply, causing resentment. The *what* of the matter makes it clear who is to blame for all of this. "We The People" are to blame. What the politicians have been doing is wrong. But, it is clear we allowed this happen by not holding them accountable in the voting booth. We have the ultimate responsibility. Now that we know *what* politicians and parties are doing, let's move on to *how* they are dividing for the purpose of keeping us docile.

# WEDGE ISSUES

Up until now we've been setting the table. We learned what facet of our nature is allowing current events to take their polarizing path. We looked at who the major players are. And, we know what motivates them. "We The People" have a wealth within our will. Major political parties, individual politicians, and members of the media are working to master that will. Nothing is too far; no cost is too dear to pay to achieve this prize. We see our table is full. Now, let us dine. If we are going to accept this foundation, upon which I've built my argument thus far for laws of human nature, we must test it first. If the foundation is true, the testing of it will prove good fare indeed. If the prime assertion I've made is correct, then the two laws of love should bear out even if we apply them to the thorniest of issues. For that reason we will take special care to apply my argument to the thorniest issues. In politics, that means we have to apply the premise to wedge issues. I'm thinking of a few wedge issues in particular. But, those who do not consider themselves among the politically savvy may be asking, "What's a wedge issue?" Let's take some time to clarify the term.

Here's a description wedge issues and why preferences matter when considering them. Let's imagine you own one car, it's all you can afford, and it is on fire. You live in a suburban area so it's not like Chicago or Washington D.C. where you can just take a bus or the metro. I ate a steakhouse in Chicago once. The food was amazing. I was weightlifting as well as enjoying the blessings of youth back then. Opportunities like eating a fine meal at a Chicago steakhouse were rare and far between so I made the most of the opportunity. I actually finished a sixty ounce filet mignon by myself, with fries, no lie. Just thinking about doing that again gives me visions of gastrointestinal distress. That was a lot of fun. Anyway, I had trouble finding the place and got lost in the process. What happened when I was ready to leave was something I'll never forget. By luck we happened to time it. After twenty minutes of asking everyone from the wait staff to the back of the house we finally found someone who knew the way to the freeway. It had actually become a game by that point in the restaurant to find someone who knows how to get to a freeway exit. You've got to understand, I'm from the heartland of Ohio. Growing up we had corn and cows, and if a car went by that day it was rush hour. If we wanted anything that couldn't be made at home it required miles of driving, even for groceries. You could imagine what a culture shock it was for me when some of the staff said they had never even been on an interstate. They walked to work or rode the bus, and found the thought of driving yourself forty minutes to work to be somewhere between comical and frustrating. It was fun. But, that will not be the case in our hypothetical. No, your car will be your means of making ends meet. It will be the link between you and gainful employment, groceries, play dates, and everything that can comprise daily life.

Just because this is a book on politics, we'll add a mix of well meaning people and not so well meaning people who are pouring an accelerant on the car, claiming that the liquid they are adding will help put out the fire. Another group of people are holding the back door open. The family dog is escaping out said back door of the house. The dog may never be seen again. If that happens the children will cry, and the adults will spend months putting up posters containing moving messages in the hope of motivating passers by to find and return their flown family member. If you talk to the homeowner about their back door and dog situation while their car is burning, I could imagine the owner screaming at you. "I don't care about the dog or the door right now, my car is on fire," they might say. Of course, they might also scream "my baby," and leave the car for to be ruined as they race to the back of house. Right at that moment, something visceral is happening. It is something that taps directly into the car owners understanding of their wellbeing. It is a wedge issue purposefully crafted to hinge on aspects every bit as central to our human nature, but not touching on moral law. It is something called a prudential matter. This way our little quandary will be more effective after we've been studying the nature of moral law. It is useful because is still illustrates the power our preferences and judgment have over our decisions without demanding a definitive answer. When a chance for a defining an answer is present various preference systems can coalesce to compete supremacy. A prudential matter is useful because in this situation if it is your car and your pet, the best judgment you posses will be the right answer for you. This way we can look at the situation and the power of our responses to it without getting invested in the final outcome. In that moment of perceived crisis our preferences determine what gets addressed, what actions get taken, and how the available resources are used. In this case your presence is the finite resource. You can either be at the car with the garden hose, or at the back door rounding up the dog. One person can't be in two places at once.

The way resources are allocated has to be determined somehow. That homeowner screaming about their car or chasing the family pet is motivated. In that moment a rational response is difficult. A person that motivated is likely to jump at anything remotely plausible as having a chance of putting fires out or saving a beloved pet. Their primary goal is mitigating a perceived threat to a dearly held preference. When a preference starts drowning out all others, obfuscating important priorities that could be fulfilled through cooperation and problem solving, that's exactly where the worst of politicians want you. The voter in that frame of mind is easily moldable, willing to implement even extreme change if they think it will advance what they've come to hold as their most important preferences. If you're a politician willing to use those tactics then you might also understand that sometimes the best way to steal someone's dog is to set their car on fire. That's just a little something to think on. People in a polarized mindset demand little explanation or follow up. They aren't using critical thinking. Rather than wanting careful deliberation, they just want more to be given to their cause, and hate any resistance to that conferral. If your response can be predictable and unthinking, well, that's what some politicians might call good for business. This is why people in this type of business people carry master keys and a steady supply of lighter fluid.

When politicians mean to amass a large group of unified, motivated voters, that group is called a "base." Amassing a base isn't easy. For everyone who wins a contested election, there are one or more people who didn't succeed. The bigger the election, the bigger the base that is required. National elections require the biggest bases of all. Fortunes are spent, and armies of volunteers are sent out to organize the public. With vast resources on the line, the issues they run on must be equal in efficacy. The leaders of each side pick certain issues to run on because of their ability to galvanize their side of the political spectrum. The dictionary I read defines galvanize as: to startle into sudden activity. I think that's right on point. Ever wonder why the same issues get circulated each election no matter who is running? It's probably linked to the reason the percentage of the voters who vote for each side remains roughly the same. But, I'll leave that conversation for another time. The same old issues get brought up in each election cycle because they continue to strike the same chord in the populace. Politicians, when trying to get elected, or when they are pushing a policy, want to startle you into acting on their behalf.

Why does it work? Well, I could say human nature again. But, that would make for a far shorter book, and would most likely be too succinct to satisfy. So, let's tease this out a little bit. If you're going to startle someone, you're aiming to bypass their rational response and get them to jump, maybe let out a scream. Anyone who's ever had a friend or relative has had a giggle at someone they know and love leaving the floor momentarily when someone suddenly came around the corner. We've all done it. I think this is best context to approach the issue in. It's safe. The response to getting startled is pre-rational. Something is perceived internally as being a threat to some aspect of our being. We respond without thought. That's the same response politicians are hoping for when they attempt to polarize us. They want to convince us something core to our being is threatened, and tie a vote for them to our response. If they have worked their craft well, the voting booth becomes an act of reflex for even the educated political consumer. Just like when someone we know and love sneaks up on us, there doesn't need to be any real threat to get the response the other person desires. We react to what we perceive. And, when we have time afterwards, we consider how we reacted. If we focus, we can reduce the time between our reactions and our thoughts, even master how we respond. We can also learn to ignore false signals. I'm sure you all knew one person who never flinched, no matter how hard the younger relatives tried to surprise them. When juveniles in the family are on the prowl, that relative with the cool composure has learned it is best to keep an eye on them. There's a lesson here. When politicians act in a way which could be considered juvenile, trying to bypass your natural defenses to foolishness, it is best to keep an eye on them.

It may distress you to find there are more than a few ways to hack the human brain. Parents who have watched their children enter maturity and fall in love have seen dramatic degradation of rational thinking first hand. We just have to want something bad enough and start making sacrifices. New car smell triggers swooning in us faster than Pavlov's dinner bell can draw slobber out of a dog. Cute shoes seem to have an indescribable power to part women and their money (I think "cute" is another word for outrageously expensive). In the political realm wedge issues streak past our defenses in a way that surpasses even the most polished sales professional's neuro-linguistic programming laden pitch. These are issues which don't rely on mental constructs we've developed to help understand life. Little life experience is required for these issues to fuel our desires. They tap into something basic to our human existence. Other means of circumventing rational thought have been studied fairly extensively. But, this kind of pre-rational motivation seems to have been largely overlooked. For that reason it bears probing at a deeper level. How does it work?

Let's start by examining the kind of ideological thought which is common in political precincts. Ideological thought between the two major parties is B symmetrical. For those who don't remember high school art class, there are two types of symmetry. There is A symmetrical. That's when both sides are identical. If you make a line down the middle of a capital A, then fold it in half, what you see will look like half a letter A. The folded half neatly matches the side it is folded onto. B symmetrical is when the two sides don't match. If you made a line down the middle of a capital letter B, then folded it on that line, it would not look like half of a letter B. The two sides would each cover space not shared by the other half. One side would be defined by straight lines and rigid right angles. The other side would be composed predominately of curves, with less emphasis on straight lines. I also think the description of each side of a capital letter B makes a fairly accurate, artistic analogy for describing each party's body of thought. There's fun thought, no?

That's the way ideological thought functions. If you were to turn the issues that motivate voters into an image the two sides would inhabit fairly different space. An image which represents the way each major party approaches an issue would have two halves inhabiting radically different space. That's naturally occurring. They get there on their own. If this is part of human nature, then the question becomes, at what level does this occur? It must be primal to affect so many people in such a similar way. That's why I compare reactions to this with other pre-rational thought. As a rule, it would therefore undergird every area of our lives.

Think about something as simple and personal as your preferences. There are a number of factors which go into what we prefer, even when the question is, what's for dinner? What turns a restaurant into someone's favorite restaurant? That's a decision based on preference. There are practical reasons involved. A restaurant that is filthy won't see as much business as one where they clean regularly. But, when all things are equal, some people like comfort food where others like high cuisine. You can learn a lot from studying the cuisine. But, if you want to start a new restaurant in an area you'll need to start by learning about the local customer's preferences. In a saturated market, that's the difference between making a successful restaurant and failing to break into the market. If preferences are important in something as simple as dinner, where would you place the importance of your given bias in determining the direction and fate of our nation?

We should probably note, this is where the analogy ends. There are some fun other fun similarities we can point out. Food tastes, like political views, are subject to change throughout one's lifetime. What you liked as a baby or a child most likely won't appeal to your adult palette. People are also usually willing, even excited to try new food experiences outside the normal. Books are written to provide these new tastes, and cable networks successfully rely on delivering the new in this arena. But, whereas one's palette seems malleable, political tastes seem to be hard wired once they have been found. Inclination toward one of the two laws seems to be one of the fascinating building blocks of being human. Even those born into regional and family traditions devoted strongly to the tradition of thought growing from the other law can find themselves pulled irrefutably to thought which grows out of the other law.

That's why I liken the thought and preferences which define these sides to a B symmetrical construct. Each side has half of a picture. So what is the point of each side of the picture being different than the other? As we covered so far, this total image depicts the totality of morality. No one person is likely to learn all there is to understand on moral thought, and its application. Our preferences create the possibility of a mosaic of "specialists" in moral thought. Pursuing the things that matter most to you lays down a track record of experience which has been pondered and tested. Communication with others allows the humble to then reap the benefit of the experience of others. Remember that high cost of education which comes with personal experience? In this way the cost of firsthand experience could be spread across all of humanity, paid by those who are doing what they love and don't mind the small cost. Of course, these are just preferences. They are the precursor to a conscience, and continually exert a pull on conscience formation. Just like you can change your diet, you can form you conscience. A person, through consistent exercise of their will, can refuse to act on these preferences. Although pre-rational preferences continue to affect a person, just like hunger for food, we do not always eat that which our bodies crave. A person who gives into unhealthy appetites long enough can even find themselves in a place where a force of will is necessary to recognize their original preferences. To continue the same metaphor, dining on the aspect of morality you crave the most, while supplementing your diet by learning from the example of others who are seeking their preferred aspect of morality, you live a more balanced and morally healthy life. That kind living incorporates moral truth form both sides of the morality big picture. When both sides of the picture combine they form a total image that looks appealing and makes sense to bother sides. That's important to note.

A concept which holds both sides as true will be universally appealing. It is very hard to find the dividing line between application of the first law of love and the second. Examples where the laws have been separated and polarized come most frequently from the fringe. Extremists craft arguments that represent themselves. People naturally inclined to one side or the other will resonate with the selectively presented truth as long as a fuller representation of the truth does not persuade them. When the full truth is presented persuasively, however, it can be very difficult for extremists to go about dividing. You will find it much easier to defend such a concept. Why, do you not hear arguments which tell the whole truth more often? If you've read this far you've seen the answer already. A population resistant to division is bad for business if your business is crafting political bases. When an issue is not presented in terms of the whole truth, one half of the moral picture is underrepresented, or not represented at all. When one half is not present, or listened to, those who believe in the underrepresented half will find representation rather than accepting placation. They will fill that craving with whatever they can get their hands on that is even remotely appealing. Even if they never find true representation, a person with an unfulfilled moral craving will pick the political party which appears to present the closest approximation to their favored law of love. It is amazing the evil a population will accept from those they approve in power when they fear a total loss of their preferred moral law's representation. Once this principle is in action a slide into moral darkness occurs. The conscience, which used to unite humanity in a common pursuit of total morality, has been repurposed by the ignorant and power hungry to lead us into greater polarization.

I like the visual artistry of the B Symmetry comparison so let's go back to that for a moment. If the side of thought preference that represents the curves is present and are not making the effort to seek balance, they will instead endeavor in self replication. The fruit of their labors will leave you with a figure 8, not a B. Try seeking beauty without a B. You get 8eauty. That makes no sense. I can't even pronounce that. The same is true of the other side. It happens on both sides. When the straight lines side tries to remove whatever opposes their narrow orthodoxy, leaving their preference in its place, they also work to replicate themselves. They will try to complete the B using straight lines, forming hard angles, with no bend whatsoever. Neither side seems able to innately know how to represent the other side. Each side must therefore make the effort to learn the form, application, and importance of the other side.

Ok, it got a little artsy for a second there. Hopefully my indulgence didn't bother you too much. Artistic expression, even when it is very poor like mine, can be a bridge to truth we find hard to define. This is a tender area we tiptoe around in day to day conversation. Our busy lives don't always lead to times of quiet contemplation. When we do have time to take stock of our personal inventory we humans tend to think in terms of what we'd like to accomplish, rather than honestly appraising who we are. We don't always make it identifying what tools we have, what we lack, and where we need to round out our understanding. It is important to engage ourselves in this evaluation. But, putting the concept of us into plain speech where we can begin to tackle this kind of evaluation takes effort.

It is about the way we inform our values. Our conscience directs what values we hold. The two laws are a big part of the way our conscience formation happens. These terms seem esoteric to some, but values, which lead to habits, help us make daily decisions. Our natural predilections put pressure on the way the tools we use to govern our day are crafted. We get to know each other, and interact with them in a normal fashion based on their actions. It's how we relate. Our actions, while not definitive, help us understand the question of what people stand for. While the process of evaluating others can be difficult, evaluating ourselves can get even more complicated. The bias we bring to our evaluation of others seems to run rampant in our evaluation of ourselves. And there's not just bias clouding our judgment. If you know anything about shaping values, you know this is a very uncomfortable, demanding process. In the same way we guard an injury on the outside of our bodies from potentially painful contact, we can avoid the internal areas that hurt. Introspection is entirely necessary. Healthy societal function in each generation depends on it. And we are the ones who will need to take a role in the process. After our parents have done their job, we take over. When we become responsible for our actions we begin parenting ourselves in a sense. If we do not, there are consequences. There is a saying I thought up, but have also heard elsewhere. Hurt people hurt people. Perhaps, it is too clever by half. If you are hurting on the inside, and you take time and effort to heal, you will most likely hurt other people until you do take the time. It is also true that we hurt others out of ignorance. If we don't take the steps to improve the state of our understanding, the result is the same. Healing and understanding are two benefits introspection can help with. To achieve these benefits we need to work from the whole picture. So what tools do we have available in the process of personal development?

Tradition and the guidance of previous generations greatly facilitate the process the process of forming our moral understanding. Of course, tradition can lead us in the wrong direction as well. It is a two edged sword. Just like habits, tradition merely makes a practice more resilient in the face of change. It makes no judgments as to whether a practice is good, edifying, or true. We could spend time parsing out the differences between tradition that helps and where it hurts. For this conversation, however, let's concentrate on tradition where it helps. Family in the form of parent, grandparent, aunt, uncle et al., plays a vital role in this process of creating and maintaining traditions. Traditions are made to be passed down. So much of this is by what we learn from the example of others. We observe the totality of the actions those closest to us take. A parent, a grandparent, a sibling, and others we look up too all contribute to our understanding of traditions. Some things we pick up easily. Others require more observation and even practice to master. But the simple yet elegant rules for interaction and conduct we learn in the institution of the family create a foundation for navigating the larger, more complex institutions in society. Members of each generation must learn the functions required in a healthy society to which they are not naturally inclined. In the best environment for learning there are an abundance of stable, consistent examples to choose from. A wider array of examples provides greater acceptance for the "black sheep" of the family. Those who recognized differences between themselves and members of the nuclear family could find another relative with whom there is sympathy. They could choose among several familial role models to find one that shared a similar worldview, yet had learned to exist and cooperate within the whole of the family. In this way answers could be found to illuminate the path to harmony through understanding.

It sounds great, doesn't it? But, tradition isn't what it used to be in our culture. We need to renew a desire for good traditions in our nation. The best way to do that is to have great traditions that entice others to share in those traditions in their own lives. That may be harder today than a generation ago, however. We face some special challenges. Families aren't what they used to be either. Consistent and stable examples have been replaced. Children today are left with a rotating cast of characters comprised of relatives they don't see anymore because they were lost in the divorce along with the car and the 401k. The world of answers for the children of today shrinks in an inverse ration with the divorce rate. Words like, "You're not my dad," and, "Will you be my mommy," play in the soundtrack to the path by which experiences today are passed to posterity. The result is a culture which reinforces hardening preferences, rather than examples of reconciliation which venerate applying the full picture.

That explains U. S. culture. We've demanded narrowing constructs of society instead of seeking reconciliation and cooperation in a shared pursuit of the transcendent. I suppose we could wrap the book here. The principles we've covered thus far could be applied by the clever reader. But, this is a safe place to experiment with ideas before the consequences of life kick in. I'm a big fan of learning from example when possible, books when needed, and experience only when absolutely necessary. So, we're going to go through some big picture examples of how it all shakes out. This is done with the intention that you'll catch on to the theme that's being played.

Some issues only motivate the concerned. Sadly, Eminent Domain seems to be one of the issues which have fallen into this category. That may just be one of my pet peeves. For those not familiar, if the government is planning to run a road through your living room, or give your land to a company who will pay more in taxes, you're likely motivated on that issue. The people who live in the next neighborhood that aren't in jeopardy of losing their houses may either be apathetic to your concern, or excited about the prospect of better infrastructure or shopping access. That's a narrowly defined issue. The only people who care are the ones motivated by principle who have the awareness to know it is happening, and the people directly effected, in this case you.

Some issues galvanize a wider group of individuals, but not other groups. The humane treatment of animals is a great example of an issue capable of motivating groups to action. No one likes animal cruelty. Well, almost no one. The only ones I know of are locked up where society keeps serial killers, or in some country where things like dog fighting is still legal. But, not everyone is willing to contribute materially to raise awareness for the cause of treating animals humanely. Groups like PETA, the Humane Society, and other animal rights supporters are willing. Some are so motivated that they advocate for this cause by creating spectacles, like depicting normally clad people taking off all clothes in public protest of clothes made from animals. The members of this group are obviously highly motivated to their cause. Usually, these exhibitionists are known for being attractive. That seems counter intuitive to me, but what do I know. I think the tactic might be more effective if they picked someone for the ads who looked like me, and then had them threaten to not put their clothes back on until their demands are met. But, that might land said person on a terrorist watch list for using tactics like that. Perhaps they should probably stick with attractive proponents. Viewers would be less likely to confuse the activists with the animals they represent.

The end result of these extreme, sometimes jarring tactics is that people who wouldn't normally consider the issues represented talk about them. Awareness is being raised in society. Political force is definitely being exerted. But, we really don't see a lot of opposition being motivated against the cause of treating animals humanely. This is true even when activists, a little too fervently for polite society, embrace their principle issue with the aforementioned fabric free fashion statement. Despite the societal lines they cross and occasional use of heavy handed tactics, I would assume most agree these groups are doing some good. They are tolerated, despite occasionally crossing generally held lines of acceptable behavior.

Wedge issues also galvanize widely across the culture. People of all walks of life can have the same strong reaction to wedge issues. Unlike issues more benign political plays, wedge motivate their side, but generate an opposite reaction worthy of a physics dissertation. And that's what makes a wedge issue different. A wedge issue is one that drives a metaphoric wedge between the voting populace. These issues separate voters into the largest possible groups of common interest. When either side brings up a wedge issue to rally their base, the motivated among the other side have a strong, polar reaction. Many times these issues are used in to rally rooms full of people who already agree with the candidate. Politicians will use these issues because they have a historically guaranteed return. But, wary politicians also know they risk motivating the opponent's base against them in the process. This risk is what invokes the political equivalent of Newton's Third Law. The conflict these issues engender, when pushed in purely partisan way, is what gives them and the politicians who use them their most nefarious reputations. These things are the power source behind the proverbial "third rails" in politics. As such, they are rarely approached directly when used this way.

They are often set up in the form of attacking a political opponent's stance on a wedge issue. The idea behind such an attack is to get an opponent to talk about a wedge issue. If they can be tricked or boxed into walking near that rail there is a real danger they will step wrong to dire effect. One side criticizes the stance the other side takes on a wedge issue. The other side now finds themselves in bind. If they defend against this charge indelicately they risk giving their opponent's base more reason to oppose them on the ballot. If they don't take a stand on the issue in a firm enough way, they risk discouraging or even crossing supporters on their own side. Voters who feel they have been betrayed on issues important to them are less likely to come out in support on voting day. Because of how they are used, and the alacrity with which both sides of the political base turn to rancor on these issues, wedge issues have gained a reputation. And, if that reputation matters to you, I'm going to ask a hard thing. I'm going to ask you to suspend any vehemence while you consider the following pages. We're going right over to that third rail so we can learn where the power comes from.

Now that we've explained what wedge issues are, let's list three:

- Abortion
- The Second Amendment
- Tax Policy

We will analyze each issue in terms of the two laws, and where the two major political parties fall on each issue. It is also important to understand that I often take a thing to its furthest logical extent to see how it fares. I liken it to taking a car out alone for a test drive on a race track to see what shakes loose. If anything goes wrong it is a controlled environment. Better to prove confidence in relative safety than to have something fail in traffic, or on a fast curve. A well built machine will purr like a kitten. A lousy bucket of bolts will complain loudly on its way to becoming an oversized paperweight. Under normal situations one might ask, in what hazardous situation could an idea possibly put me? Remember, these are wedge issues. They feel the pulse of our very sense of justice. Wars have been fought over notions like these. We may forget the power ideas have over our hearts, having enjoyed in our lives the peaceful means of resolution others have forged and tempered in their. Abraham Lincoln addressed Congress in July 4, 1861, "That ballots are the rightful, and peaceful, successors of bullets...." We take the importance of what happens on voting day far too lightly in our culture today. The potential for change happens with relative calm and ease every four years in the highest office of our nation. Before our republic was formed this kind of change was hallmarked with vicious bloodshed. The sense of justice has not dimmed, our desires have not dissipated. We've merely found a careful balance by which moral people can find agreement to govern their own nation without resorting to bloodshed. That careful balance is at the heart of the threat posed by polarization. Because that balance is achieved through our participation, we must endeavor to take on the hardest issues with a full understanding of morality. This responsibility is both for ours own good and the wellbeing of other. So brace yourself when you find you are being galvanized by what you read next. You may find yourself offended, or feeling I've gone too far. These issues are at the heart of a very vulnerable place. Such feelings are perfectly normal. We're dealing with preferences that spring from the place where we define ourselves. If there was a road to the seat of human will, these preferences would mark the way. Brace yourself.

The very act of turning our attention to what defines our preferences can cause the kind of discomfort which stems from a very private place. I beg of you, if and when this should happen find no ill in my art. I am a paltry author and this book is a study on polarization. This is about the extremes of a system which struggle to pull the middle in opposite direction. When the logic of an argument is taken to its furthest logical extent, by definition, while maintaining its educational worthiness it probably no longer describes you. These extremes describe a small minority which exerts undue influence on the majority. It is also important to keep in mind that even in these vocal minorities are found those who follow their conscience the best they know how, just as Saul did millennia ago. And, that's where the use of this study is found. Of interest is that human quality over which time, culture, and distance hold no sway. What comes together to form the conscience? How are these extreme poles that play on decision making process create the intellectual and emotional space in which you form your own sense of right? It will become clear to see, by playing these concepts out you don't just test a theory. You test yourself.

That's why it's going to hurt a little. But it's ok. When your sense of privacy struggles to gain distance remind yourself, it's just you and a book. You are on your own mental and emotional journey. I didn't include the physical, but if your pulse pounds, and a copy of my book goes flying across the room, I won't consider it disrespectful to the author. I just hope for your wall's sakes you are enjoying a paperback. And people say books are good for you. I imagine sitting around reading them all day is not good for a waistline. I've certainly gained a pound or two sitting around writing this one. Moderation always seems to recommend its own value. And don't bother telling me about the people who can read while they walk on the treadmill. I'm sure that takes more coordination than I can muster. That would only result in an embarrassing thud.

Keep your reactions as close as necessary. There's no need to share the answers you've found until you're ready. I've merely taken assumptions, which both poles of the culture have respectively asserted as solid, up to the point to where they will easily serve illustrative purpose. What comes from this is between you, these pages, and your wall.

Abortion

Conservatives feel, to date, abortion is about responsibility. They have argued an expecting mother made a choice to engage in intercourse. Becoming pregnant, they continue, is a common consequence of intercourse, for which many families hope. The conservative stance is that the choice to engage in behavior that can result in pregnancy carries with it responsibilities. Most notable is the responsibility to care for any life created in that action. Conservatives have a great affinity for responsibilities they classify as personal. A compassionate person arguing a pro-life message might speak of the great potential to contribute this human life holds. But, while you hear it occasionally, that is not the message most commonly heard out of the conservative camp.

For conservatives it's all about the individual rights of the baby, and the personal responsibility of the mother. The other side argues the case in terms of the mother's rights, and her child's inability to carry out responsibilities. The most polar extremes polarize the populace as each side builds their arguments on these respective terms. It is borderline a rule, if not definitively categorical. The two sides have been framing their positions on this wedge issue for decades. Why does each side continue to think this way? Why did they begin to think this way in the first place? Their arguments come from their preferences. The right prefers arguing for responsibility over compassion based arguments. They rarely bring up our duty to nurture other human life. Their most forcefully presented assertions leave out the wellbeing of the mother. They seem happy to leave room for the other side to claim as their uncontested province concern for the mother. The arguments of the right orbit around the demand for personal purity. Those on the far right get excited when natural forces seem to punish those who don't live by this standard of purity. Want to see this one test at full speed? The Catholic Church enforces both laws of loves in its governing message, so we'll use them as a baseline. Compare Catholic arguments against abortion, like those coming out of Priests for Life, to arguments coming out of partisan conservative political camps. Compassion for the mother is featured much more prominently in the Catholic message. Even in the harshest cases, such as rape or incest, they present abortion as further damaging to the mother by killing her baby. I've heard extreme conservative arguments justify killing the child because of a rapist's involvement. Obviously, if both sides hold the position that all life has value then the Catholics have a more disciplined approach to moral constructs. But, if your primary concern is gaining distance from any potential affront to a personal sense of purity constructed on imperfectly on only one law of love, then compassion is secondary, or even tertiary if mentioned at all.

It is important to note when mentioning compassion that failure to live the first law of love does hurt others. If your neighbor isn't maintaining their living space the pests that nest their will raid your house too. If you don't keep you moral house in order in terms of the first law then problems in your life will negatively impact others too. Both laws are necessary to build a solid society.

To get the first law right is to conduct one's self well. To those inclined more to the first law of love, principles growing from this first law and are generally common sense, doing what appears obvious. But that's not easy enough for all to find direction. So, conservative pundits make an effort to codify this concept, sometimes inappropriately. They often do this using jargon used in conservative circles which can be easily applied to behavior of which they generally don't approve. Possibly most notable is the phrase "personal responsibility." It is a catch all phrase which is used to encompass every act of sacrifice they want you to make on their behalf, and every impediment they wish you to remove from their path. Of course, this demand they make that one be responsible is not always accompanied with an estimation of what it will cost the other to act according to the conservative's will. Because the answer is always found in what comes from the self, there is a disregard, willful or otherwise, of the actions of outside forces.

Outside forces are not seen as factors in success for failure, only the self is considered. These forces take a secondary role, if any at all, such as being acknowledged in the list of obstacles which were overcome as laudatory to the self, or as the avatar of judgment on violators of the first law. This is the inspiration for such arguments as, if you're suffering it's because you deserve it. Great burdens can be laid this way on those least able to carry them under the guise of helping in desperate circumstances. And that's where they lack. Without the role of compassion, they lay burdens on the backs of those already laboring under great weight. True conservatives take no consideration of compassion when assessing culpability, or even capability. Compassion demands personal action from those who would abstain from services to others. Sometimes people need help fulfilling their own responsibilities. This need may even go beyond the material. Consider an addict who needs a support system to kick their addiction. They have innate gifts, a contribution to make to society. Yet, they cannot make this contribution fully or well when flitting between stupor and dissipation. But, to the conservative extremist, compassion is leaving the addict to the harrows of their chemical tormentor until the natural order inspires motivation. It's like kicking that addict until they fear the boot more than the pain of withdrawal, except the extreme conservative doesn't want any blame associated with owning that boot.

But, life doesn't always work that way. Sometimes, to get things started, an addict needs an intervention. Resources of time and money may be needed for the cause of their sobriety. It need not escape perceptive notice that success is most likely when both laws of love come to bear on the situation, specifically when the addict acts out the first law of love and those around the addict act out the second law of love. The second law of love requires a willingness on our part to give to others in proper time and measure. The people who make appeals to the masses by calling the loudest for personal responsibility should be careful to see that they are living under both laws of the love. It may be easier in this divided environment to build a following by making superficial demands which appeal strongly to almost half the population.

Jesus, our teacher, was quite clear on those who make demands of others. He spoke directly to those who claim authority from the laws of love without living those laws fully and first. An excellent example of this is recorded in the Bible, in the book of Luke, chapter eleven, verses thirty-seven through forty-one. In this passage, Jesus responds to the Pharisees' surprise that he did not engage in a traditional custom. The custom was engaged in by respectable people as a display of their own purity. When Jesus declined to labor under the restrictions of their tradition, partisans of that divided period considered this a breach of his personal responsibility. Jesus responded to their show of surprise that he did not make an outward display of his own purity. He did so in a way that should be considered a warning to all those who build purity tests instead of balancing their judgment using compassion. Jesus started by calling them out as fools. He then continued to tell them that if they wanted to be clean on the inside, instead of full of greed and wickedness, they should give to the poor. That, Jesus said, would work to make them clean all over. This statement strikes a blow through the heart of the conceit that a person can withdraw from the obligation of the second law of love, and accurately consider themselves acceptable under the first law of love.

Democrats, on the other hand, have a different take on the abortion issue. You may have noticed I said democrats without making any special distinction of liberality. The Democrat Party is clearly known as the party of abortion. It's official. Also, President Barack Obama, the nation's most prominent democrat, has openly supported legal abortion of a viable child in the womb. We're talking has a heart beat, feels pain, moves to it's favorite music, could live outside the womb if taken out now, viable. That's not a difference of state, that's a difference in locale. When questioned about advocating the death of human life who's most commonly portrayal is purveyed by proud parents pointing out their son or daughter in an ultrasound image, notable democrats have said things like, "A young woman shouldn't be punished with a child is she doesn't want it".

There really isn't much use in defining the difference between a liberal and a democrat these days. There used to be a distinction when the party was more moderate. There probably will be again if the progressive wing continues its ascendancy. At that time democrat will be synonymous with progressive. But, for now the terms liberal and democrat are practically interchangeable. I know I'm going to get flack from some for that, but it is fairly evident the Reagan Democrats have left the party, become radicalized, or lost their voice in the new progressive party leadership. Not many like to be called a radial. Most people I've met believer a radical is anyone more extreme than themselves, no joke. I'm not interested in getting into a war of terms over it, parsing nuances between political terms like progressive and liberal. So, I'll define it up front. For those to whom it matters, a progressive is a liberal, but a liberal is not necessarily a progressive. Progressivism would be considered a sect of liberalism. Progressives can therefore be referred to under the umbrella of liberalism, while liberalism cannot be wholly defined by progressivism except where they do not reject progressive doctrine. Just a personal opinion, but that margin seems to do nothing but narrow.

Let's focus on the differences which apply most to our discussion. That would be the differences between liberal and conservative thought. These two schools of thought, doctrines even, grow from the two laws of love. Each side claims authority based on self evident truths derived from one of the two laws to which the populace responds. The connection between the law of love and the argument each side uses becomes their particular orthodoxy. Differences between these political groups are clearly visible in where each side claims their authority is derived. Conservatives see their authority as coming from moral principles derived from the first law of love. Because their favored law of love deals with the personal obligation to moral law, they find lawless behavior especially offensive. Liberals see the grounds for their authority in principles derived from the second law of love. Modern liberal thought is defined by compassion. As such, they are especially offended by hate.

Of course, failure to follow both laws of love is a total failure of morality. Those who are the worst make a show of following their side's orthodoxy usually do so while offending the spirit of both laws. You'll find conservatives who complain about people who illegally cross a border while they themselves are violating traffic laws by breaking speed limits every day. An unsecured border carries the potential for grave costs, including fatalities, but so does a motor vehicle accident. Liberals accuse those with whom they disagree by labeling them with hateful terms. They use labels like racism, homophobia, or some other 'ism while knowing they are deliberately falsely accusing their target. This kind of slanderous character assassination is in itself a hateful act. With all their airtime progressives are getting these days, some may be asking where they stand in all of this. Progressives see their authority as resting on like minded consensus in whatever country they are found, beginning with an orthodoxy influenced by liberal thought. In effect, this makes them a derivation of a derivative. I'll explain. Progressives base their sect's doctrine on the orthodoxy developed from the second law of love. Each step distancing a body of thought from the moral laws which govern our nature allows the adherents to tolerate more extreme actions. The distance of being two theoretical steps removed from the law of love their thought and agenda come from explains why they have been willing to accept more extreme measures, like eugenics, than classical liberals. Those who wish to read more about my reference to progressives and eugenics may read the article Retrospectives: Eugenics and Economics in the Progressive Era by Thomas C. Leonard in *Journal of Economic Perspectives*—Volume 19, Number 4—Fall 2005—Pages 207–224. I'm not much of a researcher myself, but I imagine a Princeton lecturer will do nicely. While liberals and progressives classify themselves as distinct, they both ultimately seek the same ends. The variations between liberals and progressives exist in overall scope and means. As I mentioned earlier, delving into the varieties of liberal thought wouldn't be germane to this little literary endeavor. So, we'll leave it there and use the catch all term of liberal when we want to describe both. Now that we have explored the respective approach of both groups let's try it on a wedge issue.

When it comes to a wedge issue like abortion liberals are naturally inclined to think about the ramifications which compassion can address. The expenses, sacrifice, and pain of caring for a young human life come to the forefront of their considerations as well as the possibility of a life of privation for the child. The liberal mind is most pleased by solutions by which it can see itself as freeing the young mother from these cares. The radical liberal wants to be a hero in their own estimation, like many of us. The hero want to be uses their preferred system of values to accomplish their goals. Other values aren't as important, or are even considered adversarial if they challenge the preferred values system. When it comes to abortion, this may seem to some a farcical excuse to put an end to a human life. To understand how they have come to canonize this rationale, if one does not understand intuitively, some explanation may be in order.

It is important to emphasize here that both sides can make their ideology into their god. Notice the small "g" which makes the word carry only the meaning of a ruler, or supreme conception. No one is being demonized or condemned. Anyone who rejects half the morality necessary to have a civil society characterizes themselves. But, many seem to do this out of a fervent desire to live by as their conscience dictates. Maybe if more people in the middle lived that way we would all be better off.

When those on the extremes of the moral big picture carve out a part of morality for the purpose of elevating it, and leave the rest to ignore, a drift takes place. In any group or person, as understanding of the requirements of human nature diminishes, we walk the road of depravity. By ignoring, or outright rejecting the parts of morality we find less tasteful, over time society becomes less human with each generation's step. This can also be true of subcultures within a society. But how does this take place? Others modes not found in the narrowly defined ideology, which has been elevated now to orthodoxy, are eschewed. Modes popular enough to compete with the new orthodoxy are treated in an adversarial manner, even as a bitter enemy. People can be very motivated to move in a given direction when the values coming form their core are challenged. When a group or individual elevates their preferred aspect of nature in this manner, it can be easy to transgress the other parts of nature's law, while denying the dire nature of the transgression. Both of the two laws of love, from which our societal law springs, must he held in high cultural regard for the whole of society to function from generation to generation. As such, a generative societal cohesive unity which will last over time depends on a system of values which includes the fullest possible image of morality based on both laws of love.

Put more simply, people who pick and choose what to believe from human nature are in for a hurting. Sometimes you just have to put it in "redneck." My family was blessed to come from both sides of the tracks, so to speak, but enough about me. When an ideology is engrossed, and subsequently consumed, with the thought formed by those who lean more toward one law of nature, one commandment to love, without regard for the other commandment to love, it creates a dangerous blindside in that ideology. Like other immutable laws, that's like randomly choosing not to believe in gravity. Such an ideology then builds massive theoretical structures which are then used to justify real world actions on that assumption. This method of delusion has the potential of leading entire nations into truly horrible actions before the truth is revealed. Just ask the progressives of the early twentieth century how their eugenics have been used. The ideas extreme ideology create are dangerous because they can take root even among a people of deep conviction. In fact, for assumptions to be acted on which rob others of the rights self evident in their humanity deep convictions are almost entirely necessary to be present. Usually, assumptions like these require copious amounts of alcohol to create, and are espoused by that friend or relative who makes you wonder if Darwin didn't have at least little sense to him. I think my redneck is showing again. But, the road to eugenics was trod by those who considered themselves clear thinking intellectuals. So many revolutions which lead to the deaths of millions and millions were the result of popular uprising. The world of politics seems to pull this off again and again stone sober. Now that's a neat trick, if you can call it that. Maybe it's possible because capitols like Washington D. C. are populated by leaders who surround themselves with those who tell them they're always right. But that doesn't seem sufficient to the carnage we're describing. How does the one's who seem reasonable, your friends and neighbors, get caught up in something like this? If we can find the answer, wouldn't that be worth knowing? The worst part, what really terrifies and galls, is that the authority necessary for governments to commit such acts comes from that nation's people. Now what does that say? Regardless of the form, national level atrocity seems to take place behind a moral blindside, heralded by the cheers of those who call it right.

 In this blindside, it can ruled acceptable to take a human life, or ignore the value of humanity. Human life is no longer judged by its true worth, illuminated by the light of self evident truths. We've been discussing how natural preferences turn into orthodoxy, and then become used to obscure half of a people's moral understanding for political gain. Some perils have been outlined, but the stubborn who accepts this truth may believe there has simply been a lack of the right people who can make a system like this function. For those who think their favored orthodoxy won't fail, please consider the heart of the matter. Without a full understanding of this firm context, this frame of reference, humanity no longer gets its value and dignity from an inalterable place. Human life is now judged only by the ability to uphold the tenets of a partially blind ideology. This is why every blind ideology ultimately fails, no matter how well intentioned or educated its adherents. When any group or society loses the full understanding of the value of human life in its culture and practices, that people open the door to horrors and atrocities large and small. No ill may be intended. But, that's a big door. When it opens there's a lot of room for big consequences to walk through.

The second law of love governs providing care to others. When it comes to meeting needs this is great. It is a law governing actions emanating from an outward act. The great thing about these laws is that their simple construction covers a broad application. The way they are formulated makes them very hard to co-opt for selfish ambitions. Something in our nature responds in a way that directs our conscience. Somewhere between the high we get from seeing our preferences realized and the pain of cognitive dissonance that comes when we act contrary to our consciences there a life that is built. The people who seek to commandeer these forces that inform our life decisions through artifice need the broad appeal of these laws. But, through artifice and degrees of separation they re-imagine issues in ways they can co-opt. They defend their vain imaginings with political maneuvers designed to get close enough to the center of our morality to gain broad appeal, but separated enough to maintain plasticity. They want the gut reaction, but they don't want introspection to follow. A gut reaction is desired because it is fairly easy to control. It's like showing a vampire in those black and white movies the cross. The holy symbol comes out and the vampire immediately recoils in an unrestrained display of aversion. Show the target demographic what offends them, then, tell them if they send you to the capitol with lot's of political donations you'll fix it. Once in office they use the power you've invested in them and your good name to convince interest groups and individuals with money that to get what *they* want done they'll have to go through them. That's the game.

Notice nothing really gets done for the purpose of civic interest as a result of this process. The whole goal of this strategy is to put the voter in the place where they feel the need to exorcise a feeling, and then offer them absolution through an act of contrition in the voting booth. It's all about leading people to get in touch with what motivates them the most. You can't get too specific when playing this game. People come to decision in a lot of various ways. There isn't enough time to address them all so politicians have to pick issues that will connect with lots of people, and let them draw their own reasons for motivation from there. That's why the details of an issue don't matter, from a strictly business sense. All that matters is that the issue be motivating. Whether it is as benign as a building a parking lot or as serious as life and death is a question for novices. The only question that matters in the big leagues is, does it work? The effects of the issue, should it generate legislation, fall into the same category. That's a concern for the regulators, the culture, and the courts to work out. Winning is everything in the political game. The people at the top are concern with what moves the most people. As a result, the two party's exclusionary approach to the two laws of love picks the issues, not practicality, ethics, or economy. That's why nothing is spared from their touch. The only limiting factor is what will offend us. In any area where our love has grown dark, anything is possible. Where ignorance is found as to what both laws demand on vital matters, political agents use this ignorance as a wedge to divide us. Nothings is sacred, even the human life.

 That doesn't explain the entirety, however. Forty percent of the nation didn't wake up today and plot how to end as many human lives as possible *and* make it legal. So that raises the question, why do good people vote for evil things through the election of representatives who pledge to do evil? I'm not going to try to sell you on your representative's lack of evil. It is almost stereotypical how some seem to think all politicians are corrupt, and then continues voting for their representative every election. I wouldn't know where to begin on that one. We can, however, agree your neighbors aren't all even, can't we? I've got friends I care about a great deal. They are as polar opposite in some of their ideals from me as possible. But, they've rushed to my defense many a time when I've been attacked personally. When it comes to the concrete I know I have their trust as well. It's just in the abstract we disagree. When faced with issues we can reason out together, we get there different ways but often come to the same conclusion as long as each of our views is represented in the answer. That's how it is supposed to work. But that's not good for amassing numbers in campaign season. How does political spin get us to tap into what is too painful to talk about, destroying communication between us and our good neighbors who disagree? An exclusionary political argument wraps an evil which the one side cannot abide in the form of a good which the other side cannot fail to uphold. For the issue to truly be a wedge issue this must be true whether it is approached form either side of the political spectrum. Some of the act must be rooted in compassion while the rest of the act simultaneously violates rectitude. Argued from the other side it must uphold the demands of personal conduct while violating our duty to love and care for others.

With this simple rule as a starting point, a "jig" as they call it in the trades, we can drill down to how we get from good people to very bad policies. Building on the premise of this rule, politicians who want to get elected or re-elected create a narrative. To be persuasive this narrative must make sense. At the same time it must continue to keep us occupied with fighting each other and motivate to vote for the politician. The starting point may be simple, but the application lacks the simplicity of the two laws. More rules have to be created. Rules have to be created to interpret the rules. Eventually you have a sliding scale called political correctness and everyone live under the constant threat of being politically ostracized. With the possibility of bending the system to your will on one side, and the threat of political correctness on the other, any number of grave social ills can be accepted.

Let's look at some of the rules that have been built around the issue of abortion. Again, these are the kind of arguments good people let slide past them unawares. Remembering our jig, their greatest concerns have not been violated. The concerns of the unaware have been upheld in both what has been committed and omitted. So let's look at how the issue of abortion gets framed. Since babies are almost exclusively caught up in their own needs, they do not significantly uphold this second commandment in the eyes of blind ideology. They do not act to relieve the suffering of others, or contribute quantifiably to the wellbeing of another. Therefore, they do not merit notice or consideration. That's a dangerous group to be placed into in the eyes of the law.

 Viability, in the view of this ideology, is conferred upon those who contribute in ways recognized by the ideological orthodoxy. An example of this would be the Eastern Pennsylvania State Institution for the Feeble-Minded and Epileptic, also known as Pennhurst. For those looking for more than a brief synopsis found on the internet, there's a district court case known as *Halderman v. Pennhurst State School and Hospital, 74-1345 ( E.D. Pa. )* which may have the expository journey you'd be looking for. After getting through the grisly details, it is important to remember this place was created with the intention to uphold the morality of the society from which it came. This happened during many of our lifetimes. People acted on their intention to move society closer to their ideal of utopia. This was a radical form of removing those considered not to contribute adequately to society, yes. But, it was seen as an act of kindness. The hospital was a medical facility. It was believed to be a kindness to families who would otherwise give up their aspirations of carefree lives in high society for constant care required by a family member with special needs. It was intended by some to be a place where those who could never function as others might in society would be provided for in a manner deemed better than what they would contribute in return. But, as I've asserted before, when you fail to acknowledge both laws of love in your motivations you end up failing both in your actions.

 If you're familiar with the arguments for abortion, you've probably heard it described as an act of kindness. I've heard it presented often as a medical procedure which saves a mother from the burden of caring for a new family member who will require constant, substantial care. And, it is also claimed it saves the aborted child from a life of privation and being unwanted. Does that sound familiar? Fads change, fashion changes, tastes change, human nature does not change. The mother's responsibility to the child is based in the first law of love. The basis for recognizing a child in the womb who can't contribute materially to others as a viable member of society is also found in the first law of love. With this standard of viability, taking the life of the yet to be born child is seen as removing something unnoticed at best. If the child contributed to others in a way which would then merit notice in the orthodoxy which deviates from the point of the second law of love, those inclined to this orthodoxy would be offended. Granted the child may provide great joy to someone now. Hope for the future and a sense of fulfillment can be found in loving someone else, especially a child in the womb. The sacrifices we make for those we love can teach and grow us in ways far more valuable than any estimation of what they are given. But, how can we measure joy? How do you litigate hope or character development in the sound byte driven court of public opinion? That question lingering would be the best case of coexistence with ideological orthodoxy. In the worst case, the child is seen as an affront to the ideology, and punished (or freed) with removal for not contributing. And, the mother is freed from the constraint of a responsibility not recognized by the ideology. It may not make much sense to some when explained in the extreme. But, such is the way of depravity. Often we walk this road out of what we neglect, the fulfillment of selfish ambitions.

Let's wrap up the abortion wedge issue. The first law of love places a demand to conduct our personal lives in an acceptable way. To take an unborn child's life is to take on the guilt of killing, and deny the child's ability to live to their fullest potential. That's why the conservatives have a problem with abortion. The second law of love creates a compassion based demand for how we treat others. When the second law is elevated in the mind, and the first abjured, no obligation remains to safeguard life and wellbeing not in service to the ideological orthodoxy. But, would a compassion based argument for taking human life even begin to motivate if we as a society competed to outdo each other in our care of single mothers and couples in want? While one law is greater, and either law may be more attractive to some, both laws were given equal weight in practice by Jesus. Ideology based solely on either law of human nature cannot satisfactorily explain the whole of human experience. Great harm and human tragedy occur when both laws of love are not observed equally.

At this point, I had to take a moment to step away from writing. I totally understand if you need a break, too. I put a break in between each wedge issue. Think of it as an emotional rest stop where you can evaluate whether you need to take a moment, process what you've read. Just make sure you pick the book back up. This is important stuff.

The Second Amendment

We'll pick back up with the second wedge issue, guns. Rarely does an object evoke such strong emotions. The gun has transcended mundane concerns such as being a family tool for putting food on the table, protecting the homestead, or waging the occasional war to becoming an icon. Why has the firearm, as a symbol, grown beyond its utilitarian function to capture the political mind? To answer this question we need to define, at least partially, what the gun represents. We need to layer this understanding with what each side of the ideological divide is built to strive for in society. I used to use the analogy of peeling an onion in reverse to describe how this is helpful. Fortunately, technology has provided a better analogy. If we add the layers in the same way as a 3D printer, a recognizable image should start to take shape. Of this set of layers we'll start with the latter first. As you've probably come to expect, this set up is going to take a while. For those who enjoy it… enjoy. For those who are just reading this because someone they trust said it was important, hang in there. It really is worth it.

For the conservatively inclined mind, when it has given itself over to ideological orthodoxy, the most important thing is to conduct oneself in a manner which does not compromise one's own personal purity. This means there is a great emphasis on being free of inducement to act against one's conscience, or constraint from acting according one's conscience. No exception is made for those under compulsion, or grace for weakness. No mitigation of culpability is allowed in this orthodoxy. Although the peer pressure is hard, their harshest judge is nearly impossible to escape, themselves. That's why freedom is considered so important by this group. Because freedom is a personal responsibility to them, an outside party cannot provide it. One must make one's self free to conduct one's self in such a way as to abstain from impurity. The importance of this in conservative culture cannot be overstated. Human nature compels them to be free from what they consider to be reproach.

This internal compulsion becomes is something that comes before their understanding kicks in. When you are walking through an apple orchard and you see a delicious, ripe, beautiful apple, your mind will call to memory the crisp snap of the skin as you bite through the fruit. You sense of smell will remind you of the sweet smell, your taste the juicy meat of the fruit as pull it free and hold it in your mouth. You don't need to intellectually analyze the concept of fruit to begin acting. Rather your action becomes oriented around your desire, your actions and analysis subsequently ordered by it. Self control may restrain these actions and redirect analyzing powers to questioning personal desires and the consequences of acting on them. But, this kind of discipline is strengthened by practice, and often employed best where it is practiced most frequently. If a person has not practiced refusing themselves in the ungoverned desires of an impaired ideology, not thinking their actions required balancing or limitation, their internal drive is therefore more dramatically bent in its course by their limited understanding. The less understanding there is about the tension demanded in following both laws of love, the more deviated this path becomes. Since fulfilling a fidelity to one of these laws is part of their human nature, even without understanding, the drive is still there. Life is complicated, full of situations that demand answers. What we don't know, we tend to fill in with what is familiar or comfortable. We give special care to avoid contacting our most valued tenets. It's like walking through a dark, unfamiliar room. The heavy immovable stuff, like furniture, causes pain when we come into contact with it. A sore knee or jammed toe leads caution and avoidance in the same way stepping on our core values causes internal distress. Rather than charting a clear path like someone might do with full illumination, we simply have groups fighting to take the culture in a direction which avoid the sources of their own distress. That can be a recipe for societal pain. Watching this happen, or worse, experiencing this while it is happening, underscores the need for an understanding of how our nature influences our culture.

That's what is going on, bubbling under the surface. But, what does that translate into on a daily basis? You may be asking, what does this mean to me? Right about now one might be thinking of the old saying, morality can't be legislated. Well, that's true and it isn't. What is the law but the morality of a people? The extent to which the law of a nation serves justice can be an indicator of their moral state. What we the people allow defines our daily lives. We become our own judge and jury, either meting ourselves mercy or acting as our own societal executioners by what we do or do not accept. But, in the entire existence of the earth no set of laws, no matter how excellent, has ever succeeded in directing the human will to seek moral things. That's where the law fails.

What is the aim of creating laws when no amount of legislating has ever produced one moral person? What are the criteria by which "We The People" should evaluate the laws on which our political representatives vote? It may seem like I'm merely switching one word that starts with "P" for another, but I would submit that laws exist to protect rather than to produce. A just law is one which exists to protect the free exercise both moral laws of love from all impediment or encroachment without impeding or encroaching, or if it only supports one law of love it must not impede or encroach on the other. I reprise, a good law must exist to protect the actions or inaction which comprise doing our best with what we have in either our person or our property, each according to their own conscience, and the sharing of the proceeds thereof to the extent we choose to share with those in our sphere of influence, all within the bounds of both laws of morality. I concede this to be a lofty goal. To be sure, it is limited in both practice and theory by our understanding. There is even a persuasive argument in theology which describes the pursuit of this goal in its fullness as something requiring constant divine intervention. As a proof for their argument they point to all of recorded history. Like I said, it's very persuasive. Following along with this theory there is also the argument that we get what we deserve in society. Given our record this far, I'm praying that doesn't happen. I'm leaning on the hope that a people with humble hearts receive grace. Grace seems to be a national need right now.

We seem to be full of ourselves right now. Rather than demanding laws which protect the rights which flow from the font of moral law, we have been demanding laws which reflect ourselves at what some would say is our worst. I would pose the question, are you frustrated by Republicans in office? For most Democrats who care about the political process I would assume that question generally gets an answer in the affirmative. However, for those who vote Republican of late the mere mention of the powers that be in the GOP is likely enough to cause conniptions (one of my favorite words). So you may be asking, why does all this mental mumbo jumbo matter to me? Well, it explains the way those in office have been behaving. Next to men and women understanding each other that's probably up there on the list of life's mysteries. Let's try the supposition we've been laying out on the stereotypical established Republican.

It's painful for someone when what they hold most dear is publically maligned and challenged. One of the things dearest to those who prefer the first law of love is their sense of how personally responsible they are. They love to think of their mental image as clean. Political attacks have historically included calling a person's integrity into question. Conservatives really don't like that. When mud is getting slung at their clean image they start to wonder what others will think. But first, they start working through the attacks. The feel a need rule out the accusations to maintain their own confidence in their purity. To do this they need to work through the math internally of rebuking the accusation. That means they have to consider things they don't want to be true about them, not fun. And, there is the fear that their voters who are also conservative will skip all that trouble and simply dissociate themselves from anyone who is being targeted for accusation.

They could go on offense. I've heard it said that the best defense is a good offense. But, fighting back can be just as painful. There is a fear in the conservative mind that they may incur some blame in activity they would have avoided by abstaining. But, rather than take my word on it, let's consider the opinion of an affirmed conservative in a friendly forum. On the Glenn Beck Program radio show, October fourteenth, David Limbaugh said, "Political conservatives seem to be meek, cowardly, and afraid to stand up." Mr. Limbaugh continued by framing the attitude he was observing in the context of the current political environment saying, "You can't possibly beat Obama in the marketplace of ideas and in public opinion if you announce ahead of time that if you stand up it will be blamed on you." Mr. David Limbaugh clearly framed the frustration created by leaders on the political right who won't fight. Even if they feel they can win a contest with the left, what if they get accused of going too far? What if they say something that isn't accurate? What will people accuse them of then? If you abstain from activity you can't be blamed for something you did is their mantra. The left may be concerned with failures to do enough for the liberal cause. But, likely voters who conservative leaders seek to attract seem to have been more interested in a shiny exterior than a heart worn and scarred from fighting the good fight. They have elected leaders in their own image. For an office holder with a strong natural affinity for the first law of love, but suffers from vanity or lacks humility, the very thought of blame can create fear and emotional suffering at a visceral level.

You see, these are transgressions of commission. That's when you do something that shouldn't be done. Generally speaking, the purity minded conservative side is more concerned with transgressions of commission.

This is fairly general, but as a jig it helps in explaining the understanding of how conservatives act. The kind of failing a conservative hates most when they evaluate their own conduct is an error of commission. It is this failing they feel vicariously through their political representatives. People tend to avoid pain, and associations which cause pain. That's why republicans in office typically run from political fights.

On the other side, a transgression of omission is when you don't do something you should have done. The compassion minded person cares more about transgressions of omission. Being blamed for something they failed to do is much more pain inducing to liberals than being blamed for something they did. That's why when one liberal is under attack the other democrats circle the wagons. The liberals aren't judging each other on form. Even if the accusations are true, supporting a fellow traveler while they are under fire is ostensibly an act of compassion. Any act of compassion seen in a positively light. A violation of purity is dismissed, sometimes violently. It's just not what they care about on the extreme edge that knows how to resonate with a liberal base. Let's get further into this. We need to really analyze what makes a politician effective.

To be successful, politicians need to rally as many people as possible to vote for them. This is not an easy task. Running for election successfully means convincing the public to let him or her spend their money, make rules of law which will be enforced on them, and send their children to fight in war. It may be gauche to put in a sentence, but their performance needs to be at a professional level. Like a professional athlete, it's not enough to have a solid work ethic. There needs to be natural talent. Politicians who possess talent must refine it through training. There also has to be a structure behind them, a political machine. But, even the most impressive organization rests on the ability of their candidate to connect with their base. They've got to have talent. A basketball player knows where the ball is going to bounce. A running back knows where to find the holes in the defense. A star pitcher might have a hundred mile an hour fast ball. But how is political talent described. It includes being closely aligned to the things which motivate the largest number of potential voters possible. When a reporter sticks a camera in their face at hour 16 of a day spent campaigning and asks the most irritating question they've spent all day coming up with, that campaigner needs to be able to speak off the cuff to the core values of their voting bloc.

In the Republican Party, the motivation in the voters comes mostly from arguments which lean more heavily toward the first law of love. The politician must be aligned in this way to make convincing arguments on those unexpected questions. They need to respond, spontaneously, in ways which will sway others who feel strong desire for this body of thought. Those are the people who they need to get, who will go out and motivate others. It is absolutely vital to a strong campaign. Motivating, and not offending their base, is the classical way campaigns build momentum. When it comes to amassing voters in ways that will not offend, someone has to know what line to tread. One of the ways conservative politicians are personally and strongly motivated is by the desire to be free from reproach. It's vital to reaching the party who rally around this value. Some just want very much to be *seen* as free from reproach. But, that's what it takes. To succeed on the right, they have to be believable in their role of motivating their base through championing this value.

But, plot twist, they don't always realize they are built with a personal desire to be viewed as free from reproach. It comes before they put concepts into words. The parts of our person which our values are built from are tender. It hurts when you go poking around in there and do it wrong. People generally try to avoid pain unless they discipline to the encounter, like a runner would. How is someone who is motivated to avoid the appearance of error, but to some extent unaware they are wired this way going to react when they are being accused of things they desperately don't want others to believe about them? What will they do? In the face of a direct assault on their foundation, even those who understand the way they are wired may need a minute. They will need that time to face their own fears that the accusations might be true. If they are not well prepared for the assault, they may just stall entirely.

We've seen that happen in plenty of primaries, where the contestants are all using what works on them to try to take down similarly built opponents. In sports, that is referred to as "choking." When someone chokes they let their fears dominate their thoughts. When Republicans choke it is often because they feel if they proceed their accusers will have more ammunition to portray them in a way they don't want, and fear others will believe. That's what is often going through their heads when you see their backs hurriedly getting smaller in the distance.

Many times, facing an accuser means joining a fight. Being in a fight means there is a high likelihood of getting hit. If your primary concern is maintaining your lily white façade, then fighting is definitely out. What if confronting an accuser only encourages them to fight harder? Confrontation could risk exposing the conservative to more mud slinging. What if more people join the fight and they get dragged into a massive brawl? This is a scenario that can be highly undesirable if you are internally motivated to keep your external image clean. No, for the conservative extremist fighting is only an option when the opinions of the people who's opinion they care most about, including their own, are never put in jeopardy. This motivation remains even if facing and publicly defeating the accuser would bring about desirable long term goals.

No, much better to let someone else do the dirty work. Someone else does the convincing, and someone else takes the blame if things should go poorly. If no one steps up, and nothing gets done, at least the most important priority has been preserved, at least in their mind. Now, these judgments are all subjective on the part of the extreme conservative. Notice I said stacked the priorities by the way they see them. This is often where the confusion comes. When we evaluate their actions, we do so from the position of our point of view. We evaluate their actions based on our own priorities. Fire burns. Water is wet. Take care lest you drown. Considerations like these which come from realities we are forced to live with the consequences of hold no sway over liberal or conservative orthodoxy. The people who make the decisions have been severed from the sacrifices. Those who are doing the sacrificing respond in the affirmative to the pang of a little understood moral core inside them, in lieu of a better way. Even if the leaders and those making sacrifices for the cause come out looking like a villain in everyone else's eyes, according to their own orthodoxy they've acted with virtue in their own eyes. Those in the orthodoxy follow their favored course, ignoring all other pangs of conscience which conflict, to gain the favor of their fellows and exterminate all diverse discourse. The orthodox conservatives, in accordance with their orthodoxy, are all too often willing to make "a sacrifice on the altar of expediency" to avoid personal confrontation entirely which may threaten their self image. In conflict that doesn't directly serve their personal orthodoxy, the preferable outcome they pursue is a hasty, and I stress hasty, end of aspersion. Most often this seems to be affected by retreat or blame shifting. But hey, that's politics.

Of course, there are some conservatives whose occupation puts them in the center of debate on a regular basis. Those who swim upstream balance their lives more than others who are equally ardent. These conservatives can be every bit as far right but don't understand why elected conservatives don't put up a fight. Like the rest of us they are constantly galled by elected conservatives, usually in the establishment, and their bent for myopic self preservation. Of course, these mental gladiators also run the risk of developing their own sect of the conservative orthodoxy. That can be easy when so many who call themselves fans would happily install a cult of personality upon request, or even against complaints. And, like anyone who begins to identify their self image with what they do, constantly defending their values can lead them to see their self image in the defense they present. That seems easy to understand since so many of us see ourselves in terms of what we do.

Now we have answers for heretofore timeless questions which had been favorite sources of debate in conservative bastions of thought. Have you ever wondered why elected republicans fold when the other side starts throwing mud? Ever wonder why republicans turn on themselves, rather than roll up their sleeves and get a little dirty fighting back? Well, now we know why. But wait, some may be saying at this point. Conservatives are positively vicious in their own primaries. If they're so averse to fighting with liberals, why do they fight so hard against their own? The answer is rules. Every conflict has them. As the time honored truism says, in any conflict the aggressor sets the rules. When both verbal combatants are try to please the same base they will stay mainly within the bounds of what that group considers estimable. Lying and throwing mud like a liberal may not offend an increasingly polarizing base which care more about offenses against general compassion and less about trespasses of specific purity. In a primary with a large conservative voting bloc compromising your own integrity to sabotage a competitor is one of the fastest ways to the bottom of the poll rankings. These types of attacks are usually employed by candidates who think their fifteen minutes of fame are past, and they're aiming to spoil another candidate's prospects out of revenge or disdain.

Conservatives certainly don't mind competing amongst their own party for the crown of most conservative. Pretenders to the perspective candidate's perceived ideological crown are, by their very existence, an affront. I'd go as far to say being recognized the most conservative person standing is a need they feel. But, the language and strategy by which these conflicts take place follow the lines of their own ideological orthodoxy. There's no need to appeal to another mindset. The combination of the desire to be recognized and the sense of comfort with the rules of conflict free the conservatives up to go on offense against each other. Primary contenders are often dealt with harshly.

It can be frustrating if you're waiting for these types to fight for something you believe in and they campaigned on. In the primaries when heat is applied the get positively indignant. In the general election or once they're in office they wilt like old lettuce in the sun. From what we've learned, if merely passing the dogmatic shibboleth is all that's required for them to grasp the power they desire, well, there's not dogma on their side that says you need to win, just keep clean. Something existential has to be facing an immediate threat to get these types to risk their reputation taking on a challenge, or face the pain of processing political allegations. Even if there is a real need for them to weather some blows in support of a colleague under fire, or a much needed bill that may backfire politically, don't hold your breath. The two words to remember are existential and immediate. Other terms may apply, but these two together can often create the kind of threat needed to draw out action from an entrenched conservative extremist. And, they'll be thinking the whole time about a way to get out of the situation. It's like riding a horse that hasn't had much saddle time and just wants to go back to eating in its stall. You've got a bit in its mouth and heels at its side, and even then every few feet that horse will test you. It will keep pulling back towards the barn, regardless of where you're trying to go. The only difference is that horses can learn. Politicians, well, I'm not big on spurs, but I don't even think spurs would do it. As a matter of fact, a few have even ended up in trouble by getting caught paying for that sort of thing. If you let go of the reigns for a second, that horse will head back the trough. Just like the horse that hasn't been out exercising, a politician's record will determine their performance when you take them out of the voting booth. Well, that's a depressing reality, given our current political situation. But, remember, we're looking at what goes wrong when you only respond to half the high call of being human. Yes, people may start more oriented to either side. And, bad things follow if they never even out, it doesn't matter well educated they get. But, even the worst cases can and do accomplish truly great things every day when they humbly commit to love fully. On the conservative side, they just need to look icons of conservatism who are also humble people willing to commit to loving others compassionately through their life and work.

I know it seems like a lot go through. But, this really is the set up for understanding the conflict surrounding the second amendment. Once we get all the groundwork laid, the conflict will seem vastly simpler. And, there is a certain pleasure derived from dissecting a group which, until now, has spent a great time of time and money learning how you can be forced to function for their benefit. I think that covers it for the conservatives. Let's turn our attention and meditate on those who deviate at the point of the second law of love among those inclined to the political left. After that we'll understand how both sides approach a thorny issue. Then we'll apply it all to understanding the conflict that ensues.

The second law of love is that we love one another. The first law governs actions which have God (for those who believe) and the self as their object. The second law of love governs actions which have others as their object. For example, it is common when someone talks about the concept of "fair" in a society they are talking about courses of action directed at others. If you listen carefully when "fairness" is brought up in politics you'll hear a complex system of rules used for litigating cases in the court of public opinion with a big payout paid for by the taxpayer as the award. Some want to reduce this fairness game politicians play to mere emotion. But, this reduction would be in error. They are tapping into something in the way we are made when they use these arguments to gain popular support. We are triune beings. That's a fancy way someone came up with of saying we are composed of body, mind, and spirit. All three are important to consider if you want to truly love someone else. The needs of all three must be engaged. They are the doors through which compassion enters into another's life when we wish to show love to them. Love in action is known by us through acts which meet needs of body, mind, and/or spirit. I'm sure you can recall some examples you've personally witnessed. Think of an encouraging word, which soothes worries. Or, how about can make in a meal when you are hungry and used to doing without. Maybe your example comes from your work experience. Think of an expert in a field who humbly and gently spends their time patiently teaching the untrained. The knowledge that person passes on will be used to meet material needs. The desire in praxis to help another person improve their circumstances is an act which could be called love. Perhaps the experience which comes to mind is from your formative years. An athletics coach who builds athletes character in the areas of perseverance and self discipline is showing love.

To understand a liberal mind you have to notice how all these expressions involve an outpouring to others. There is a directionality here that can be classified as a mode of doing things. I've heard it said before that doing follows being. The more influence this mode has over a person's thought, the more some types of behavior are prioritized over others. Actions common to liberalism are actions which fall within this mode, and appeal to liberally oriented likely voters. That preference system informs every decision. Tradition, culture, and other ambient factors can provide a wider palette of solutions to choose from, increasing likelihood of finding an answer which will minimize unwanted unintended consequences. Teaching a liberally oriented person the importance of moral thought stemming from the first law of love, or vice versa, can and does have a balancing affect on their preference system. But, this is a book on love and the danger of polarization. What happens when that balance isn't there? If the importance of the individual conduct as stressed in the first law of love is taken away, what is remains and what is missing? One is left with the belief that the only acceptable means of doing anything is as an act directed to others.

Taken to the extreme, there is no heed whatsoever in this orthodoxy for service of self, or the intrinsic value of personal wellbeing. It doesn't even need to be a deliberate course of action that is pursued. For those operating with this preference structure actions taken on behalf of the self are deferred, while actions directed to another are preferred. Among those given to liberal ideological orthodoxy, actions given to serving the first law of love are considered apart from there moral foundation and deemed selfish. It's that simple. In the binary political world of wins and losses, budgets rising or getting cut, those actions not spent in the preferred way are considered in competition for time and resources. We as a nation can only do so many things at once. We're called the last remaining superpower, and we can arguably do a lot. But, when your item gets turned down because of everything else that's already in the national budget you begin to realize even a "superpower" has its limits. Those who feel beholden to this extreme ideology are not satisfied until all resources are sacrificed on the altar of their agenda, and all actions are made in service to their preference structure.

From the perspective of an ideologue on either side, time should be spent practicing the orthodoxy. Anything else is bad for business. Whichever analogy you use neither one likes it when something competes for their base. When something else comes along that competes for their core, they rally their supporters against the encroaching group. As the extremes on each side grow in strength they leave less and less in the middle. That's why the more this competition heats up and the more polarized things get, and the more they try to eliminate the competition. It's a self perpetuating loop. Both sides are doing it. As the cycles play out and intensify both sides must become more extreme to maintain a sense of urgency in their base. That means both sides harden their positions, becoming more exclusionary of alternative ideas.

In liberal orthodoxy, this creates a culture where those who wish to receive acclaim will make a spectacle of contravening the first law of love during acts of service to the orthodoxy based off the second law of love. Entertainers being called courageous for doing something conservatives find objectionable courageous comes to mind. While we're on the subject, let's discern the answer to why so many liberals are in the media, entertainment, news, and otherwise. The media is an obviously liberal industry. Why do you think that is? The answer, I think, is in the directionality. A compassion based morality system has others as its object, even when it goes astray. A purity based morality system that is broken no longer has God as its object, or in the case of a moral atheist it never did. The focus is on acts which have the self as their object. Providing content for consumption to others fits more easily with one of those two directionalities. There's no need to filter out unwanted perspectives. Over time, the people who care most about providing the best content will beat out the less motivated. Better content comes from greater focus on others. Eventually, the people on the top are composed of one point of view. As they refine their craft they also can create an echo chamber where they and those they respect all have the same opinions. Incorporating diverse thought becomes a challenge, rather than a given as the people in charge become more and more mentally monolithic.

Fast forward about one hundred years from the beginning of the age of moving pictures. Add some meddling from the political parties, and you've got where we are today. You end up with two sides, implicit or explicit, you have Us's and Them's. There are two commonly used ways of appealing to either side in an oppositional dynamic. You can appeal to the side you want to please, or upset the other side. The most efficient way is certainly to achieve both goals simultaneously. As a result, many times those who have ambitions in the media will endear themselves with decision makers in their industry by making choices which offend the conservatively aligned. Whether is a talk show host carrying the politically correct line or actors and actresses pushing the bounds of the movie ratings system, they are heralded for ribbing the right in their pursuit of pleasing the leaders leaning left. Why were they heralded as courageous? They pushed a boundary those who can help or hinder their career never cared about anyway. I submit it is because they acted in support of their side's preference system, while striking at the other side's preference system, so a superlative was picked which described the act in terms of advances in the cultural war. The topic isn't one of the most moving communal acts a body is capable of performing being recorded and disseminated for commercial purposes. It is the directionality turning the national fabric into tug of war cord. After all, isn't sex an act by which a person can make another feel good? Even the most conservative theologian would classify the act in its most perfected form as a mutual giving of self to the other. If your preference system is narrowly defined to exclude considerations stemming from the first law of love, and your background or tradition of understanding sex is not greatly informed by apologetics common to religious teaching, it's hard to find a problem with promiscuity.

Whether you are a talking head on Capitol Hill or pushing something racy, the media makes sense when you look at it through the prism of preference systems emanating from the two laws of love, written into human nature. You might be saying about now, what about the conservative media. That could be called the exception that proves the rule, except it's not really an exception. Anything who's ever listened to or read a conservative pundit with a major following should be able to quickly discern it can be described in three words, cult of personality. What most people don't readily see is that the personality is a universal one within conservative communications. They're all taking the role of the myth of self sufficiency, which is the exact same thing in effect as the raunchy movie scene. What offends those who find meaning and satisfaction in acts targeted towards more than someone asserting that their actions range from useless to harmful. That's the definition of self-sufficiency. The people who's cognition revolves around adding to the self, great when one is working on patience, often don't even understand how they are frustrating and enraging the one's who's actions focus on others, and vice versa.

I mentioned before why republicans fold so often when under fire, rather than enduring or rallying to each other's aid. Those on the left are more prone to do the opposite when a member in good standing with the party is facing political heat. Understanding the liberal orthodoxy makes it clear why democrats "circle the wagons" when one of their own faces controversy. The rest of the committed liberal establishment is more than willing ignore a compromise of personal integrity. A compromise of that kind is not addressed within their preference system. A compromise of personal conduct is minor factor, if a consideration at all. The liberal orthodoxy doesn't acknowledge conclusions derived from the first law of love. That's why when one of their own transgresses a tenet of a stable society drawn from the first law of love, there is little concern. In denying the importance of such an infraction they perceive themselves as upholding their liberal orthodoxy, by rejecting a competing orthodoxy.

Those who have wholly embraced liberal ideological orthodoxy don't consider compromising one's personal morality to be a transgression at all if done for certain reasons. As long as the person is supporting their side's preference system, much is permissible. It's all about what is good for business. The major parties have repeatedly used wedge issues to separate the voting public into the largest two groups they can manage using the methods they use for the purposes of perpetuating themselves. Supporting other preference systems is not what they are in business to do. Ideas are persistent things. Cross-contaminating ideas into a group they've already carved out with their bombardment of political ads and messages meant to drive a wedge is counter productive to their plans. For the left, taking the morality of the first law into account creates a precedence that could dilute the united message creating the force with which they drive their wedge, and vice versa. When one of their own becomes embattled over something rejected by another preference system, like getting caught in adultery, they rally to that person in support. Losing an influential figure who can further their preference system would be bad for business. Failing to uphold the values of the followers of some other preference system, who aren't going to donate to their cause, or vote for their candidates, isn't bad for business. The ironic thing is that they don't even have to win. All they have to do is keep their base donating and powerful people who can influence industry believing they could be back in position eventually to shape policy.

It all seems pretty dark and cynical. Who would support such a system? Do the voters who vote for these compromised candidates have morals? Of course they do. How often does one find the perfect political representative? What candidate has it all? Some say Reagan, other say Kennedy, still others say Lincoln. Washington was called the indispensable man because everyone agreed on him. Without that agreement the colonies would have broken apart, never to be united. In party politics designed to divide through expediency we don't often don't see a candidate come through the system with a complete moral formation. A representative like this would draw supporters out the base of both parties. It's bad for business. If any voices like this which do get through to holding office, every attempt would be made by both sides to effectively drown them out. Through selection and marketing, voters are carefully presented choices the parties want them to believe define the entire field of possibilities. A false dichotomy between the two pillars of morality is presented. Each party claims their preferred candidates are the only ones who can defend their side of the false choice. The political dance ensues from there.

Sometimes a candidate comes along with a full complement of the moral image, capable of appealing to both preference systems simultaneously. Often, these figures are much beloved long after their day. Ronald Reagan famously won reelection with the help of the "Reagan Democrats." John F. Kennedy is beloved by the left. But, policies he advocated, such as tax policies, are echoed and cited by the right even now. Leaders like this are too often the exception, rather than the rule. Voters who aren't paying attention, and have not been attentive to their own educational needs, are more easily left with a false choice between the two laws of human nature which are both necessary to have a healthy society. Hopefully, that is changing. It is my humble aspiration that this book will be part of this change. It is my even more fervent hope that you will be part of positive change too.

This emphasis on one preference system over the other presented in this false choice provides segue to another political puzzler. The Republicans feel the need to pretend they aren't putting their party concerns above the needs of country. If they were to come out with their role in perpetuating the political dance there are those who feel such an admission would end them as a major party. Democrats seem unconstrained by this concern. I'm often asked why committed liberals are willing to craft spurious arguments to win political battles. Why do they get away with it when one blown lie can doom someone running from the right? President Obama racked up more lies than his flacks know what to do with. President Obama even promised the insured of the nation they could keep their doctor and their insurance when that claim couldn't possibly be substantiated at any point in time. Before him, President Clinton's political adversaries complained he was getting praised by the media for how well he lied. The most memorable lie probably had to be when he falsely claimed to have abstained from certain relations with an intern wearing a blue dress. Both men are still considered powerful and influential men in their party. Both served two terms. President Herbert Walker Bush promised he wouldn't raise taxes in a "Read my lips" moment. He eventually did raise some taxes. Many feel the failure to keep his word on that one issue was the reason he didn't win reelection. It could be argued, based on these examples, that a willingness to lie is advantage in liberal circles, and career ender among the conservative base.

 My favorite example of this variation in standards is something that has become a tradition in politics called the "October Surprise." Every four years the pundits in the know are always on the lookout for a pre-election game changer by said name. It goes like this. A specious charge is made in October of an election year, typically when control of the presidency is at stake. The false claim has enough time to circulate. The goal is to leave voters with an unanswered question and a bad taste in their mouth at the voting boot which damages the reputation of the opposing candidate, normally a republican. Because of the last minute release of the insinuating to flat out defamatory information, there isn't enough time for the defamed candidate's rebuttal to circulate. That means those aforementioned people in the voting booth hear the mud without the perspective granted by having time to see if it sticks. That makes it very hard for the targeted candidate to clear their name with everyone who heard the claim before Election Day in November. People go to the poles having heard the lie, but not the defense. Of course, it gets cleared up after the election. But, by then the presidency has been decided, and the failed nominee is largely forgotten until presidential power begins to wane in the sixth year, if the president elect is fortunate enough to win re-election. That raises the question, why does one side get away with pulling this so often it has become an unofficial election tradition? And, how does this factor into controversy surrounding the second amendment? The answer is simple by now. It isn't about the issues. The issues are the symptom. Like a patient with appendicitis, we aren't going to get well by curing the symptoms. Human nature is the cause, and what we need to understand to encourage the healing process.

 These examples make it clear that we are dealing with two overarching ways of thinking. One of those modes places a high degree of importance on actions toward others, with little to no importance placed on personal conduct. When you consider the ramifications of using a gun in a defense which irrevocably removes something from another, it's the only explanation that fits. It only further confirms the directionality of the preference system when you look at how accruing favor takes place. The most acceptable way to receive importance in liberal orthodoxy is as others assign importance to you by their action and approval. I've noticed, in my own observations, the more liberal people involved, the more highly the approval is esteemed. That's how those who are keeping score on the left pad their self image, or affirm their self esteem. I imagine that's why liberals are always giving each other awards, like Tony's, Oscars, Golden Globes, tenure, Peabody's and Pulitzers. The list goes on. But, that last bit about awards is pure conjecture on my part.

The necessary ground work has been laid concerning the followers of the two laws of love. Let's get into the second amendment as a wedge issue. We will contemplate the meaning of the gun. There is an old saying. God made man, Sam Colt made them equal. That facetious truism infers that a gun is a means of individual empowerment. If you think about the direction, power is flowing directly to that individual. Those who have been paying attention through the preceding pages may feel the hair on the back of their necks begin to raise a little right about now. The galvanizing affect of the wedge issue is kicking in.

The portable, repeating firearm means an individual can assert their will in a situation where they would otherwise be at the will of others. Before, the social order was governed by whoever could rally the greatest number of allies. You can call it the feudal compact, or whatever you will, but the king with the biggest army usually got to exert their force as they desired. Conscripted vassals would act out the total will of their domain with cumulative force. The concept here is that many gather together in sufficient numbers to deprive the impact of a smaller group, or that of an individual. Numbers carried the day and the side with the big army usually won. Even though monarchs ruled the often identified with aspects of social order to maintain power, describing themselves as serving protectors of their realm or involving themselves deeply with the religious beliefs of their culture. Then, a group of colonists across an ocean used personally held firearms to repel a monarch and arguably the most powerful army on earth at the time. Of course I'm skimming over a lot here. There was some masterful diplomacy on the part of Benjamin Franklin. First the British kicked the French out, and then Franklin convinced the French to help the colonials kick out the British. Of course we're like family with the U. K. now, God bless the queen, but it was pretty hot at that time. From then on, the ability for a smaller group of individuals to repel a king sent a shockwave that was felt around the world. One could argue guns made it possible. A farmer defending his home and household who hunted regularly for food with the family rifle could be every bit as deadly on the battlefield at that point in time as a soldier who had spent their life in training. They just needed some basic education in warfare and a little experience. That would have been unheard of in the Bronze Age, for instance. If you were a Greek hoplite warrior from Bronze Age Sparta, the thought of a merchant or carpenter presenting any real opposition was laughable.

The firearm, even a single shot muzzle loader, greatly empowered an individual. Numbers were no longer all that was required to significantly mitigate the power of another group or person. A prepared individual armed with firearms could inflict significant harm, or even make a victory over them pyrrhic. The threat this armed individual or smaller group now posed could be sufficient deterrent to dissuade larger aggressors entirely. There are other ways to look at this subject. But, none of them can totally obfuscate this way in which the gun is conceptually understood. This meaning is almost ubiquitous in our culture, and plays out again and again in our art. Even actors and actresses who speak out vigorously for anti-gun laws make movies in which guns are portrayed as a magnifying effect on their character's expression of will. The gun is seen as a tool of empowering an individual.

Now, we apply this garnered meaning to the two groups. Do you see how one group may be more inclined to an expression of personal power, while the other is more inclined toward group actions which are believed to empower the collective? Conservatives are obviously the former, while liberals are the latter. Conservatives are inclined toward being good stewards of their own personal faculties. One of the favorite topics of conversation among conservatives is self improvement for the purpose of expanding independence. That doesn't mean building a patio or deck on the back of your home to improve the resale value. When they talk about self improvement, it generally refers to improving skills they consider to be of value. These values come from the part of their core which leans more towards the first law of love. So loving God, how do you think one might measure such a thing? What, do you think, might one use as a measure if one was inclined to judge success in self improvement? Hopefully, such a person would measure personal growth in areas such as patience, gentleness, kindness, self control, etc. If that was the case, we could leave the right out of the literary endeavor entirely. But, this is a book about a nation on the road to ruin. It is a book for people who want to make a one hundred eighty degree course correction on that road, a metaphorical u-turn. The dysfunction that affects all of our lives negatively resides on both sides of the political divide. So, we're going to talk about where conservatives go wrong too. As the saying goes, there's more than one way to fall off of a horse.

Comparing one's self to others as a way of measuring is an easy answer for those who have taken the love out of their hearts. And now you know why hard line, far right conservatives are so preoccupied with competition. The whole world is a means of proving self worth, in their eyes. To them, competition is a way of rating self worth. Unfavorable comparison that competition readily appeals to their sense of self improvement in what ever area matters to them. That's why the love capitalism. To them, "the one who dies with the most stuff wins" is more than a bumper slogan. Of course this is generalizing, but people are complex. Something simple like a stereotype or a parable can be a more facile means of conveying truth to a varied audience than a specific case study. When it comes to guns, anything that empowers conservatives in this search for self improvement is looked upon fondly. That's why a fight over the second amendment carries such wide interest on the conservative side. For those of you thinking right about now that your job is over and simply getting the word out about this is all it will take to improve the culture and political climate, you're wrong. Without you taking both laws of love to heart and carrying them as a living witness into the culture, I can tell you how the partisans, asleep in their orthodoxy structure, will take this. The right will ignore this work since they think their own personal interests are all that matters. The left will use what is described here as a study on human nature and how to further control others. Being the aggressors, they will slowly advance this control while their occasional overreach causes push back from the right when angrily roused. One extreme is soundly asleep in their orthodoxy while the other is sleep walking in their side's orthodoxy. Both orthodoxies end in tyranny. The left will gain ascendency, and bloodshed will follow. Just look at socialist regimes of the twentieth century for and idea of the body count and extent of the cost to human life and dignity. Or, the right will react violently after being pushed too far and bloodshed will ensue as they take power. That's why the difference between tyranny and freedom is so often you.

 The right greatly values that which can be used to defend their ability to conduct themselves as they desire or see fit without interference. They greatly value even the fantasy of defending things which stem from their core beliefs. These core preferences even determine the preferred mechanism or way this defense takes place. Their focus is on personal actions. Again, the firearm allows them to take personal actions which enact an effective defense. Given a high enough caliber weapon that holds enough ammo, beneficial terrain, and the proper preparation, they enjoy the fantasy that they could repel all likely advances rather than call on help from someone else.  A popular saying among conservatives of all kinds is "I am 911." It is also interesting to note that a personal defense weapon is seen by this group as the last line of defense against a violation of the self. It's no wonder conservatives, even ones who have never used a gun nor perceive a personal need for one, value the personal firearm in the abstract. That's why some conservatives who have never owned a gun will fight for freedom of access to ballistic weapons so powerful myths have been spun about the military restricting them to use on equipment, like a car's engine block.

 Liberals act out of their own preference system too. Unlike the conservative preference system, this statement of dichotomy is possibly no truer than on the issue of who gets to carry a weapon. Liberals can go so far as to feel weaponry which empowers individuals to harm groups as an imminent crisis, no matter how meek the person carrying the weapon. This applies with greater magnitude as they embrace their side's preferred orthodoxy. "Why would you need a weapon," the question is asked. "We don't recognize your right to act on your own behalf," is inferred in this statement. This, of course, is the problematic core of the second amendment conflict. One group prizes personal action as a means to achieving all ends. The other group prefers actions taken on behalf of others, to the point that they see actions taken on behalf of the self as uncivilized, even barbaric. The orators of both side craft arguments to sway the masses. Commentators call those who throw themselves into the wet embrace of the other side's propaganda, "Kool-aid drinkers" as if they have a problem with propaganda when they're really just objecting to the flavor in the glass. By the way, "drinking the Koo-aid" is a reference to Jonestown that I think is unfair to Kool-aid since, as the erudite have often pointed out, they didn't actually drink Kool-aid with their life ending poison. But, drinking the Kool-aid seems to be the mainstream thing to do these days, along with being a favored phrase in politics. A lot of people still love Kool-aid, so I don't borrowing the term has hurt the brand. If anything, all this talk of flavored libation is making me thirsty.... A possible consequence of any use of the gun as intended on another person is the ending of a life. Consider that end from the point of view of someone whose conscience is hard wired to focus on actions which are directed toward others. A gun is a tool which fires a hard, metal mass with penetrating force sufficient to cause a cavitation wave in soft tissue, and crack bones. It intentionally causes injury and death. These are things this group will likely highlight in their assessment of a weapon's use. Yes, this tool functioning as intended is abhorrent to how this group is internally ordered. At best, this weapon is a nauseating necessity.

Without a significant degree of internal preparation and deliberation this nausea can be a high hurdle to overcome. Even when a tool like this is considered necessary to protect dear family and home, it is often relegated to carefully constructed niches. Usually, these niches are constructed out of the means accepted by the liberal's preference system. For example, liberals prefer group action since they prefer scenarios where no one person is acting on their own behalf. If you prefer that actions have directionality towards others, you prefer groups and not individuals making the decisions for individuals. That means a group must be in charge of how a gun gets used. A sheriff in the Wild West handing down law by the barrel of his gun would be eschewed. A review board that reviews how an officer involved in a shooting followed the policy set by the city and police department would meet with greater approval. If the review board, a group, disapproves of the use of a gun altogether, that's even more palatable.

A political orthodoxy exists to advance itself. Over time, it's not enough for the liberal orthodoxy that a group to make the decision. That group has to be subject to liberal thought. The city leadership needs to be liberal, the metropolitan area needs to be predominantly liberal, the police department leadership needs to be liberal, and the police union needs to be liberal for liberal orthodoxy to feel comfort. Contrast this with our military, a group which exists for the purpose, and which every member of swears an oath to defend the constitution. Not just the parts of the constitution that appeal to liberal orthodoxy. Every jot and tittle, including the guaranteed individual rights, must be defended using the biggest guns known and most effective weapons known to mankind today. Now we're starting to understand why liberals have gotten a reputation for hating the military. The military even uphold our nation's interests against over other nations, socialist nation who are closer to the preferred mode embodied by the liberal's orthodoxy. What's worse, the military supporting our nation is operated by an independent leadership which reports to one man, the president. Even though only congress can declare war, and those in the House of Representatives have the power to restrict funding for anything they don't like, this is still considered antithetical. They both use guns. But, now you can see why liberals are constantly trying to defund the military, but praise and enjoy support from police unions.

It is important to note, both poles profess a certain morality, albeit deficient and one sided. And, the political parties make every effort to ensure their bases are spared, as much as possible, the pains caused by their support of unbalanced politicians and policies. If you have any doubts you can do a web search for the definition of a slush fund. Here's a quick summary. It is money, sometimes obtained illicitly, which is used as a means of placating a group. For example, let's say a supportive union is about to collapse under the cost of their pension obligations after years of promising more than they can give. The party who regularly receives campaign donations from said union might arrange to pass a spending bill for the purpose of funneling money, your money if you pay taxes, to prop up this union and keep the campaign donations flowing. That union is going to keep supporting the party that is supporting them. The partisans may be hurting the future, but their use of your representative power is helping the union maintain power and solidarity now. It is easy to cling to an incomplete moral image which pleases the ear but has no efficacy when the consequences of such preferences are not personally felt. It is the history of the world.

Those in power, time and time again, will shrug at the suffering of others while clinging to untrue notions simply because those notions appeal to their worldview. Our values direct and actions, and is painful when they are challenged. Finding fault in our values makes it very easy to see fault in ourselves. Even when we are confronted with a truth that will further free us and advance happiness in our lives, we can experience pain in the process. I liken it to the debridement of a wound. The thought that our way can be toxic is painful because we associate our will with ourselves. There is possibly no more personal expression of a person than an expression of their will. Like a tender wound that is sore to the touch, we protect our will. When debridement takes place dead tissue is removed from healthy tissue so that the live will be protected and fill back into the wounded space. The death is removed so that life can fill that space. I'm told it is also one of the most painful things that can be experienced, depending on the severity and location of the wound. That's why the best teachers are humble and meek. History is replete with People in power going to great lengths to avoid that kind of personal pain. A king may rise to power that is wise and wins the love of their nation. The next king may not share the same personal convictions and life experiences. That makes it hard for them to make wise decisions. If someone with power doesn't want to face the pain of introspection, and does not directly feel the pain of their own failure, how will they be stopped from continuing in things that hurt others? The longer a person in power exercises their failed will on others unchecked without feeling the pain caused by their own actions, the worse a society will get. That's why the founders of our government created a system which endeavors to give those who feel the effects of governance the keenest the most say. Our Constitution spreads the power out over the populace so that one stubborn fool can't rule others without their consent. And, when the people tire of suffering a fool, they can remove their afflicter or afflicters in the next election. The closer power stays to the people, the less likely bad laws which ignore suffering remain. Creating a bulwark around this principle is the whole purpose behind the tenth amendment, but I digress. We're discussing the universal effect of the second amendment.

When it comes to the issue of the gun, it can be easy for some to place the wellbeing of others as secondary to their own personal preferences. With even a nominal understanding of history, such as my own, this is clear. So where does a practicality clash with political orthodoxy over the second amendment? Possibly the best example is in the case of a weapon designed solely for safeguarding the personal security of the person carrying it. Often cited is the repeated rape victim who wants to obtain a concealed carry weapon. For the ideological orthodox on the left, no argument can be compelling. As a defense against victims turning to personal firearms, they would claim the weapon would be used on that person when the next attack happens. Tthe heir demeanor demands that their hypothetical defense be taken as certainty. In the hardest cases, this demeanor remains unchanged even when their hypothetical comes face to face with real victims. The commitment to liberal orthodoxy does not even permit this hypothetical to be considered in the light of what will doubtlessly happen to the victim again if they are deprived of an adequate defense. Victims of repeated abuse can face a growing threat of death over time, compounding the abuse as their abusers become bolder. But, the allowable actions which change important states, such as breathing to not breathing, must be initiated by others to find validity in the orthodoxy. When it comes to something as important as a life threatening action, the assent of a great many is required. And, they approve action only under the strictest ideological control measures.

 Here is where the conflict becomes clear. One side sees the gun as a great, glimmering boon. It is the guarantee behind the hope of conducting one's self as one see's fit. The other side sees it as an all but unnecessary evil. Only in what it removes can a gun be used to support the law on which all liberal thought is based. Using a gun and intended carries the possibility of irrevocably placing the target beyond the reach of all earthly compassion. It is therefore easy to see why the orthodox of each side are wholly unwilling to compromise on the issue of the gun. The base of both sides finds the issue deeply motivating. Each side responds to the drive of human nature within them as it branches along the lines of the two laws of love and their own personal makeup. Politically, both sides seem devoted to using how the second amendment is applied to antagonize each other. There's something to be in pandering to either outraged group. Only those who submit to both laws of love can chart a clear course on a wedge issue.


Tax Policy

Smart financial planners know the way to tell what a person considers important is by looking over their checkbook and their datebook. Putting it that way may show which side of thirty I'm on, but your money and your time tell the story of your heart. Today we have debit cards and cell phones running calendar apps. It is a principle that has weathered well. Every store and service under the sun seem like they are trying to get you to use their private label credit card. It is entirely possible to buy everything you need without ever leaving the house, pay for it all on credit, and have it shipped from your door. If you've created a profile with you most commonly used services, you don't even need to enter your bank or credit card information. They can automatically debit the information on file. All you have to do is point and click. For some people, shoes are an unnecessary accoutrement to their average day. If you have direct deposit, and work from home over the internet, you could theoretically live your day to day life without even leaving the house. You could also go months without taking the time to look at your financial health.

That's a far cry from the time when it took a basic knowledge of accounting to navigate the credits and debits of your account, all tracked in pen and paper on a register. Pencil was a risky gambit, since pencil markings sometimes wore off. And there is the line delineating the generations. It could have been the aforementioned check book or a circuit box. Readers of a certain age are probably laughing right now, recalling the high price of education when they first learned the perils of pencil. Balancing a checkbook seems to be a forgotten skill in the digital age. And, the denizens of the new age likely haven't owned homes long enough for the writing on the circuit breaker labels to fade. If your imagining a bewildered person in the dark and at there wits end with no idea where to start fixing their situation, well, that' what happens when you don't keep track of your finances. It will probably happen in the circuit breaker situation too, at some point, if you don't go back over those things in ink. In a world where services are provided in the blink of an eye, some skills can get overlooked. Banks offer up to date tracking services for your account through your own personal page on their website. I love the services they provide. Used in conjunction with classical tracking methods they can provide a greater degree of protection and oversight. Some may feel inclined to let the service they use keep track of their credits and debits for them. Some may never develop the skills they'll need to take control when things go awry. It's a bit like calculators. My great grandfather spent much of his adult life before calculators existed. I remember visiting him in his hospice care room during last few week of life. In his nineties, weeks before he passed, if you asked him a complex math problem he would have the answer before you could get your calculator out of your pocket. We made a fun game of it while we spent time with him as he looked forward to joining the love of his life. He didn't last much longer after great grandma passed. Those two were meant to be together. What a special generation. We haven't developed skills like that, by and large. It is easier to pick up a calculator. They are ubiquitous. It is a maxim that what you don't use, you lose. Since we're not using these skills often, well, it's like algebra. I think many parents who tackled algebra in school experience palpitations when trying to help their kids do their homework.

If we're not looking at our finances regularly, one has to assume we're losing a facile understanding of how accounting works. If we're not organizing a calendar to track the dates of our expenditures over time, do we really learn the impact of a dollar? We live in a society where attention to our account balance peaks when standing in front of the object of our desire, and is used to determine what we can pay for in that moment. Understanding of our financial future is based on the date we get paid. As a society, are we going to notice when the price milk goes up sixty cents? And, if we're missing the rising cost of essential things like food and energy, which we see presented in front of us every week, will we be equipped to decipher spending in our government? I have the answer, we'd better be. They're taking in more and more money while the average household income is declining. What are they doing with the money? What would you do with it if you really saw all those resources as *your* money? Would you want them to respect your money?

Where and how we spend our money says a lot about us. When explaining the concept of money to the younger generation, I've often described each dollar earned as time, and each dollar spent as a vote. Sacrifices need to be made to earn money. It's the way of the world. Some sacrifice more and some sacrifice less. But, every dollar made represents a sacrifice someone made. That's why reputable charities are held in such high esteem. They faithful transmit the sacrifices of some so that the needs of many can be cared for. Not everyone gets that in depth with money, though. For some, money is what they get after doing work for someone else so they can go out later and do things they want to do. They may enjoy the work they do, in which case money is a nice after thought which allows them to keep coming to work every day. I don't know too many young people who have found themselves in that situation already. They may be showing up to work every day because electronic entertainment can be cost prohibitive if you don't have a job. I've found that if you learn to love working, the job fades into the background and employers praise the work that you do regardless of what you're doing. It's about understanding the value of our daily interactions, and the fruit of our labors. That's why I love it when people get involved in charity work. There, you are hopefully getting an understanding of the labor it takes to support your preferred cause. Desire and exertion meet to create a better world. There, you take the reward of your service and use it to perpetuate blessings in society, which you have enjoyed, in the lives of others. Your monetary gift empowers a worthy cause to meet the minimum functions necessary for existence. Those who are objects of charity in turn give you a gift of character that no accumulation of funds could ever obtain by presenting you with an opportunity for service. Of course, not everyone votes that the same things should continue to exist. When you've served a meal to someone who would otherwise go hungry, or sorted through the clothes that will keep families warm in dignity, you really understand the importance of the voice you have for what will and will not exist in a society.

Money spent is a vote for what will and will not exist in our lives. There doesn't even need to be a plurality. Just enough votes to pay the bills. The various preferences people have, when traced through the flow of how they choose to spend or not to spend their time and finances, represent a focus on certain things and a disregard of others. Not everyone is canny with how they use their financial vote or aware of this reality, but that's politics. Some purveyors are quite canny in how they market their products to win your financial vote. Terms like organic, fair trade try to influence factors that have nothing to do with the quality of the product, or your need for its use. Tags citing where things are made reveal to the savvy eye designs to influence your decision on whether or not to buy. The vote made by your dollar is substantial, but do your realize how important your vote is? Do you put much thought into what the choices you make when you buy say about you?

Some find the exercise of examining their expenditures quite flattering. They apply their income, no matter how meager, in ways which will see their means expand and the hard times hurt less. For others, their spending says they are disorganized, driven by impulse, and ever at the mercy of their payday. If panic is setting in right now as realization dawns on you, this isn't a book on finances. But, I won't leave you fearing for your personal financial future. I'll point you in a good direction. I recommend practically anything written by Dave Ramsey for getting your finances in order. Back to the point I'm making. Few are paragons of thrift. Most of us fit somewhere between spending like a drunken congressman and running a ledger like a professional accountant. For everyone, however, what they do with what's left after bills which are absolutely necessary for their continued existence tells anyone who cares to look what they consider important. Why is this important? The same approach is true of tax policy and the approach of government on spending. What do we do after we've paid the minimum to keep the roads paved and the threats at bay? After we've made sure the best materials are being used in the safest and most efficient ways through intelligent decisions, what else will we pay for?

Most of us could doubtlessly agree it would be best to verify intelligent decisions are being made and our tax dollars are being respected. To do that we would need at least basic accounting skills, wouldn't we? To further the conversation, let's assume everything basic is being spent wisely. We're straining credulity for sure, but we'll never make it to the next point if we don't take a leap from here. We'd be stuck at point one without making it to where the wedge issue kicks in. When all the infrastructure and defense has been paid for, what comes next? The question is then raised, what should our taxes be used to pay?

There are always necessary tasks to undertake which require constancy without the promise of profit. There was never any expectation that going to the moon would make us rich. There was no business model for that accomplishment. But, I would argue going to the moon was good for the economy. The capabilities we had to develop to achieve that accomplishment put a whole world of possibilities which would bring a profit within the reach of U. S. industry. How do you achieve things as a society that everyone recognizes the importance of but no one wants to go poor doing? National defense falls into this category. There's also the need for institutions central to our existence to endure. As a whole, markets may be fairly stable. But few institutions in the private sector achieve constancy. In the markets of the free world, businesses rise and fall. Fortunes are made, lost, and made again. Events and individuals come together in ways that create new growth, and clears out the rubble of those companies who could not perform. This undulation cleans our economy of stalled dreams and removes the wreckage of poor choices. The excesses of pride shortsightedness are broken down to become fuel for those with vision. It works in much the same way as a controlled wildfire, which turns dead brush and debris on the forest floor into food for new growth. But, to carry the analogy further, if you prevent all controllable forest fires, eventually the tinder and debris builds until a spark can ignite a conflagration hot enough to kill even mature trees and volatize necessary nitrogen. If you stall the ebb and flow of the economy, a recession can turn into a prolonged recession, or even a depression.

So why am I comparing markets and trees? Infrastructure like water, power, roads, etc., and the military cannot rise and fall with the tide of industry. Forcing them into the marketplace and then propping them up so they do not fail could cause even farther reaching implications as the laws of the market reassert themselves. Services like these must be constant, or all will suffer their loss. Don't get me wrong, I'm a big fan of incorporating free market influences into the system to push their excellence and keep them sharp. The military wouldn't very effective if they had to build their own weapons. Without private companies competing for defense contracts there would be a stark difference, complaints about the military industrial complex included. Private companies will come up with better pavement material where government agencies would fail. I'm advocating each sector, public and private, be used where they can make the most positive difference. We don't want the constructive undulation of the private sector ending services we depend on, or putting the power to topple nations, or defend our nation in the hands of any one person. Think about it, just because the last remaining heir and owner of a company decided to leave the entire inheritance to the cat is no reason to close inner city schools, or defund the production of aircraft carriers. In choosing to serve certain societal needs through government action, we trade the efficacy and efficiency of the private sector for the promise of stability.

That doesn't mean the government will always get it right. That's not even a guarantee the government will get it right *most* of the time. Look at how the government turned the Vietnam War into a political football. Enron was a black eye for government oversight of energy. Our State Department was blamed for getting a diplomat and others killed in Benghazi while claims circulated that there was ample evidence and warnings ahead of time to the danger. Sometimes, the hybrid system that I mentioned earlier is preferable to hold the government accountable. Charter schools go into the same neighborhoods as failing public schools and produce better educated students out of the same population with less money. In most cases, the government functions best when those who carry the brunt of its shortcoming have the most say in it administration. This is done by keeping as many functions as possible at a grassroots level, to the fullest extent possible. This is not achieved by retreating from the use of government services entirely. Some people aren't going to like that on both sides of the political divide, but it's true.

 Generally, the government guarantees there will be roads to drive on, schools to learn in, and power to keep the lights on while industry ebbs and flows. All this costs money. There's no getting away from it. The roads won't pave themselves. Fresh, clean water won't pump itself into our homes. Intelligent and assiduous workers have to be paid. Technological wonders must be purchased from the private sector. All manner of tasks must be performed to maintain the standard of living to which we have become accustomed. I come from a blue collar background. I struggle to think of an uncle who has not renovated or built a home at some point. My father built the home I grew up in. In my family growing it was a commonly used phrase that you need to use the right tool for whatever job you're doing. This is about using the right tool for the job. There are some problems the free market is not built to resolve. Think about child labor laws. A completely free market actually incentivizes using children as a pliable labor force. "Morganizing" in the twentieth century contributed to the rise of unions. Unions don't exist in a totally free market. It's funny, free market advocates always want to talk about products of industry in terms of property rights. But, they start throwing up caveats if you talk about the property a person has in their intellect, or in their labor. Government steps in to protect workers of all kinds in our mixed market economy on a daily basis. Some people may find it distasteful when the government starts infringing on the free flow of an economy, but so is telemarketing, another gift of the free market. I've never heard one complaint from someone who doesn't work in sales about the government enforced "Do Not Call List." Don't get me wrong, I love and enjoy the power free markets have as they have improved our standard of living. But, like any competition, there have to be rules to keep the players on the field instead of causing collateral damage in the stands. If it was legal and a business owner objected to interrupting your supper with a sales pitch, his competitor would undercut him right out of business with money he made off the people who are willing to eat cold meals. In an industry with thin margins, a little edge can be all it takes to make a company uncompetitive.

You may say telemarketing is a minor concern, and child labor is morally extreme, therefore not comparable to telemarketing. In my experience people like that tend to discount the slippery slope argument, but will go on to explain how Adam Smith's invisible hand is a real force. Try squaring that circle. It's nice to think that somehow morally reprehensible things would never thrive on the open market, even if a raw dollars and cents approach incentivized it. But, slavery is comparable to child labor when you consider that children die in sweatshops every day. And, economic forces incentivizing slavery in the first hundred years or so of the United States were so powerful in they soon became the basis of the south's economy. The southern states had become so dependent on the vile, archaic practice they were willing to start America's bloodiest war over keeping slaves. Economically empowering an evil like slavery was a problem so large it required a, "President of the United States, clothed with immense power (Abraham Lincoln)," to solve. The government has a specific role and enumerated uses. If you would like to know more about the specific uses of government, I recommend reading the Constitution.

Some may not believe me when I say government helps uphold your standard of living. That's fine. Pretend waste disposal doesn't exist. Figure out what to do with what piles up without making it someone else's problem. Will you turn to an unregulated private waste disposal company? Now zoning restrictions of waste management facilities don't exist. Whose neighborhood are they going to dump that waste in? In a totally free market system the answer is probably wherever the land is the cheapest. Now, multiply that problem by three hundred million. Take away environmental protection regulation regulating what runs off landfills into the groundwater. How far is that problem going to spread? I don't think you want what you smell in your trash ripening in a hole while whatever breaks loose works its way towards your water. Maybe some start up company in the free economy buys the house in foreclosure next door to your home and turns it into a literal dump. When the garbage piles up, making your home stink, you'll understand how the cost of maintenance is a universal truth. Let that be a lesson to you. It's not just the up front cost you have to worry about. The greater cost, many times, comes in the form of maintenance. Sometimes, there isn't any profit left to go around after the cost of maintenance is paid. Take the cost of national defense. It's not cheap to maintain the finest fighting force on the face of the earth. In earlier times the Romans offset that cost by conquering and looting neighboring lands. We're not really the looting type of people. When we go into foreign lands we leave things like roads and schools behind. How do you find a company willing to take on the cost of maintaining a first world military, but not let them loot? Then, make them spend more money to build schools. There is no profit in that scenario without a government check forthcoming. In a totally free system that military would either not exist, or be unchecked in doing horrible things. I challenge any who disagree to prove me wrong....

Taxes are required to fund the government coffers. Wise people are required to spend the money well. By now these two statements are self evident. Accepting these truths inevitably brings us to a whole new set of questions. Who will pay these taxes? How much will they pay? What method will we use to determine how much people pay, and whether they are paying what has been determined? What will our money buy? How much will we spend? How will we select the people who determine what we buy and how much we spend? Will it be elected officials, or will administrators be allowed to regulate these decisions? Congress has the constitutional obligation to make money decisions for the nation. But, I'm pretty sure congress would be shut down by paperwork if they had to approve every pen and paper clip purchased by the administration. How do we determine the difference between an administrator working within a budget and congress abdicating their constitutional authority? Questions like these have thorny answers, and can be seen very differently from the far ends on either side of the political divide. When the things you care about become a political chew toy for politicians looking to make a name for themselves by stoking your outrage at the other side, what do you do? Wouldn't you like to know the answer to that question before your emotions are involved, and someone you wouldn't trust to hold your wallet starts tugging on your heart strings? How do the ideological orthodoxies, of which we have been learning, try to corner the answers to these questions?

Let's begin with the first question, who will pay the taxes? That's actually more involved than a person's faculties might lead them to believe. Do we all pay? Right now that question is a little murky. You see, politicians fight over who does the paying in society. Each side has their stereotypical stance. Some say fifty-one percent of the country doesn't pay federal taxes. That's really just a game. You see, there's more than one tax, and that's where they get you. Here's a brief summary of what's going on in Washington. Congress will create a new project or identify a need that will require constant funding. Then, the will create a tax and a fund to pay for that identified need. Payroll taxes often fit into that category, and everyone who draws a paycheck as an employee pays those. The problem comes when the government decides fifty-one percent paying taxes aren't enough, and they raid one of these specific funds. Now, do fifty-one percent of people pay taxes at that point, or are tax policies being used to say one thing and do another? Again, it goes back to the principle that government governs best when those who bare the cost of its bad decisions have the most authority. Those who feel the consequences of those decisions first and keenest must be able to make informed decisions with the power to change bad policy. So what do politicians do if they want to spend money *and* get you to pay for it without you getting outraged? They tell you someone else is going to pay for it, and try to prevent you from making the connection between their actions and your pain. So, they create another category. They try to convince everyone the cost is worth any pain. When that fails, they start moving money from to things you do approve of and are willing to pay over to the policies they want to fund. Or, they try to hide what they are doing altogether. I think the Value Added Tax is one of the most infamous examples of this strategy as it has been applied here in the United States.

If you haven't guessed, I'm a big fan of the flat tax, with the possibility for some exemptions on what gets taxed instead of who gets taxed. The current system, in my reckoning, fleeces the people in the bottom, middle, and top while telling them nothing is happening. Clarity would only help this process. As long as politicians think they can pass new taxes the subterfuge and innovation they won't cut spending as a primary recourse. That could outrage the interest groups who got the spending passed in the first place, costing voters and donations. If you simplify the tax code to one number, and rule out things which poorer tax payers rely on such as food from what can taxed, you end up with plenty of money and far less uncompassionate hardship on lower income families. I lived on ninety dollars a week for a while. That's three dollars a meal, enough gas to get where I absolutely had to go, and precious little left over. I remember I would eat my last meal of the day right before I went to bed so that the pain of hunger wouldn't keep me away. It would have helped a great deal if gas and food didn't have a tax cost associated with it. It may not have made any kind of difference to the wealthy. But, that's the kind of help which would have mattered a lot to me back then. At least in that kind of society we provide opportunity to help those with the least in society. The grocery store still has to pay taxes on everything from the hats they wear in the deli to the pallets they store goods on in the back. But, in a competitive market they have less cost to pass on to consumers because we just lowered the cost of feeding people. In a competitive market that means lower prices. People with less can afford to eat healthier, fuller meals and rich people are still paying taxes on their yachts, not that I have anything against sailing on yachts. That would be fun, sailing on a yacht. With a flat tax which is either applied to a category of sales or it is not, the people who consume more could pay more while the people who have the least can be taxed proportionately less. Since the power of the free economy is there, some of the most lucrative sectors of the economy to work in would be the areas that also provide needed services to the poor, since those areas would be taxed least. The promise of profit brings the ingenuity and competition which raises quality of service, and by extension the standard of living in those areas, without overburdening the forces creating the kind of jobs which raise people out of poverty. It is a comprehensive approach to tax policy. But, did you see how I did that? I added elements from both value systems until the whole withstood the scrutiny of both laws of love. Respecting both sides will take you a long ways towards crafting better policy.

The questions we've been asking in this chapter define fiscal policy that protects the financial welfare of our communities. Although one system is the result, we are seeing that each side sees that system in a radically different light. For example, if you are chasing the ideological orthodoxy which deviates at the point of the first law of love, you are probably pursuing the myth of self sufficiency. I can tell I hurt a few feelings there on one side, while the some on the other side are trying to figure out what could be hurtful in that statement. Remember, if you find yourself feeling offended, hang on until I take the argument to its fullest logical extent. Then, we'll see what we will see, agreed? Right now I'm pointing out how sensitive we can be when our values are challenged. I can guarantee that for some, this will be a rough ride. But that is part of what this book is about, challenging inclinations. Some people prefer to make right turns, but that won't help them in the times when their destination is on the left. Inclinations can be good or bad. When an inclination becomes lifted to the level of moral certitude problems will follow. Our inclinations have been built on our values, which are built on our conscience and what informs our conscience. That's tender territory. Just looking at one's own value structure hurts. We're prodding around how it connects to what is even more personal in the hopes of finding common ground to unite a people, stay with me. Consider what you will get out this kind of exercise.

If you are a liberal, take a moment to appreciate what your conservative friends are facing personally. Unite over the feeling of having your values challenged for your own good, rather than on the particular value that is being challenged. Otherwise, you're probably not going to find much interest in this next bit. Here goes. If you are staunchly conservative, you are most likely struggling to reflect in your life your sense of the perfect self. For some, this means a search for beauty and truth. Just go through the list of things attributed to God in theology, and that's most likely what you value in life. But for some, they have gone beyond pursuing beauty and truth. Some may have cut some corners and made compromises over the years, but are still looking at aspects of the self sufficiency and either claiming them or aiming for them. This trail of idealistic trial and error end up shaping their sense of self worth, derived from the extent to which they perceive themselves to achieve this notion which is called self sufficiency. Instead of beholding and reflecting beauty and truth, they consider themselves to have apprehended and become the measure of true beauty. We're not talking physical beauty, but of ideals. This idyllic self they think they have achieved, or are remarkably close to, requires no others to meet its needs. I'm not a philosopher, but in borrowing some terms one might says these people aspire to be all actuality without any potentiality. They move the world, but are not moved by the world in this concept. Of course, like all of us, they want to world to react in a way that is positive to them when the move it. Who doesn't want to be responded to positively? This kind of self image creates a specific worldview. In the eyes of the individual who claims to be self sufficient and has the self as their focus, the world around them and the events contained within exist to acclaim the greatness of their self. Ideologies like this are competitive by nature, each member seeking to outdo the others. And, we all have pride. What measure would those of this nature employ to measure the greatness of themselves after their basic needs are met? The closest comparison one might draw could be the person standing next to them. If world and its happenings display demonstrated approval of the self then contrasting the great need of others to the small measure of their own need presents a means of calculating their own achievement. Of course, that's like grading on an extremely lenient curve. And, the people who do this tend to steer clear of real challenges like a Mother Teresa of Calcutta, a C. S. Lewis, or a Billy Graham. It may seem obviously farcical to an outside observer who is not playing that game. But, remember what they are chasing and how they are different. Everyone is unique. Some people share more similarity that others. But, no one will be as good at being you on their best day as you are on your worst day here on this earth. You were created to fulfill a unique space, and we're all impoverished if you do not live to your fullest because who you are and what you give can never be replicated. That's why any kind of comparison against others for the purpose of determining self worth is fruitless. Exploring who you are when you're at your best is the only pursuit of self worth your time. Comparison with other is worthless except to encourage you on to go where only you can go. Any person not caught up wholly and lovingly in this pursuit is living a tragedy, just like any person not contributing to the overall wellbeing of another is a tragedy. If a self sufficient person is a one who moves but is not moved, what does that say about self sufficiency? Going beyond the philosophy, how can you really be human if you are not moved to tears by the plight of those in need, and do not move in reaction with the aid and comfort that only you can bring? There are many instances where Jesus, to whom we look as a teacher for this literary work, did amazing things after feeling compassion. I would encourage those who still prefer maintaining unfavorable comparisons to their neighbor but respect our teacher to read to read Luke chapter six, verse thirty-six.

It is easy to understand how those who hold an ideological worldview on the right commonly see benevolence in government as a negative, or something which obscures their greatness. The welfare actions of the government are constantly ruining the contrast. From their perspective, government reduces their own total wealth in the form of taxes, and gives an unfair advantage to the less affluent who are losing in life in the form of entitlements. Granted, I think private charities do it better, and should be incentivized greatly. But, I'm not a fan of totally removing the "societal safety net" either. I think the ones who are in favor of this are the people who have gone beyond the moral imperatives of the first law. I'm not talking your average "preppers" here. I'm talking about the full blown self righteous. You usually hear these types complain about poor people having big screen televisions or fancy cars. Let's get some perspective here. As a nation we are massively in debt and doing nothing to improve our situation. Our education system spends more and gets less than comparable nations. The surveillance state is getting out of control, getting caught spying on everyone from your neighbor, to reporters, to members of congress. But, someone on the bottom living "ghetto fabulous" is what vehemently sticks in their craw. Think about that. A person not living up to ideologically orthodox ideals and not receiving the affluence believed to follow makes it to the top of their short list of social ills.

 You rarely, if ever, hear these individuals compassionately speak about the heavy toll of not being able to actualize one's dreams, suffered daily by the poor. I've been there. It is hard. I couldn't see any way for my economic state to change, at various points in my life. But, that doesn't mean it couldn't have happened. We're fortunate we live in an economy where people still move up and down the economic scale, rather than a caste system from previous periods and places in time. It may be history here, but you could have been born a few hundred years earlier and elsewhere. We just need to stay compassionate as a culture so we keep creating opportunities for others. Overlooking the state of the poor, and the way they feel trapped, goes beyond a desire for fiscal thrift. It often comes from a belief that one is excused from benevolent compassion because life punishes the unworthy, and publically displays the worthiness of the successful with excess. Life is then reduced to a system where actions like "hard work" and "clean living" can be mystically used to guarantee one's status in life. Of course this doesn't withstand scrutiny. There are tribes living in the Kalahari who work extremely hard every day just to subsist. And, never mind that our role model for this book, Jesus himself, was homeless. While no record of wrong ever existed, Jesus was mocked, tortured, stripped, and publicly nailed naked to a tree for his message of love. So much for the magic of hard work and clean living, while both are wonderful neither hold power over the future.

 There is no reason to put any faith in the claim of self sufficiency posed by the ideological right. We have debunked it in the preceding paragraphs. No grounds are sufficient to uphold self-sufficiency, whether logical or emotional. Philosophically speaking, we are beings of actuality and potentiality. One could easily argue, and many have, that only God is or could be pure actuality. Therefore, that makes it impossible for any creature in the universe to be truly self-sufficient. If you have a higher emotional quotient, desiring to consider the matter in a different way than someone with a high intelligence quotient might, consider this. Understanding the myth of self sufficiency on a very human level allows us to reduce the concept to an easy question. For those who still believe in self sufficiency, when's the last time you looked at a suffering or homeless person and recognized their resemblance to Jesus, Mother Teresa, or any of the other paragons of virtue we admire?

You will never convince true ideologues of the fallacy in their orthodoxy. You can get a lot done by talking to them in front of an audience. They usually double down on their desires, providing an excellent foil for point you're making to the audience. Ultimately, though, I've found that people believe what they want to believe. They may even know what they believe isn't true. But there is still a difference between knowing and believing. Belief is part choice. At best, you challenge desires that miss the mark and take someone in a bad direction. They've got to want to give it up on their own after that. Walking away from the truth of the second law of love has left a gap in their nature. The affirmation internally created by acting according to the second law of love needs to be filled with something else when it is lacking. People oriented conservatively are naturally introspective. They don't always notice it, but personal pronouns come up quite a bit in conversation. Now I've done it. I'm sure there are enterprising readers going back now and counting uses of I and me, etc. to find out who they're dealing with. Just remember, this material applies best to those on the politically active extremes. Classification and application starts getting fuzzy the closer you get to the well balanced middle, or when these concepts are applied to specific individuals rather than people acting in groups. The people attempting to herd the masses don't think of the people they are influencing as individuals. To quote a sales axiom, it's a numbers game. One person equals one vote. In order to flex political muscle, a political group has to get a large number to buy into their narrative. That means a good narrative is like a multiplier. One vote is still just one vote. One vote times a good narrative equals many votes. That's something with which they can accrue money and power. The narrative is what matters. It doesn't even need to be honest. The narrative they spin just has to be a big enough multiplier to build political power. Are you upset when politicians don't care about you? Find ways to get them to care about every vote. Notice I didn't say, "Find ways to get them to care about your vote, or your group's vote." When you personalize it to a person or a group you've only created a competing philosophy. People don't generally want to buy into that sort of thing. That may be part of the reason voting participation is so low in this country, given what politics has become. The ones who want to buy in to politics as a team sport already have a team and their team plays in the big leagues. They're not interested in an expansion that's going to lose for its first few seasons, to borrow a sports metaphor. If you are just trying to build power, like the two major parties and all the other existing minor parties, you are starting from the wrong side of the equation. (1 Vote x narrative = political power) doesn't work well for you when your narrative is selfish ambition. This may come as a shock, but not everyone is interested in your ambition. The people who are best at dividing the population based on selfish ambition have divided us into the two biggest groups possible. The only way to form a larger coalition now is selfless service. (1 Vote x narrative = political power) works when your narrative is composed of principles which serve both laws of love. When everything you do politically advances freedom to pursue both laws of love without violating either you create a winning narrative. And, I would argue you create a better world in which to live in the process. That equation is more power than selfish ambition, since selfish ambition necessarily divides, and, "Every kingdom divided against itself is laid waste, and no city or house divided against itself will stand." That quote is an ominous one most all of us has heard, and had fun repeat at one point or another. That quote is also Jesus from Matt 12:25. Abraham Lincoln borrowed from these words of Jesus in his speech on June 16, 1858 at the Republican State Convention in Springfield Illinois when they chose Lincoln to run for the U. S. Senate. He was talking about how our nation would be torn apart if we did not put away an evil that was causing greater polarization and treat all men as equal. That's a lesson to us. Like Abraham Lincoln called for, and Jesus before him, we find uniting principles rather than profit from division which devalues and dehumanizes others. If we stop polarizing practices when they are small by defending the laws in all areas of society we do not reap the harvest of division. If we are vigilant in filling the gaps created in our society where we do not love fully with fidelity to love as Jesus describes it we will enjoy unity and prosperity. Our nation will thrive. If we go about filling the gaps with something else, political orthodoxy that mimics the appeal of love but has none of its uniting power for example, events will occur which are far less desirable. People may get some power in the short term if we let them, but the eventual cost will be devastating, vastly pyrrhic beyond description.

Filling gaps in what love we lack is not something that needs noticing to happen. If only on an instinctive level, people know they need to fill that gap. The question that rises then is, if not the love for which that hole was made, what is used as filler? The vanity of self sufficiency is as much a lie conservatives tell themselves, as an orthodoxy they preach to others. It explains the presence of internal emptiness in comforting terms which are easy for them to accept and tempting to believe. They need pour into that gap continually in order maintain their own sense of wellbeing. Love is best because the more you give, the more it fills you. A wonderful paradox comes from love where giving it away means you are continually filled and at the same time always desiring more. Nothing else I know of gives fulfillment while simultaneously sharpening desire. This is true of living both laws of love. Without the fullness and fulfillment love brings we are left with a need for fulfillment and pursuits which are more desirable in expectation than in having, leaving us restless. Natural inclinations take over, directing where our restless hearts wander. On the right of the political divide, conservatives each consider themselves and their household to be the best investment they can make, in that order. Taxes are a nuisance which hamper investing in the self. How can they not react vehemently when the believed means of bringing peace to their restless hearts is sapped and given for other purposes?

On the other side is a different approach to the decisions that define tax policy. When you're more inclined to that part of human nature defined by the second law of love, government is not merely a means to an end. There is a luster and shine to the edifice on the hill directing the business of the people. Government is a worthy end in itself. Those who base their ideology on the second law of love believe you should give to others. They see taxation as a means of keeping track to make sure you're giving enough. Notice use of the word "enough" rather than a definitive percent or amount. Government is also the force with which they enact their concept of "enough." As I've stated before, when you elevate one part of nature to the status of an idol, and dismiss other laws of nature, you create a massive moral mess. Those who hold their private interpretation of the second law of love as their idol, and dismiss the first law of love, do not see an end to how much one should give to government. Logically, this is where it falls down. You see, for those who hold to this persuasion there is no such thing as "enough." Whenever they are asked how much a person should give the answer is certainly "more." Those who have gone to extremes in the liberal mode believe the only legitimate way to receive something is for others to give it to you. And, they see themselves as fit rulers of society. If you have built something for yourself, but did not do it in a way they approve of, they may decide you have taken from the total societal resource in an inappropriate manner. This belief is the core from which liberal statements such as, "you didn't build that," grow.

The love of money represents the ability of a person to impose their will in society. It is an evil which corrupts both sides. When it comes to political people who love money on the left, the end game is always the same. It doesn't matter whether they are Marxists, socialists, communists, progressives, or whatever else. Ideological orthodoxy follows a similar line of thinking. Ends don't matter. After all, at the moral core on which they base their orthodoxy is a law of caring for others. Caring for others does not have an end point. It is an ongoing lifestyle. So, to motivated liberals, the means *are* the ends. That's why liberals are stereotypically bad at pursuits which inherently require an end point to be a successful, like balancing a budget, or fighting a war. That's why this discussion, so far, has rotated around means, without evolving into ends. That's how the mindset works. It becomes a way of doing things of which they highly approve, and they seek to impose this way on others.

So how do we understand liberal theory? Some would say it is the nature of bureaucracy. It is also important to point out that all of the "ism's" break down into groups. That can get confusing. So, let's break this down and evaluate this at the macro level. It's getting kind of confusing, so we'll make it more interesting by starting with the payoff. Those who have deviated at the point of the second law of love turn their orthodoxy into an idol. We know they will seek to subjugate all others into the service to their god. Despite dire, repeated warnings and failures, those who seek to run a society under this god will not heed consequences. In time, the laws of nature reassert themselves. Kipling described it well in his poem on what happens when our gods fall to the laws of nature.

Sticking with the big picture and bringing it back to taxes, for those who craft their own orthodoxy on the departure point from the second law of love, when it comes to money, there are two things which matter. That you give, and that the money is spent in service to their mode is all important. That's why elected liberals in government are always demanding ever increasing taxation. The base which empowers them reacts instinctively when they are distracted to demands promoting an outward focus. Let's take this home for a second. Someone in the house is trying to do something that requires concentration. It could be a family member, or even yourself. While you're trying to focus, something else is going on which demands your attention. A loved one may be feeling neglected and making more noise than usual so you'll get the message. Loud, audible sighs progress to cupboard doors slamming and pots banging in the kitchen if not caught early. Younger kids may be screaming. Older kids may be fighting. The cat is throwing up a hairball on the rug. The dog is barking out the window at a terrified mailman who, just this moment, developed a keen interest in the tensile strength of whatever is used to make screen doors. In that moment, maybe you snap. Shouting comes from a place of frustration that others are not what they should be doing, and now you have to stop what you were doing to address the situation. The things that are said likely would never come out if you were exercising full control of your faculties with these loved members of your home, or at least would come out in a gentler fashion. But, that's not what happens when your focus is shattered by circumstances demanding attention you weren't prepared to give. Liberal politicians demand increasing spending as a percent of gross domestic product in areas of which they approve. But, unlike the kids or the pets, politicians break your focus every election cycle in a premeditated fashion, redirect your rage, and stoke it while holding your peace ransom until all the votes have been counted. The wife may get a day at the spa after you snap at her. The husband may go out and get a new grill. Politicians turn your inattentive reactivity into momentum for a new spending on their pet projects. There's nothing that will check the liberal approach to tax policy if you don't. Liberals are motivated at their core by the second law of love and the values which demand fiscal responsibility in spending are derived from another law. As polarization continues the likelihood that the solution will come from the left side of the political divide becomes diminished. Neither side has any desire to do something unless it builds the party, is good for business. The people on both sides that want to genuinely serve country instead of party keep getting drowned out by the partisans on both sides who want to perpetuate the games they are running on the citizenry. And, the press today seems to go along, rather than exposing the major players.

The issue of U. S. border protection is a prime example of the discrimination against spending that is not within the mode of either side, and has been brought up in many talks about taxation but the situation allowed to continue to fester rather than being resolved. Currently, there is just enough attention being paid to the issue to raise money, but not enough attention after the money is raised to fix the problem. That is possibly Capitol Hill's favorite kind of problem the way it is being run lately. When someone who has been doing bad thing repeatedly on the wrong side of the border does something really bad, or a company is exposed for offering working conditions to migrant workers well under what we consider moral treatment, outrage sparks in the populace. Politicians pretend to do something by voting for a spending bill. But, once the money is there the run a wedge through the voters until both sides are disgusted and gridlock is achieved. Time passes until the press has moved on to something else and with it the pressure. I like to think that the press is the country's biggest pressure group, as intended from the outset of our nation. All that money is still available for spending. It didn't go anywhere. Claims are made as to what has been done on the border that later are proven untrue. And all that money the people in charge said they needed to fix the problem, well, the problem isn't fixed after numerous such efforts. Where do you think the money went? Was it spend well? We don't. We stopped paying attention too soon.

 This is an obvious example of the break down in taxing and spending as a whole, so we'll invest further scrutiny. We'll start with the left. Securing a border does not fit into liberal orthodoxy. It's a necessary task. It may prevent repeat criminals from coming across our borders and committing more crimes. It may greatly reduce the influence of harmful drugs on our streets and the kidnapping, murdering gangs that sell them. It may prevent terrorists from one day sneaking a bomb across our borders and into a major city where the damage would be unchecked. But, spending money for that purpose still does not fit the ideology. It's not about the consequences of action or inaction. It's not about pragmatism. It is about service to an orthodox set of ideals. This is its own religion. One of the wonderful things about good religion is that it does not change. When societal whims push fads in every direction, religion is one of the anchors of society, along with tradition, which keep us generous, gentle, and provides barriers to crossing the lines of human rights violations. Religion is a beautiful thing when its chief concern is feeding, clothing, and housing orphans and elderly widows, for example. A bad religion, like one that instructs its members to strap bombs on and commit suicide in an effort to maim and kill others, and is decried by members of the same faith, has a detrimental effect on society. Notice I delineated between religion and faith. Religion is praxis. It is important to note that two people who both believe they are serving the same faith may be severely at odds with each other. We have that a lot in our politics. Or, two people who share no faith whatsoever may pursue the same ideals in practice. It is important to talk about religion. Faith is a bit touchy. To believe in a faith you need to have faith. Faith is, or should be, grounded on experience. Even artfully placed words have a hard time swaying a person's life experience. Religion produces results, both in the observance of it and the people who those observances affect. Whether a religion is good or not can be argued by looking at the affects it practices have on others and in the lives of its adherents.

On the conservative side they dismiss the possibility of normalizing the flow of workers over the border by creating a process which would protect them, as well as our national interests. We could have a safer, experienced, motivated, reliable migrant work force. These workers would be spending money in our restaurants, stores, and hotels, which would all be taxed at the same rate as every citizen of our country under my idea for a flat sales tax. I just wanted to point that out. The money they send back home to Mexico would give us a tremendous bargaining advantage with that country, if it were routed through documented, official channels and subject to U. S. Law. All you need to do is put a hold on all money transfers to Mexico for a period and suddenly listening improves. I'm not saying we should be looking for more levers against our allies, or not. We're talking about conservatives here and what motivates them. If we're going to convince them to act on an issue they hate we're going to have to dangle something they like. Conservatives like levers. The charitable aspect alone of the plight of the migrant worker makes action worthwhile. But, for conservatives it isn't on their list of things to do because it's not what their orthodoxy focuses on, and that also makes it bad for business.

In either case on both sides it is about the field of preferable actions. Natural laws help form the conscience. Cognitive dissonance pushes us in a direction which is in keeping with our conscience. Politicians fabricate scenarios, whether intentionally or out of their own misunderstanding, presenting a false choice between upholding one moral imperative and ignoring another. Voters feel they have to choose between two sets of values rather than honoring both. The point which is targeted to be leveraged here is the conscience. Politicians are getting personal. Why? They are incentivized to make arguments which affect the widest swath of voters possible. As long as we are not savvy when it comes to our own moral currents, the way each of us understands and approaches morality, they are going to keep exploiting our ignorance to great effect.

A conscience can be formed through continual acts of will. A well formed conscience, which sees the whole image of morality necessary to govern a civil society, is a stalwart defense against this kind of voter manipulation. If we don't have a complete moral image, we self limit our choices to those preferred by our natural preferences. We reinforce these preferences by giving our will over to them again and again, forming our conscience. Our conscience reacts painfully to perceived threats to our natural preferences. The key word is perceived, because if we don't work to incorporate both laws of love into our lives we aren't very wise in this area and can be fooled into thinking they compete rather than coexist. An incomplete sense of morality is easily offended and easy to trick. When one political side uses these kinds of fabrications and finds success, it creates a competitive advantage. If the other political side does not use at least equally effective tactics, they will function at an extreme disadvantage in a system with two major parties. A party either wins or loses in a system like that. You don't have to win every race, but you do have to keep it close to maintain credibility with political donors and other interests which are good for business in politics. The political party using methods that motivate a wider group of voters will succeed. And, a reactive voting base is good for business while an engaged group of voters with a balanced perspective is harder to distract. So, what do you think happens?

In a polarized society the far ends of the political system show up to vote and the moral middle feels under-represented. This is not to be confused with the political middle who calls themselves things like independents or label free. There are those craving a more fulfilling and complete moral representation in their government on both sides of the political divide. If a figure or group rallies the under-represented in a polarized society by presenting a complete moral image they can gain the competitive advantage. In effect they would be sapping votes from the other side. Crafting policies and conversation which upholds both laws of love inoculates against the pangs of conscience, providing a solution to pain caused by politically induced cognitive dissonance in voters on both sides. They say the best way to sleep well at night is to live well during the day. If the major political powers in a system of government have built their power on half truths that polarize, they aren't going to sleep well if you're telling the whole truth. In a polarized system, the best way to enjoy success while eroding power from the competition may be as simple as a good night's sleep. The options we face, by my reckoning, are as follows. If no one steps forward, and the other party doesn't fight back effectively, a preference system which does not meet all of societal needs will ascend to supremacy. The nation then slides into decline under tyranny. Sometimes this decline is accelerated, other times slow, but always it is sure. If both political parties use morally divisive tactics, dividing between these two widest preference systems, the population then becomes polarized. The end result of this division, if not rectified, is a potentially catastrophic impasse. As the definition of an impasse informs us, this can end in conflict. Or, as we've been learning from our teacher, if we stand for both laws of love, fully embraced in our society, we can save ourselves from learning through costly mistakes end enjoy the wonderful life which follows success.

People who start on either end of the understanding continuum that rests on the two laws must strive to gain a full understanding of morality. A full understanding opens the field of possibilities up which we as human beings will pursue. We need to turn our continuum into a Mobius strip. Sometimes we will deepen our understanding of a law of love through following our passion. Other times it is found through self discipline. It just depends on how you are oriented and which body of moral thought to which you are applying yourself. I'm not kidding about self discipline. Just to understand how great the divide is let's engage in an exercise describing how a simple preference for one of the two laws can be pivotal in our approach to life.

The same person who told us loving others was one of two paramount laws, also told us the poor would always be with us. So, for liberals, it can't be about the end. Focusing exclusively or even predominately on finite or empirical things, such as how something ends, would drive someone naturally oriented in this manner to conniptions. They would be trying to end something that can't be ended, if that were the case. That would make no sense. If it really is true that there will always be those in poverty, then to judge success in serving the poor by their presence or absence guarantees a judgment of failure. It logically doesn't follow. Right now I imagine there are liberals who are cheering because I just explained the compassion logically. To focus on the needs of society where their nature directs them to look, ends must be secondary if considered at all. This approach is a natural one, and therefore indiscriminate. They apply it in all areas. Without self discipline, this even includes very linear and objective areas, such as tax policy. In such rigid fields as accounting and budgeting an unchecked approach where the answer to every problem is always more spending causes serious problems. Those who do not labor in broadening their understanding of prudence may find little motivation to pursue a healthy economy.

I pointed out liberals a little so let's pick on conservatives too. It must be said that while staid and steady judgment based on the quantifiable is to be lauded, there is something about caring for others that constitutes a basic human need. Although intangible, its measure is in the goodwill and cheer created in those who serve each other. Like the wind, or gravity, charity it is most easily observed in the objects upon which it acts. Charity is measured in the anxiety it relieves from those in need, in the suffering it relieves from those without consolation, and in so many other ways. Charity strengthens us, and a strengthened people make a stronger society. Those whose preferences naturally direct them to consider others generally find an inborn way to measure and the value of these intangible things. Those not naturally inclined towards the law demanding we love our neighbor find it harder to understand the currency of compassion. Those people need self discipline to apply the second law of love in their lives. Without charity for others, they build through their neglect what liberals build through their excess, a broken society. Lower taxes may encourage those who need or desire money to work, as defined by the Laffer Curve. But, whether or not people are working, the health of the economy, these are secondary at best. Our national disposition towards prudent compassion, by wisdom, will determine the future of the nation as well as our present. Divided, each side uses their own motivating factors in their personal evaluation of governing philosophy. The energy of the nation must be directed in a manner which reflects a balanced, better way.

# AMERICAN EXCEPTIONALISM

It's a phrase we've all heard. Although not quite a wedge issue, the words American exceptionalism have been the grounds for many a conflict in U. S. politics. On the hard right, some conservatives make it sound like the reason for everything we do in the U.S. that's good and worth doing. For the hard left, many liberals deny the very existence, complaining that every nation is exceptional. Obviously, that makes no sense since equal exceptionalism spread out through every nation would be the definition of uniformity. But, how the United States got the nickname America makes about as much sense as calling Canada or Brazil America. It's especially ironic when you consider a German clergyman named Martin Waldseemuller is the one who got the name America to stick, and named the continents after an Italian navigator named Amerigo Vespucci. If you want more confusion go through your friends and family asking them one by one to define American Exceptionalism. You may get a different explanation each time you ask. No two people seem to have the same understanding of the meaning but it is a phrase that still works to unify the parties and fires passion on voting day, and every other day if you include talk radio. That's why I call it a quasi wedge issue. What is American exceptionalism? For many, it represents an effort to define the success of the U.S. in the twentieth century, as well continued primacy of the U.S. in its role as the sole remaining international "superpower." That's where the conflict begins. One side likes the idea of a society they see as being built on empowering the individual and protecting individual freedom being the dominant power in the world. The other side wants groups to hold power and the wellbeing of people to be considered in blocs rather than as individuals. Those people are willing to amass power to an individual if that person promises to enact that system. I didn't say it was rational. People will go to some strange places for their ideology.

The U.S. is a representative republic. What that means is the founders who constructed our political system of government studied the failing of other systems that came before them and used all their art and skill to protect against government gone awry. They looked at a simple democracy where fifty-one percent of the population imposes their will over the other forty-nine percent. If you think that is a good idea, consider the pet rock fad. It was a marketing dream. People actually paid money to get something they were digging up in their garden or passing on the side of the road. What did the pet rock do? It sat there. It was a rock. It's worth repeating, people actually paid money for rocks. It's not like bottled water where bottling companies actually offered an arguably better product that what comes out of a tap. Evian may be naïve spelled backwards, but I've never had to avoid my bottled water because some chemical or bacteria made it unsafe to drink like my tap water. And, it's delicious. Unless you're building a very expensive wall, that rock was anything but utilitarian. That's what mob decision making looks like. Now let's pretend that instead of a ridiculous rock and a brilliant marketing strategy giving us some fun for a while, that same decision making that led us to spend money on a rock is used to repair roads and fund the national defense. We know what mobs can do when it comes to dispensing justice. In the past it has involved a rope and a terrified innocent's death. Mob rule is terrifying, but that's what you get in a majority ruled democracy. That's why we have checks and balances in our system which slows the process down just long enough so that by the time fading passions lose momentum and die out they haven't left a slew of ridiculous to disastrous national decisions in their wake. I don't mind the pet rock product, it's hilarious. I don't want to have the pet rock government.

That's a situation where the mob has too much power. But, there's also a danger in the government having too much power. In the case of a king, all they need is a bad hair day and worse character for people to start dying. It may seem extreme, but history is replete with examples of bad monarchs. Think about the best person you know, and imagine their grandkids getting everything handed to them along with life and death power over you and your family's lives. Even good people die, eventually people do that. When one generation passes on the next takes over. How do you avoid investing power in the bratty kids who kicks the cat and pops the heads of their toys? How do you remove ultimate earthly power from someone who doesn't turn out to be so great after they get a taste of said power? That's regime change. Often, the people who ran nations previous to our constitutional republic system showed a high degree of reluctance to regime change, to put it mildly. When we wanted regime change at the time of the founding of our country we had to fight the revolutionary war to get it. People don't always realize it, but every four years there is the opportunity for regime change in the United States, and no one has to die over it. Think about the differences between the Clinton administration and the following Bush administration, or the Carter and Reagan administrations. Prior to the U. S. Constitution that kind of change required an army and an insurrection to enact. President Obama ran on the slogan "Hope and Change" and people changed. In 70 and again in 130 A. D. when the Israelites, whose understanding of moral law we based our government on, hoped for changed the Roman Empire responded by burned the city with their temple to the ground and dispersing Israel's inhabitants. Rome was ruled by an emperor. When our president's approval drops in the polls here in Ohio we don't fear our homes will be bulldozed and we'll be shipped to Kansas. It's good to limit the power of government, to slow down their action long enough to deliberate on them by spreading that power through various branches of government and imposing checks to its use of power.

It's not by accident we've succeeded in avoiding these extreme abuses of power. Simply put, it's because people wearing powdered wigs some two hundred years ago put together something special. Various types of government and economies have been developed since then. Socialism and the free market system exist on the far ends of the governing philosophies jockeying to fill the void left by lagging faith in the ability of monarchs to rule all aspects of society. Major nations slowly moved away from purely being ruled by a single person or family. Now it seems like only the poorest countries that can still afford a military cling to dictators. And we're somewhere in the middle between a strong government and a strong people, a free market and a socialist system. Although we all pay taxes of some kind or another, personal property rights are still maintained and respected. We have a constitutional republic. If you want to know what that looks like, read our Constitution. The economy is not a pure market economy like Adam Smith might have envisioned. But, it's not socialist either. If you're looking for a name, our economy is a mixed-market economy. There is a mix of both value systems which fuel the extremes within our governing and economics. That kind of balanced philosophy provides a degree of satisfaction to each side, providing stability and the kind of environment where opportunity is created. If everyone is protected while enjoying the maximum freedom to pursue what they consider important then everyone is invested. That means a nation with a talent pool of ideas that is larger by percentage than nations where all but the inside crowd don't believe the things they care about can become real and be established. It's the kind of system that's good for the economy, and good for a nation. But, that kind of equanimity is not good for business among those who make money and prove their power by aggregating a political base. Division is the tool they use so that others will come to them for their influence. A unifying system is a roadblock to power in their case. The lasting power of our national system has been proven in its ability to thwart the ambitions of disruptive power seekers. Our founders created a kind of political buffer system in the distribution of power throughout the branches of government and between government and the people that appears to work like a buffer system in chemistry, which maintain a balanced ph even when an acid or base is added to a solution. It's stunning to watch as you look back through U. S. history, especially when compared to the dramatic failing of other revolutions and constitutions since our nation's founding.

In addition to the ambitious seekers of power who willingly detract from national stability in pursuit of personal gain for themselves or their group, there are also some people who just don't see the other side of the political spectrum. You could think of them as the politically color blind. Some people can't see political blue, while other people can't see political red. They may never have been taught to consider other points of view, or, they may have been taught not to consider a certain point of view. But, the result is that neither side of the politically color blind sees the same thing a balanced person sees when they look at the flag of the United States. That explains some of the confusion surrounding a charged phrase like American Exceptionalism. It also makes the politically color blind easy targets for the ones making money off dividing us into voting blocs. That makes you wonder, which came first? Did someone figure out they could make money because a lot of voters aren't paying enough attention to see past a campaign slogan and a red or blue poster? Or, did groups of slick political operators actively work to separate out and groom voting bases, conditioning them to charge like a bull when someone waves a red or blue cape at them? You can try to figure out the paradox. It's like the question of whether the chicken or the egg came first. I vote chicken. Instead, let's do something productive by taking the debate out of the hands of those advancing purely personal interests. We'll move the conversations away from polarization into something better. We know that our society achieved sole remaining international superpower status in a little more than two hundred years. Other cultures and societies have roots going back for thousands of years. We don't, and despite their head start we have still manage to achieve such prominent status. It is important to take the better path and be humble about it. After all, we didn't build something out of nothing. We based our culture which created aviation and computers off the success of nations throughout time on the other side of the globe, and built it all on the foundation laid out in places like Deuteronomy. Using this basis allowed us the understanding necessary to create a nation where the two most fundamental laws of human morality can be expressed more fully by our nation's population than at any preceding time in history.

In the United States more people are freer than at any time in preceding history to express the desires of their heart, and see their desires actualized. I choose the word actualization because it is a good word for describing the purpose and existence of American exceptionalism. Self-actualization is a psychological term for the achievement of one's full potential, thus the exceptionalism. After all, the average person being able to pursue their dreams is fairly exceptional in history. In previous places and previous time the message would have been, dream anything you want, as big as you want, as long as your dream is what your caste, king, culture, etc. find acceptable. The American part of the phrase is that you make sure you play well with others. They don't get to crush your dreams, and you don't get to inhibit theirs either, as much as is possible in society. Some might say that if your dream is to be president there's going to be some competition. But, that comment would stem from confusion which is at the heart of the dysfunction between the parties today. The problem with political talk today is that it treats means as ends. For example, people compete for political office regularly in our nation. The highest office is President of the United States. Being the president is a big deal. But, being the president is not an end. It is a job comprised of a collection of powers granted by the people for their governing. If a president uses the presidency to promote peace between law enforcement and the communities, especially minority communities, that's an end. Cooperation, understanding, and the office of president are means to the end of advancing peace. Another example, if a president uses his office to negotiate trade deals which provide new resources to the United States economy while lifting developing nations out of poverty, then that president is using the tools of the job to achieve ends. But again, neither negotiations nor the office of president are an end. Security is an end, both in our economy and in nations struggling to normalize their food and employment structure. Holding the office itself is not an end. The American half of the phrase American exceptionalism only works when you have a proper understanding of ends. Creating an environment with maximum possible potential to pursue both laws of love is the ultimate end, and the result of the famous "American experiment" our founders began. It is the idea behind America. This freedom is the American dream. In my opinion, an environment with maximum potential to pursue both laws of love in a society is the recipe for America to prosper, because only in this condition does everyone feel the desire buy in to the future of the nation, and achieve their own potential.

 There is something about the human condition that desires to explore our potential. Psychology has proven this desire to be a powerful and motivating. We know this now. But, even before modern psychology existed, a group of rebels from a king huddled around a small room in colonial America and signed their names on a document that would ensure hardship for them and peace for us today. For the sake of their desire to be free and pursue their dreams they penned their names on a constitution which would see many of them tortured, bankrupted, mocked, and killed. So many other revolutions have ended in bloodshed and tyranny. Means and ends are very different things. Means are flexible. They can be used by a wide variety of people to achieve any number of purposes. The disposition of our hearts bleeds out in the overall context of actions when we obfuscate or motives. Sometimes we don't even know the vagaries of our own disposition. No one wants to be a villain in their own eyes, and we can do terrible things which we will later regret after our attempt at the apotheosis of our selfish desire. Ends are stubborn and inflexible. Their very existence limits the tools which can be used in their creation. This very quality is what makes them undesirable to political leaders as tools for managing their base. Unlike means, and end does not allow much room to operate between people's perception of the end and the objective truth of the end. When there is peace we feel it. If we are insecure we feel it. We may be told peace exists, but if it does not then merely presenting an image of peace will destabilize any credibility built on the illusion of peace. Means are vastly more flexible. Hypocrisy is the very definition of means being used to send a message opposing the true nature of a hypocrite. Campaign promises are made to be broken, some say. Some campaign promises are meant to be stretched. Political leaders promise to take up all sorts of means. Because people in the voting booth have placed means in the place of ends they vote for people whoever pays the best service to their preferred means. The politicians know a political show can be substituted for results and is far less costly for their business of milking the American public than actually achieving the end which gives the means it meaning. If producing the ends solves a problem and removes the need for the associated means it may even be counter productive to produce and end. And all that happens within the constraints provided by the U. S. Constitution. It's far worse when nations in history without the constraints on government we are protected by lose sight of the difference between means and ends. I hate to take it to Hitler, especially since other totalitarian leaders killed more in raw numbers. But, everyone recognizes the Nazis as a problem so let's start with a place we all agree upon. When Hitler was on the rise to power he needed support so he told people he was Christian. When he got into power Hitler threw dissenting religious leaders like Dietrich Bonheoffer in prison. After he gained power, Hitler tried to dismantle religious institutions in an effort to prevent people devoted to ends of Christianity like love, joy, peace, patience, kindness, goodness, faithfulness, gentleness, and self-control from opposing him. For Hitler, religion was a means to gaining power. One of the ways he was able to fool people into giving up their sovereignty was by cloaking himself in religion. People didn't looking past the means Hitler used to see if he was working towards, valuing, and supporting good ends until it was too late to avoid war and bloodshed.

The founders of the Unites States of America managed to set up an enduring state. That state didn't just survive, it thrived. Now, we better understand how this nation has endured. That's exactly what happens in a society built to protect the citizen's ability to express the values which move them deeply. You can see it in the rise and fall of Rome, a republic which included elements of Greek democracy. Although democracy was in its infancy, they had a senate until they gave their power to an emperor. Unlike Rome, who empowered only a few by limiting citizenship and progressively consolidating power while conquering others, we've made it our aim to push empowerment farther into our national fabric as we've grown. To defend that statement, Americans were at the forefront of major international powers working to abolish slavery, a practice as old as any except maybe gardening and marriage. At that time, abolition was the shocking new trend and slavery the historical practice. American abolitionists like Abraham Lincoln and Frederick Douglass along with Brits like William Wilberforce publicly carried that charge during their respective times in history. And, they changed the way national powers look at freedom to this day.

The domestic policy of freedom to pursue desires which come from the heart, within both laws of love, is also the best description of our foreign policy. This conversation on domestic policy may be the talk we need to have first in order to establish national interest in foreign policy. It can be very hard to get a polarized society to listen to a conversation of foreign affairs. To attract and maintain the interest of foreign nations you really need to be predictable as a nation. They have to know what you'll do before they take actions if you want them to try and win your favor with certain national policies and avoid offending you in how they select others. Nations don't turn on a dime. Anything big enough to need the resources of a whole nation is going to be slow in starting and hard to turn around. An ambivalent nation racing between ideological poles may be able to limp along domestically, but will not send a clear enough message for other nations to trust the investment of their resources to your considerations. When they look ahead in planning their projections for an ambivalent nation will land all over the place. Not even a Las Vegas casino would take that bet. Partner nations can be found who want to build something great together. But, no one wants a fickle partner in the exercise of building a foundation for their future. Too much is at stake and the consequences are too severe. That sets up a scenario where national interest doesn't normally interest the nation. That sounds like an oxymoron, right? There's big, fancy word. I just like it because it has moron in it. We're talking about a situation that is not as advertised here. It's a little ironic that a nation fighting over means like they are everything, which has forgotten how to recognize good ends, eventually, loses all interest in a thing called national interest until something erupts overseas. So many times you hear things called ironic when they really aren't, but I think I actually got it right on this one. I thought about doing this one as a discussion topic. It's got that high interest factor, you know? Everyone seems to really care about it when there is a flare up somewhere. Entire presidential debates purport to focus on it. But, any relationship is about context. A book kind of needs to have a timeless quality unless you plan on putting one out every time something happens, and that may be a bit more than I want put into this. I'm doing my part, but I've also have grass that needs mowing, plumbing to fix, trim to put up since a chipmunk decided the old trim was a great place to try chewing his way into the warm house, and a long list of other things that need doing. So we'll take this in a different direction where change happens a little more slowly. To get context, you need to have history. If you don't know history, you don't know the context, and you're really not going to care. Everyone who watches the news knows about the conflict in the Middle East and our ally Israel over there. If you don't know, it is pretty easy to get the general idea. Conservatives Christians love Israel. I contend that's because the conservative Christian culture draws those who lean more strongly toward the first law of love. Israel is culturally understood to be a place where Jews can defend themselves, and fulfill their personal obligation to God. That very strongly aligns the argument for the existence of Israel with the way of thinking which comes out of the first law of love. You don't need to know much more about the situation to understand why those who base their ideology solely on the second law of love, to the exclusion of all else, would have a problem devoting national resources for that cause. It doesn't help that in an effort to rally their base to the cause the conservative wing of U. S. politics has so effectively couched the argument for U. S. support of Israel in terms of service to conservative means instead of national ends. I could start a whole discussion on whether that was just politically color blind or intentional, aggressive politicking. But, we know now to look past those kinds of unproductive arguments to see and speak to uniting ends which stir the hearts of both groups. Step one is recognize the problem. Once you know what is going on, step two is to speak the truth which will unite as many problem solvers as possible in resolving the problem. Step three is to sit back and wait for opportunities to serve the real experts on getting things done with whatever they need in resolution process. Those would be the people posing or enacting real solutions that are showing promising results. That kind of discernment obviously needs to come from someone who is not acting in a partisan fashion or politically color blind. As an exercise in understanding this process, let's start with step one.

Yep, there it sits. The nation of Israel, in the mind of the American populace, stands for the right of self defense and freedom that people to honor God as they see fit. By this point those terms are probably jumping off the page at you as provocative to either side of the ideological divide. The conservatives want to elevate those ideological actions of defending one's self and seeking personal freedom to place them on a pedestal. Service to their ideology needs no further justification in their minds, and any further discussion lands on the border between heterodoxy and heresy. The far left, including the liberal media, always seem to side with whichever aggressor is currently working to wipe Israel off the map, usually Palestine. They don't like the idea of using resources that could be used to pursue their liberal orthodoxy on conservative buzzwords. Anything which thwarts compliance to their ideology should be removed from their point of view, whatever the cost. Once sources of competition have been removed, the only remaining choice will be their ideology. Of course, this never works. We humans are remarkably creative and stubborn. Human nature doesn't work within political machinations. People trying to direct conformity through the illusion of choice find their keep metastasizing as human will branches out in new directions. Both sides like in a struggle to see the fading vapor of ideology made real in a world far more complex than their simplistic understanding can master as nothing gets accomplished. For those who take objection to including Palestine in that statement, find for me where Palestine has committed to Israel's right to existence. For those who don't know, look for them to deny the justification being used to continue firing rockets over the Israel/Palestine border. I'll point you to Schools on the Jewish side of the fence where moms pray their kids don't die in the classroom from terrorist rocket fire. Given the amount of free advertising that area of the world has received, if it was peaceful it could be made into a jewel of the Mediterranean. Just the taxes on tourism alone could raise Palestinians out of poverty if it was used to build the area. If peace were the goal it could be achieved. Peace isn't the goal. Removal of the Jewish state is the goal. But, if you're completely devoted to liberal thought in the U. S., you would see a nation described as existing in devotion to the competing moral preference system as a thorn in your side, rather than a chance to help a nation impoverished from paying for weapons of war and a war weary nation living in constant vigilance against terrorist attacks. You would fire back against the propaganda using that nation as a political galvanizer and fundraising cause. Wedge forces would kick in and the fight would be on.

 That's about as deep as it gets as far as our approach to that area of the Middle East goes. Circumstances change, but our approach really doesn't, even when the circumstances demand we alter our positions. Not much gets done with that kind of obtuse approach. People don't seem to know their own history let alone what happens outside our borders. I'm encouraged to believe this is changing. But, ask your neighbor how the Monroe Doctrine was implemented by the United States to deter European colonization of the Latin world and see what response you get. Since we had some irony earlier would you like some more? The administration of President Barack Obama, believed by many to be anti-colonialist, declared through Vice President Joe Biden that the Monroe Doctrine was dead. Of course, that probably because Reagan used it as a basis for repelling communist expansion in the Americas, and communism is looked on more favorably by the liberals in American politics. But, it's still a little ironic. If none of that sounds familiar perhaps we should try something more contemporary from the same part of the globe. If you don't know, ask someone why Miami Florida is popularly considered the capital of the Latin world. I you don't get an answer about how money and power moves internationally to and from our southeastern peninsula it will tell you something about general awareness as to how international activity is affecting us in the U. S. If we don't know what is happening just inside our borders, how can we claim to know anything of the rest of the world we live in? We don't know why we stand where we once stood, what has happened since, what people on the other side of the world have done, or what is going on in our own hemisphere. Without at least a basic understanding to provide context, how could we possibly care?

 In the past we've sent people into office that we trusted to learn how best to protect our interests abroad. But now polarization throws even this assumption into chaos. If the people elected are as polarized as the voters who elected them the policy will vacillate wildly when a different party get elected and the administration is not going to make balanced decisions. A foreign policy can take decades to come to fruition. It can have long standing consequences for the future. We still have military stationed in Japan and Germany. What started with a war has ended with enemies becoming staunch allies. These allies now allow us to extend our defense of our citizens and interests around the world. When you can make friends out of enemies I call that a success of foreign policy. If there was no harmony in the decisions of our national leaders then entire nations who have been our staunch allies would have been written off. These are national who have acted in the past when we called upon them to help keep international peace. Their trade agreements have helped us prosper. Their partnership in security has helped us gain information vital to our defense. None of that matters to an ideology. Just like any other contender with the capacity to influence the field of potential actions to be taken, when they don't fit the preference system the orthodoxy will call for their exclusion or removal. Foreign policy is as subject to polarization as domestic policy, if not more so since it can look so far ahead. If a bad tax is passed domestically the population complains as quickly as it takes for politicians to collect the tax money from them. If another nation is pushed onto the road to currency destabilization that will take place a year or two down the road, will we notice when our own markets fluctuate? The two events may not even be linked in the general knowledge base. It is a political principle that the more power experiences the consequences of their actions the better the quality those actions will be. Power in the U. S. is held in among the citizenry with their ability to vote. People in office may make the decision, but if they make bad decisions they'll be replaced by someone else. That's why foreign policy seems to degrade the farthest when the people are polarized and not paying attention.

Foreign policy may even paint the clearest picture of the failings inherent in an incomplete moral structure. Convincing arguments can be made by either side in domestic policy for reducing the burden caused by regulation or using an entitlement program to care for the elderly. While both sides push their agenda the U. S. Economy continues to create wealth and opportunity. There is still a market system where people who have means are pursuing their dreams. If the non-essential part of government shuts down because the legislators couldn't agree on a budget, the vast majority of the nation still gets up in the morning and goes to work. That's reality. Trucks full of food still make deliveries at grocery stores. States repair roads. Schools stay open so children don't miss classes. If clarity is lacking in foreign policy, there is no market keeping it going. The "market," if you will, consists of nations competing for resources, dollars, and opportunities. It's kind of like the way our states compete for jobs, only there is no international federal government laying down ground rules, nor should there be. At most, international rule promise pressure not certainty. Within the United States, if California wants Nevadan silver they're not going to line troops up on the Nevada border and wait for an excuse to invade and take what they want. If Russia wants something on the other side of a border, the only thing that has historically checked their aggression is the potential for sufficient unified global opposition. That's what worked to maintain sovereignty in the nation of Georgia, different than the U. S. state of Georgia. One could also make a case for the Afghani mountain ranges as a historical deterrent against foreign aggression, but I digress. Unification requires cooperation. Cooperation requires a shared goal. When you can't get your own nation to agree on a national goal, it's harder still to convince other nations to enthusiastically support a policy. Given the number of participants and agendas, clearly and firmly presenting a unifying goal is usually necessary for international action to have long term success. If they doubt your nation's support or conviction how can they be persuaded to add their own? It's like someone at the office who gets everyone talking about lunch, forms a delivery pool to pay for the lunch, and them pulls their money out once everyone else gets excited enough to contribute their money. Do you really want to order a meal with someone who is going to change their mind once the food is ordered and leave you with the bill? Those aren't the kind of partners we need, and other nations don't want to buy our lunch either.

So, how do you craft foreign policy? More specifically, how do you build a policy that all sides can get behind? One side is reactive. They value their concept of their own personal purity. The kind of thought they value comes from the first law of love which defines morality. That's the premise on which they build everything. As such, they tend toward isolationism or the enforcement of their worldview. They care about affronts to their concept of self. They are reactive by nature. They'd rather watch things come in, and then decide from a distance what they should do. More often then not, they just reject everything they possibly can get away with. If you take that distance away, they'll be willing to engage. But, they'll be looking for exits that allow them to gain enough distance to deny responsibility or anything that goes wrong. Their preference system focuses primarily on faults of commission. If you want to rattle these folks, simply criticize them for doing something they didn't do, and watch the fireworks. I'm not recommending it. If you do this with a friend your friendship likely won't survive the experience if you maintain your accusation or they take you seriously. Put another way, conservatives judge their own sense of moral wellbeing by the things they don't do. It seems like the only things they care that people do are the things which showcase the things from which they refrain, or the things which show how good they are at complying with their ideological orthodoxy. On the converse, try accusing a conservative of failing to do something they truly neglected to do, and don't want to do. Accuse them of what would be called a sin of omission. A purist who fits within conservative orthodoxy will most likely tell you they don't care about whatever it is you're accusing them of neglecting. Any follow up on their part will be to try and figure out why they should care about whatever neglect of which they are being accused. Apathy and slight annoyance at the accusation of failing to take a proper action is a far different than the outrage and indignation you would get if you accused them of taking an errant action. They care more about the part of moral law which has its foundation in the first law of love. In their eyes, the less you do, the less opportunity there is to violate that ideological preference system. In foreign policy they figure that if you don't do anything abroad you can't be guilty of anything. It's nonsense. There's such a thing as a failure of omission. Hiding under the sheets in a bed may work for children hiding from imaginary monsters. Hiding from real problems in the work world won't make them go away or any less real. Whether it is natural disaster, dictators like those in the twentieth century who pulled the world into war, or terrorists who maim and kill innocents in an aim to use fear as a weapon, the world has problems. They may walk around on two legs, but history tells us time and time again that monsters are real. If we're going to resist the devil in an adversary we need to find and get to know the angels we can be.

A purist of liberal moral orthodoxy will pass judgment based on an opposite criteria. This is where liberals have their primary contention with conservatives. Liberals are more proactive in nature. They tend to evaluate themselves based on what they do, as opposed to that from which they refrain. This means to feel good about themselves they always want to be doing something for everyone. Restraint does not factor into this assessment. Only activity the presence and magnitude of activity blessed by liberal orthodoxy matters because those are the actions they care about. Our nation borrowing money we may not be able to pay back from another nation so we'll have money to give to a poorer nation is a good example of how this plays out. Of course, they're even happier if this aid comes with strings that coerce the poorer nation to push liberal causes like contraception and abortion among its population. This kind of spending is considered a virtue among liberal groups, even if we can't afford it. There is an environment of cradle to death entitlements provided by the government and paid for by others which liberals consider ideal. It is an idealist's environment where all resources are fed through the matrix of the government. In that environment all solutions would come from acting on behalf of another. Magnify this to foreign policy and internationally a liberals desire to extend this environment around the globe. Contrast this with the conservatives who want to pull back to keep distance and focus on what individuals are doing. Then, consider the added weight of each side elevating their political preferences to the level of moral imperatives and you have a fiery mixture. Remember, these moral principles motivate at a level which comes far before degree or circumstances are taken into account. When both sides dismiss the imperative to live the law of love they prefer and the law of love they feel less inclined to they repel like they are magnetized, and pull any material which they can grab to align with their respective magnetic fields.

When you apply yourself to living a moral life experiences teach you best how to apply each law. Because there are aspects of morality we are not born understanding, without good education we have to learn through trial and error, like we are grasping in the dark. Government, however, is not an entity which learns from experience. Government is a social agreement to leverage the combined force of a people toward certain ends. It cannot convey the benefits of experience to its acolytes either. Whether it is learned from observation, from studying such as in books, or our own experiences, education is a personal thing. That means our government only has what we all bring to it, and is only restrained by our applied wisdom as a nation. Our power remains, but our ability to guide that power is limited to our understanding and ability to communicate well with each other in loving, productive ways. It's a little scary to think what a nation as powerful as ours could do if we don't figure out how to communicate with each other, or never even begin to pay attention to what is happening. That's why our founders set up a system where the power *and* consequences for the use of power would reside closest to the people. The people are placed in a position to learn from the mistakes of their government. The liberal orthodox remain in power by playing on the most commonly felt chords. They wrap themselves in their base and are insulated from their failures by the very people suffering the consequences of their actions. The conservative orthodox use their money and power to insulate themselves from consequences they don't like. Because the established in both major political orthodoxies don't directly feel their consequences, they won't stop until the people have rejected them and impose consequences the political establishment will feel. When that happens they'll scramble to get back into power. Some will apply themselves to learn a better way. Other will simply learn how to say things that sound like they are trying to do better, but that's politics. And, that's why we have to continue paying attention. The cost of paying attention is far less than the cost associated with education through personal experience.

At this point some are wondering what's wrong with a world where all decisions are made for you, and the only actions allowed are those taken on the behalf of others. It can be hard for some to imagine suffering coming from a world devoted exclusively to systems developed from a good and true moral law. We'll take this as an example for what happens in both ideological systems. Remember, each system based on the internal fidelity people feel to a good moral law. What happens when they started building their idea for how things should work on this good foundation is where things start to go wrong. Rather than assert myself here I'll turn to yet another person who is greatly respected as a moral teacher. As an accomplished writer I think C. S. Lewis described the negative effects of this kind of unbalanced system best in his book "The Screwtape Letters." In it you'll find things like the recognizable liberal term "social justice." This is not the term social justice coined by Jesuits and practiced by the Catholic Church meaning to give others their due. When used in liberal politics the term social justice is jargon for Marxist philosophy. C. S. Lewis opposes it vigorously throughout this book. A sub plot to the book is that eventually his protagonist rejects communism. If you're still looking for a way to put all we've been reading in perspective I recommend reading C. S. Lewis. To wrap it all up in a simple package, a conservative will be concerned with being judged for what they've done. A liberal will be concerned with being judged for what they've left undone.

The direction of these two preference systems places them in competition for supremacy when both are not practiced equally within a population. Both laws of love have to be venerated. The political base of each side votes so their values won't be ignored. If each side only supports their own orthodoxy, how do you craft a policy which gains ecumenical support, pardon the pun? Good people whose values are derived from either law of love want to see themselves represented in whatever policy is created. The best foreign policy comes from continuing the best of our accomplishments. The United States was founded on a system of equal representation. That means everyone's values were intended to be represented in the future of the nation. Everyone gets a vote. Checks and balances are in place to uphold the importance of every vote. This is our national understanding. The idea had to be advanced beyond gender and racial boundaries. We as a nation must continue to be committed to advancing freedom and the representation of all. And that's what makes us exceptional. That is also what must define our foreign policy for it to gain sufficient support to be enacted effectively. We need to be about exporting this kind of exceptionalism. Whoever accepts it will find more of their people engaged in the prosperity of their own nation, increasing the value of our alliances.

Back to foreign policy for a while. Although it is often discounted, this really is the toughest subject in politics to tackle. So much of it feels far removed by geography and time. We humans find solutions when we apply effort. We find them even faster when we act in concert. That reality is the genesis of the saying, "where there's a will there's a way." We're certainly not all powerful. But, we can get a great amount done. Hopefully, everyone from wonks to those unfamiliar with political intrigue is starting to see how all these factors are coming together. Foreign policy is crafted with the building blocks of national interest. A nation interested in what happens outside the boundaries of its borders affects life inside those domestic boundaries. This can be as specific as maintaining access to the Panama Canal to reduce the cost of moving goods and services to various parts of the homeland, or as general as factors affecting the average price of crude oil around the world. Many times national security involves resources and the support of allies. Solutions and problems hold no respect for latitude or longitude. An avalanche isn't going to stop at customs and wait for approval. And, a village hit by an avalanche isn't going to need less help if the relief aid has to come from a neighboring nation to get there in time to make the most difference. Our ability to influence all these events and many more outside our borders depends on our strength at home and our reputation abroad. The understanding of equal representation under the law that we were founded on is the mortar in foreign policy which holds these building blocks together. It gains and maintains the will of the nation and the benevolence of other nations. A unified nation is a credible one and a good cause elicits support. When those two are added together there are less reasons not to support such a nation without providing offense, also an effective way to get things done. So that should be our doctrine. A doctrine is another name for a specific foreign policy stance held by an administration. A doctrine that upholds both laws of love solidifies the public will. Whoever thought a mushy conversation on love would be a concrete factor in dealing with foreign powers and projecting domestic interest? But, it is unavoidable that maintaining the consent of the public is essential to good foreign policy.

An important point to get in all this is that much of foreign policy involves preventing mistakes that can't be unmade. Let's take this to an extreme place logically to see if it holds up. If war breaks out and a town is destroyed, there's no way to reset the field and get the town back. Homes have been destroyed, people have been displaced, and massive equity has been lost. Domestic policy deals with so much self interest here at home. Rather than threats of what will happen later, policy is pushed and pulled by interested parties seeking to determine direction rather than what happens after an action is taken. Another way of looking at it is that the margins are more manageable in the policy we craft within our borders. Even minor changes like cutting back on the rate of entitlement growth to make it more efficient gets heated push back.

Bigger changes may pass for a day, but will be delayed and diluted to the point where they are hardly recognizable by the time they get fully implemented. There are signs and turbulence before we steer the nation into the storm. Domestic policy often has self evident returns that come with warning signs. Those in government make it very clear what you'll be missing if you stop the spending which supports their agenda. They commonly make it clear by taking away something you've been enjoying in part so you'll get the point. Because the government has control in that area, they have the leeway to put on such a charade. They are happy to make sure the public must temporarily do without some auspice of government because they've seen the proven return that tactic brings. Even wasteful spending is prolonged due to the certainty of this principle. If there is a movement to cut spending, the first place bureaucrats cut are the most visible areas. They'll close national parks which see heavy traffic at the height of the busy season. When you and your neighbors can't get in to see the park after traveling miles you may call your representative to tell him or her exactly how unhappy you are. They will respond by pointing your anger at whatever funding they'd like to be spending. As soon as they get their funding, the bureaucrats open the parks back up with little long term effect to their overall plans. That is generally the rule. A case for a foreign policy differs. It must be explained.

Foreign policy often prevents the loss of resources and abilities which require the continued willing involvement other parties. This kind of benevolence protects access of our defense forces to bases located around the world. Foreign policy has consequences just as real and life effecting as domestic policy. But, is often marked by what we prevent from happening, rather than what we see continue in our daily lives. When foreign policy fails there is not always a fanfare like the political theater regular played on Capitol Hill. There may not be warning signs, like when your favorite public attraction closes, that let you know life is about to change if a clever solution is not reached. Reversing the consequences of foreign policy is not as simple as letting the general public back into a park. There's usually a period where bad domestic policy can be reversed and the damage largely mitigated. Bad foreign policy can start a war, or allow the creation of an unstable nuclear threat in the world. There are future implications as well. Other nations interact with us based on our national reputation. That reputation functions just like your reputation with your creditors, or your credit rating. If you have a bad credit rating, entities like banks will charge you more money, in the form of higher interest rates, to do business with you. The better our national reputation, the less expensive our transactions get with other nations. We build and maintain our reputation as a nation through foreign policy. Supplies, equipment, vehicles, troops, all must organize somewhere and have a place to regroup to before they are deployed in protecting our citizens and property. Trade agreements allow us to enjoy circumstances which lower prices, or even provide goods we would otherwise not have access to, while improving international stability and peace. An effective information gathering network allows us to know things before they happen, like when a terrorist network is planning an attack on a U. S. city. The information gathered to prevent these kinds of attacks is many times part or wholly information which was shared with us by other nations. We have to maintain good international relations to maintain these all agreements. The deals we make with other nations who engage with us help prevent the cost of living from going up, keep us safe, and maintain global peace, benefitting everyone down to the people struggling just to make a living. Foreign policy can also bind us, like in the form of a bad treaty. All the things it helps protect can also be jeopardized if national consent is given without wisdom and preparation. If bad foreign policy goes too far the worst can happens. Our lives, liberty, and property are threatened and we reach a point at which we are prepared to go to war. That point is established further away from likelihood and held at bay through the use of aggressive foreign policy.

Any national interest which upholds both laws of love can be enacted more forcefully and fully through wider support. An America fully committed to a policy will rally allies in support. The U. S. gains credibility when other nations believe we are serious. Solid foreign policy can also undermine an adversary's opposition in mere application. A policy which draws on the most primary elements of human nature is attractive both here and abroad, after all. Gaining allies and isolating enemies becomes easier with good policy. Turning enemies into allies becomes easier. This is the definition of obtaining the moral high ground, and the reason why it is so coveted in diplomacy. This is also why polarization is so disastrous. It isolates our nation in the world. If we grow polarized and become unstable we can no longer enjoy picking allies based on our values, what treaties, and what resources we need to prosper. Let's gain and maintain the high ground through our message of unity. That's what makes America exceptional.

# PAYING THE PIPER

Here's the chapter I had to prepare myself to write. It's not because the material isn't engaging. I definitely feel engaged. It's not because the material is hard to write. The words practically jump onto the page. But, when emotions run high I find they seek their own way out. A page is a willing recipient to our ardent fervor. It's not because the research was particularly esoteric. The sources for this chapter are easily accessed. Most are within the realm of common knowledge. Even if wasn't common knowledge, I get a kick out of esoteric. That wouldn't slow me down. It would have the opposite effect of enticement. I hesitate to write because I like happy stories. I've seen and lived enough unhappy stories in my life. I don't particularly want to see more. In my experience, live isn't easy. But, it's like country music. When I was younger I was a happy guy. I don't know why. I didn't have it especially good. I grew up what many people would consider poor. I was picked on my share in school. I was fascinated by a lot of things that we just outside the realm of my opportunities. But, none of that got me down. I was a joyful little guy. At that time I didn't like country music. It was just noise and whining. That wasn't for me. Then, the hardships came. One after another, piece after piece was taken away. As more was taken from me, and my faculties failed slowly, I began to like country music. I remember asking some ladies at a job I work at in my youth why they listened to such sad songs. I won't forget their reply. They said, "Because it makes us happy." I can't explain it, but after the life I've lived there's something about real country music that makes me happy too. Maybe there is more to a sad story than learning from what other people have done before us. There's a solidarity we crave in those circumstances. That solidarity may lead to hope. We don't know where the next chapter we are writing now in American history will lead. The story of our time and generation isn't yet written. But, many don't like where we are now. Hopefully our sad story will be the birth pangs of a happy one we'll be glad to tell those who follow after us. We're not completely clueless. We've seen this done before. Preceding generations, even in recent memory, have had to make weighty choices. There were points in time when society experience painful consequences which developed an impetus all their own. Sometimes that snowball was caught before it rolled too far. Other times, in developed into an avalanche which took countless lives and sapped the wealth of a nation, or more than one nation. In either case, there have been times that an event or events carried sufficient momentum to noticeably bend the arc of our nation's history. And, the way it played out was ultimately determined by the consequences presented by the factors involved, and how our predecessors responded. Sometimes our response was not to act. To tell our story, we have to go back to when the consequences we currently face were first set in motion.

When I was very young I learned from nursery rhymes, fables, and fanciful tales. I enjoyed stories crafted for the purpose of imparting the benefit of experience without imposing the need to suffer its rigors. What a wonderful concept. Somehow, with a certain genius, writers throughout time have accomplished this transference. Through stories they managed to capture even the whimsy of a child. By reading a collection of tales called Grimm, princes and princesses were the vessels which taught me lessons about treating everyone like royalty. A man named Aesop used creatures as humble as ants and grasshoppers to teach me the importance of planning and industry. The worth of inspired stories, passed down through generations, cannot be overstated. They teach us important lessons of what our human nature is capable of, both good and bad. Children who learn lessons in moral and ethical educational genres pass on these lessons. Stories heard when we are young make passing on values to the next generation much easier. These parents hope to have children of their own who do not need to learn the value of "love thy neighbor as thyself," or, "Thou shall not kill," through personal experience before acting on these principles.

 Some writers in this genre are surpassing in value. Some texts are better than others. What a great field we have before us in which we may endeavor to find something excellent. The most illuminating accounts, I've found, which have no match in efficacy for educating on human nature come from the Bible. The values espoused and stories told in this collection of books are my favorites. But, like Grimm and Aesop the Bible has lost the place it once held in national public discourse. Schools no longer teach about human nature. The Bible is no longer used as a tool to teach us about, well, us. It can't even be mentioned among other sources. The subject matter involved has been banned in practical effect entirely. Where are we to turn to learn about our nature? What study or work has replaced it? Our culture has morphed and been fractured by the polarization affecting us. Each side of the political divide has a set of values considered for their ability to support a platform rather than on the potential public service a message provides. Do we as a people even believe we have a nature anymore? One has to wonder when the concept of human nature is not taught with math and science. The humanities which are taught seem to point to a career in psychology or are about as effective as the civics classes they are teaching these days. Tell me, what does a whip do in congress? How is the number of seats in the U. S. Senate determined? These may seem like odd questions, but both deal with the vagaries of human nature. The answers to both questions are roles designed to bring form to human will in a productive fashion. A good civics class would provide both answers. A good humanities course would explain why these roles are needed. The very thing upon which our founders built our nation, the laws of nature, have been despised on account of some who refuse belief in nature's God. After all, if you can remove the God of nature, to kill him in our devotion, some believe man inherits the power of God to decide for themselves what nature will be and what natural laws shall rule us.

This rebellion against what our forefathers described as self evident has not ended with manuscripts handed down and defended by the religious. The use of using stories as a vehicle for educating children on human nature seems to have largely faded from our culture. There are some exceptions but have you noticed the American tales told in the new millennium seem more interested in affirming than revealing? If you know the stories we used to tell that loss may be cause for melancholy, but it's not surprising. Superman is a story that was first told to children whose roots are truly unique to American culture. He is a super powerful character who is nigh impervious. He is obviously gifted with powers that go far beyond other people. The author was not going for subtlety on this one. So far he's a conservative dream. In the 1948 Columbia Superman serial starring Kirk Alyn, Superman's adopted father Jonathan Kent explains the moral imperative to him that with great power comes great responsibility. To a true liberal, that's a rallying cry. It is a story that comes from a time when we were united, not polarized like we are today. After a society has waged war on God for the purpose of removing him from his throne in our hearts, challenging a storyteller who highlights natural laws is not that big a feat. People who build kingdoms of their own in the public square are working to enforce their will and salve their pride through the consent of many. Stories reminding the people they attempt to govern of natural truths exist as a challenge to the denial personal kingdoms are built upon. Stories may be considered child's play and dismissed. But, the stories we tell our children as a people also describe who we are, and our hopes for the future. That's not fancy, it's reality. The stories we tell young ears will help shape their image of who they are, and what they will achieve. The history we fail to share, or even withhold from the next generation may represent harsh realities which previous generations learned the hard way. It is a familiar refrain by now that there can be a very high cost associated with education.

In a case called Abington School District v. Schempp in 1963 the foremost tool provided to us in history for revealing human nature, in my humble opinion, was banned from use in public school curriculum. The United States Supreme Court decided school sponsored Bible reading was unconstitutional. Now, don't get me wrong. I'm not saying that it is the job the public educational system, the Supreme Court, or any other federal jurisdiction's responsibility to teach morality. Traditionally, that has always been a job for religious institutions of a society and the leaders of is culture. If you are a member of the majority Christian culture in this nation and you think your church is carrying the load of its educational burden, please, without looking it up explain to your neighbor how your missiology directly contributes to and is also motivated by your eschatology. Perhaps you will agree that this is a problem which is not limited to stopping at the steps of the Supreme Court.

We're looking for trends in our society and there's a saying that the Supreme Court votes with the culture. In addition to cultural trends taking place, it's also true that removing the best tool for teaching human nature and morality that ever graced humanity from the schools will have consequences. Once again, for those who didn't catch it the first time, that is not the federal government's job. Keeping infrastructure running that a profit driven company wouldn't touch is a yes. Feeding, training, and arming a technologically advanced military when peace removes the free market demand for such services is a yes. Teaching kids how to think morally is a no. What's important to note is that the culture was beginning to change. In the early to mid sixties a seed that was being planted in the culture at large. Gallup has an article on Gallup.com dated April tenth, two thousand nine titled, "This Easter, Smaller Percentage of Americans Are Christian," where they report that the number of people who identify themselves as Christian has fallen since the mid sixties. In nineteen sixty-three the percentage was in the nineties. From there, the percentage fell to the seventies in two thousand eight. Whether you think that's a good or bad thing, it is obvious there is a trend taking place. Pardon the tangent, but my curiosity is getting the better of me. I wonder if most Americans know it is illegal to teach from the Bible from a position in a public school. With a nation that traditionally polls high in identifying as Christian you have to wonder. Either the nation has been distracted for a while, or Christians on the whole care more about your freedom than they care about their own proselytizing. Anyway, the Bible has been banished from government sponsored forums. The best teacher still needs a good curriculum from which to work. The culture began to change in that same period, coincidentally enough. There just aren't that many other reliable sourcebooks out there. There are many writings which are useful in various areas of human understanding. But, the Bible sets a high bar. It is a collection of books, letters, poetry, and historical accounts which has been painstakingly preserved for use by not only the writer's generations but also posterity, sometimes at great personal cost. The collection of knowledge it contains spans wide across the human experience, unmatched by any other work in its breadth and depth. Now, we are told we need to find a comparable replacement. To achieve the same standards any replacement will need texts which have withstood intense scrutiny over thousands of years, one which explains the moral underpinnings of our government in the way it was designed to function by its founders, was written by credible figures, and maintains its relevancy throughout time. After all, we wouldn't want to pick a text that will be unable or unworthy to stay contemporary with the challenges of the next generation. These lessons are going to need to inform and guide our nation's children well into their adulthood, and their children after that, and their grandchildren, and so on. This search could take a while…. We're not even legally allowed to work from what we had until we find something suitable. So what do we do? Those who hold religion sacred are in complete agreement with those who don't even believe there is a God that the government has no place teaching the Bible. That's fine. The solution doesn't have to come from the federal system. We're looking at what happens when a culture loses what have been the traditionally effective tools for teaching the next generation how to have a balanced morality. Good or bad, right or wrong, my concern is that a powerful force working against polarization in human hearts was removed.

Instead of a finding a suitable replacement we chose a fad. That's not surprising considering the enormity of the task, and the apparent motives of the people who retired what worked from formal use. It's kind of difficult to start making your own rules for human nature when there's still a very visible butt on the seat in human hearts called the throne. If you can't kick out that seat's current resident, you erect a wall between that seat and the door so the people looking in won't recognize what they're seeing. So much for teaching about human nature, or understanding nature's laws as immutably set by nature's God. It just wasn't fashionable anymore. Virtues used as mile markers on the road to meaning in life were discarded with the previous year's hairstyles and wardrobe. They were labeled restrictive and passé. A new thing called the Self Esteem Movement was replacing the study of human nature in schools. This method, coming out of California from as early as the late 1960's, promised to cure society's ills by simply making everyone think more highly of themselves. I'm not kidding, that was it. Humility was out. "I'm ok," and political correctness was in. Anyone who engages in critical thinking can figure out where this would end. It made great fodder for comedians. That's not hyperbole, some of the funniest stuff I've heard from comedic greats was on the changes in education at that time. One could go as far as to argue that comedians were some of the only ones who benefitted from this change in educational approach.

To expound on the Self Esteem Movement a little, it amounts to telling the classifiably ignorant that they're special. This was done while refusing to educate them about what makes them special. The worse someone behaved the more special we were supposed to tell them they are. Anyone who criticized a person that was acting badly had the kid's specialness explained to them. Anyone who criticized this approach was politically incorrect. Those people weren't told they were special. It was broadly explained to other people that they wouldn't be special either if they interacted with the malcontent. If that didn't back the complainers down they were ostracized, black balled, and faced the worst penalties that society could bring against them without beginning criminal proceedings. Sometimes there were criminal proceedings, but this was generally reserved for the people who couldn't be silenced through social pressure. Political correctness lived on but the Self Esteem Movement is now widely considered a failure. It failed to cure society's ills. What was discovered, much to the surprise SEM experts, is that telling bullies how special they are does not tend to stop bullying. But the failures of the movement didn't stop there. Apparently, telling children they are supposed to have better self esteem than they do has about the same effect on young impressionable minds that pictures of waif thin cover models in beauty magazines has on women. This is especially sad when you consider children are not equipped with an adult's capacity to ward off those kinds of messages. A slight digression, you're probably curious about how adult women, the prime readership of fashion magazines, reacted to the messages sent by those cover pages I mentioned. Currently, there is a push to find fuller figured more "natural" looking models. I guess the fashion industry has experienced what happens when they cross a line every guy in a meaningful relationship with a woman and an iota of sense knows to avoid. Say it with me guys, what's the answer when your darling asks you if her outfit makes her look fat? You look beautiful! The rewards of answering that question correctly are wonderful, the potential negative consequences of answering it wrong formidable. It seems the fashion industry ended up on the business end of women's capacity to ward off negative messages. And the result, they have come to the realization that understanding the beauty of the natural promotes better self esteem. Welcome to the party, fashion people. You're a little late, we guys have known this forever, but we're glad you're here. The repercussions of episodes like this can be hilarious, and more vastly respectful than before. But, this kind of push back is beyond developing young minds in the classroom.

I bet by now you are wondering how this all comes together to make a point. For those who have figured it all out, I salute you. We've got thematic elements coming from all directions at the moment. So, let's take a moment to tie it all together. Starting in the 1960's, children were denied what I consider to be the best material available for teaching human nature. They were then inculcated by society to seek whatever inflates their own desires. Learning from The Apostle Paul, we know moral laws are intrinsic to human nature. Thomas Jefferson agreed, so he and the founders built our system of governance on the best moral understanding they believed to be available, the one described by Jesus. They wanted our system of government to last so they developed checks and balances to reign in the destabilizing desires of human nature, while also developing pathways and protections for desires and opportunities to fulfill desires which contribute to stability. We know from Jesus that all laws governing human nature under this moral understanding stem from one of two laws of love, both of which are equally important in practice for public good and the health of a society. Jesus called these laws commandment, instead of "you're going to do these anyways." That implies some sort of effort is necessary to uphold both in society and in our lives. My assertion is that politically active people in the U. S., including likely voters, are naturally more inclined to the tenets of one law or the other. Those more inclined toward one law of love will require work and cooperation to learn how to live well the law to which they are less inclined. The rest of us have to work on both laws of love. Emphasizing pursuit of whatever we feel like doing from a young age has had a polarizing effect. Those naturally inclined more to ward on law of love have turned it into their idol. Those in political power have, knowingly or unknowingly, developed two entire pseudo-religious systems on the two moral laws, by which supplicants can pay homage to their idols. Reading that over makes me glad I put it after over a hundred pages of explanation. It sounds ridiculous, perhaps even radical if taken out of context. But, by now you know the rational grounds for the statement. The emphasis on personal political orientation in our culture has provided added fuel for political wedge issues designed to separate us along the lines of the places that hurt to tend and we are likely to remain ignorant. Lack of educational discipline in the tender areas which we are likely to avoid has been compounded by telling ourselves our avoidance is right. As time has gone by, more and more of our efforts as a nation have gone in oppositional directions. This has lead to people in our culture pulling farther apart from each other.

A generation was taught to indulge their desire, to measure all by their appetites rather than to embrace self discipline. You see, self discipline, not self indulgence, is what's needed for setting aside one's own preferences and embracing an understanding which calls for the appreciation of others, even the ones you don't like, especially the ones you wouldn't otherwise care for. It's an important step in learning from others. Those who deny selfish ambition become walking examples of a better way of living. That's very attractive. If we also have a text pointing out how to recognize and attain the best in life we can expect to create a society where all have a chance to enjoy a better quality of life. Not everyone will choose to follow the good examples they see. Selfish ambition is very hard to part with. But, that's the choice we all make on this earth. Hopefully, since we humans are relational in our learning, more good examples will lead to the creation of more opportunities to succeed. It's just like creating the environment that leads to more and better jobs in an economy. Hard work, plus wisdom, plus opportunity equals success. Other factors come into play. It's not wholly dependent on us. But that's the part we play. If a society decreases cultural understanding of human nature in that society, and emphasizes what one personally esteems, they've just weakened the wisdom component and the hard work component of that equation. There will be division within the culture along the lines of the two laws. When a society loses the cultural practices which strengthen it then the proverbial effort to mix the two sides ends. Free agents within that society must then be relied upon to cause the kind of agitation which brings us all back together. If that fails, when an older generation who obeyed the commandments to live both laws of love passes so does their influence. If no cultural institution is set up and handed down to the next generation, what options do they have for opportunity? Lacking that much needed agitation, gradually, each element separates and culture experiences decay. There is not a stable rate for this decay. As knowledge of both commandments and their need fades in a society, over time you will see the forces causing separation to accelerate. If you gradually reduce the effect of mitigating factors, eventually there will be a point where the two groups undergo complete dissociation. After that there will be two distinct levels, and a clear line in between.

Those with naturally split preferences in a divided culture are like oil and water in a glass container. Teaching the understanding that you must live under both laws of love is like shaking the oil and water mixture. Shaking the glass keeps them both mixed at all levels. Shaking the mixture represents the forces stabilizing a society. A stable society is like a polished gem, having many facets. The role good tradition plays in a culture is one facet. Living by both laws requires discipline that comes from good character, another facet. Good traditions pass on knowledge to the next generation for cost of paying attention rather than paying for experiences. Tradition can be another facet. Stories and other educational methods also can pass on knowledge. Factors like these and more need to be in place to avoid what happens when the pre-rational urges coming from the core of our decision making process impact a world and other people who do not fit within our own personal way of doing things. In a polarized, distracted society without these factors the desire to live in a world we understand that reflects our values remains, even if our values are poorly formed and will tear us apart. That's why it is important to know what you believe. If we keep reinforcing the need to embrace and live under both laws of love through our cultural practices we will have a solution nearly everyone desires. That's our perfect solution. In that society we can stay fairly well mixed with our neighbor. Yet, members of a society where each member conducts themselves honorably and loves others as they would want to be loved retain their own identity. You can be sure of this because the two laws when held together demand freedom. That means you are free to be you. When a society which lives by both laws of love advocates uses their collective power in the form of government freedom is still present on all levels.

The division caused by polarization causes social pain, misunderstanding, and conflict. The current polarization we face is no different. It's a thing of nature which does not bend to our wishes or require our understanding it to retain its efficacy. It is a seed that once planted will begin to grow until it matures or is uprooted. I believe we saw the beginning of this current social pain break the surface during the presidency of Bill Clinton. Children who sat in U. S. schools in the 1960's and 1970's were then fairly established and of voting age. Called Baby Boomers, they inherited control of the nation, and viewed events according to their experience. As a generation they had been told that their way was right, and if two people had a conflict they fought it out in court. The president was caught lying about a sex scandal. Rather than resign, or express shame, President Bill Clinton appeared comfortable with denial in a way which affronted those who valued the obligations of the first law of love. Each side clung to their own way. What had been going on under the surface was now visible and the nation split.    Those more oriented to the second law of love saw it as an issue of giving pleasure to another person. It wasn't a problem for them as long as Mrs. Clinton wasn't complaining. She stayed supportive of her and her husband's united ability to enact their political goals. Liberal voters were not concerned. Their preferred law hadn't been crossed. Despite the infidelity, if no one was claiming grievance, they didn't see a problem. A president who lied publicly about the affair to the world was seen in the same light. That president wasn't violating their favored law of nature. To this day President Clinton is admired by many liberals for what he did to support liberal causes, even with the power inequity between him and his choice alleged of sex partner.

The followers of the first law of love were incredulous and irate. Using the power of the presidency to deliberately and publicly lie was bad enough. The president represents the nation to the world. A public affair in the nation's highest political office was seen as an open repudiation of this nation's fidelity to the first law of love, which they cared more about. In the eyes of conservatives, their values and self image had been challenged in the highest halls of the nation. What's more, the core on which they built their sense of morality had been publically discarded by those on the left who said it was not a non-issue. Then, it was disdained in following days by one who claimed at home and abroad to represent them. That's why I call this a turning point for our nation. I would say instead that it was the first fruits of a harvest we planted a while ago, the first time the fruit was ripe enough for us to eat. From that time, the culture seems to have gained speed on its path of continued deterioration with a rift that is ever widening. Now, years later after lawsuit has been filed with one presidential candidate suing another, and claims of lawlessness throughout several executive institutions we are eating our fill of those fruits. Certain news channels have begun open political advocacy. Successive presidents seem to be competing with congress for the lowest approval rating. Congress repeatedly fails to pass a budget. Scandal after scandal has made the news headlines.

We need a return to respecting the laws of our own nature. We need to find a place in our society for the study of that nature. Laws such as these are immutable. They do not break. They do not even bend. It's like jumping out of an airplane. If nothing has happened yet it is because we're picking up speed, not avoiding the inevitable stop. We can ignore the ground for a while. But, ignoring terra firma does not invalidate what happens when we impact it at a high velocity. We wish as a society to enjoy a better world. But, we cannot realize this ideal while ignoring our nature. That's like jumping without a parachute. To illustrate this point I'll close the chapter by taking the analogy further. Studying human nature can be likened to learning the laws governing physics along with principles like lift and terminal velocity in order to discern the nature of gravity. It was by studying these laws we learned that propulsion and aerodynamics could free us from gravity's dire consequence. We've enjoyed a fantastic ride. But, lately we've picked an unfavorable direction. The plane is sputtering and low on fuel. What we take with us when we jump will determine the manner in which we'll land. Will we dive through the skies until we ride our parachute to a landing that we can walk away from, freely able to ascend to the skies again? Or, will we continue our acceleration until the time to safely decelerate has run out? In our flight from the study of human nature, it is not the fall which concerns me. In matters such as these protraction produces progression. My care is whether, in the time since shedding our wings, we've spent too long falling before our sudden stop.

# RUNNING

I've been told there are two things which make us creatures run. Those two things are fear and desire. We run *to* what we desire. One of the most powerful forces guiding our actions is our desires. When we desire good things we find contentment. You may have heard it said that contentment with little is great gain. Of course, we don't always desire good things. I'm reminded of the couple that wants to buy a house they can't afford. They fight because they have money troubles. They never go anyway to do anything fun, going out costs money. They only have enough gas money to go to work and back home. They'll be eating the most inexpensive food they can find. They better like that house a lot, because they'll be spending all their time in it with each other. When we learn the things we chase can temporarily elevate our mood it doesn't matter if it is a superficial high or a deep, intrinsic emotion like the feeling of a job well done after a hard day's work.  If we spend the best of our strength running after a desire long enough then desires go from being a menu to a cage. Like a drug, those things become more and more fleeting the more we devote ourselves to them. Even slow burning desires which come from good things can leave us feeling wanting if they go from means to achieving daily goals to means of feeling right. It doesn't happen all at once. We have all want to feel normal. We feel security in what has worked before and what we know. Sometimes, when we don't know how to feel right, we double down on a fading feeling. We hope that if we invest more of ourselves we'll know the thrill of life once again. It is a point of diminishing returns. More effort gets us more feeling, but not equal to the amount of effort we put into feeling good again. As more and more effort is required just to feel good we watch as the exhilaration of life slips through our fingers. Years and years of what started as chasing desire ends in an emotional crisis. This crisis comes with the realization that what we've been pursuing with our resources and the best of vigor moves farther out of reach with each step we take in its pursuit.

We also run *from* fear. Our fears could be the presence of a current aggressor. Many times we find ways to live in spite of current realities which can be temporarily endured or ultimately overcome. The most motivating fears may be the ones we can do nothing about. I think that's why horror movies involve people tied to chairs, locked in rooms, or being chased through places with which they are unfamiliar. The moment when fear is at its apex seems to be the moment when the future looks most grim. Some choose change their behavior now because of what they believe can happen tomorrow. As fear takes over, more and more of life is spent in that mental state depicted in the horror movie when the monster is just on the other side of the door and the victim is waiting. It sounds awful, but many times we do it to ourselves. We invent things we can do and tell ourselves that if we give enough of our strength and devotion to those activities we'll be granted the ability to influence things we can't control. In politics this could be a conservative "prepper" who has lost touch with all healthy relationships for the sake of making a zombie apocalypse bunker, or a liberal who believes in appeasement as a tool controlling mad dictators and wants to empty the treasury into the pockets of foreign leaders working to destroy our nation. I don't want to hear any complaints from Max Brooks's fans on this one.

The future isn't the place we create a home in our hearts for irrational fears or uncontrollable. We can also fear the past, and the hold it may have on our present. Think about anything you're ashamed of, and imagine someone from that event walking into the middle of a conversation you're having with a person whose respect you cherish today. The things which have happened to us in our lives can leave emotional scars which direct our actions today. I knew a man who starved when he was young and so he overeats at every meal years later. Things happen in lives which are beyond our control. Privation is always a possibility, but not one which should control our lives through fear in times of plenty. Fear is not wisdom, which is a much surer defense against lean times. The overeating man has a greater likelihood of heart failure through obesity than of starving again. But, he was ruining the body he has in service to a fear from a past he no longer lives.

Desires are healthy. They serve as guides on the path to fulfillment. Practical concerns can be healthy too, where there is trust. They serve as warning signs, if we will heed them, for dangers ahead. One of the keys to this process is that our emotions are serving us, rather than us living in servitude to our emotions. No other creature lives in service to their emotions. Other creatures are ruled by instincts. So, what makes us different? I would say what differentiates us is our capacity to choose. We can act contrary to the inclinations we are born with. We also have the duty of learning to respect and uphold the good and true things we are not naturally inclined to keep in our daily practice. Before I upset those who believe animals can choose like we do, let me ask you this. If you treat a dog well, giving the creature all it needs according to genus, species, and breed, will you not enjoy all the affection this pet can possibly give you? If you treat a person the same way, they may not return you affection. They may take your care for granted or even spurn you. For us, love is a choice that extends over how we respond to others. It also determines whether or not we spend our time running in service to things which will take the best we have while giving nothing in return. Any ideology we posses will direct our actions. Our actions flow from the principles and values we hold. That flow takes us to one of two places. We will either spend our time and energy in service to efforts which will bring greater prosperity and freedom. Or, we will give our devotion to selfish inclinations which enslave others and ourselves, inhibiting our ability to experience our self-actualization in our world.

We're reached the point where a story normally has an ending. But, in that regard I feel pleasantly uninhibited. This story doesn't have an ending, at least, not one with a time or hour that anyone on this earth could point to and say, "That's when it's going to end." Our story goes on, presumably with many chapters left to write. You, dear readers, will be the ones writing the next page. That's the fun thing about U. S. politics. Even during the most dire events, when we've really made a mess of our home and offended our neighbors, when we've failed to live freedom as well as that wondrous gift deserves, if the people choose wisely and well life can get better.

There is a road that seems right to every person,
but ends in death

.-Ancient Middle Eastern Proverb

Proverbs 14:12


Today I have given you the choice between
life and death... Oh, that you would choose life,
so that you and your descendants might live!

-Moses

Deuteronomy 30:19


My purpose is to give them a rich and
satisfying life.

-Jesus

John 10:10b